PSYCHOLOGY
for everyday living

PSYCHOLOGY

for everyday living

by

Dr. Leonard Blank,

**Ph.D., Psychiatrist
and Dr. Kenneth Lewes, Ph.D.**

ERRATA

For Dr. Leonard Blank, Ph.D., Psychiatrist
read Dr. Leonard Blank, Ph.D., Psychologist

Front jacket; title page; copyright page; and
back jacket flap.

MAYFLOWER BOOKS
New York

PSYCHOLOGY
for everyday living

By
Dr. Leonard Blank,
Ph.D., Psychiatrist and Dr. Kenneth Lewes, Ph.D.,

Produced and prepared by
Quarto Marketing, Ltd. and
A Good Thing, Inc.

Designed by
A Good Thing Inc.

Editor
Anne Ziff

Production Manager
Tammy O'Bradovich

Published in the United States of America and Canada by
Mayflower Books, Inc.
575 Lexington Avenue
New York, N.Y. 10022

Library of Congress Cataloging in Publication Data

Blank, Leonard
Psychology for everyday living.
1. Psychology. I. Title. [DNLM: 1. Psychology
—Popular works. BF145   B642p]
BF145.B48   150   79-4471
ISBN 0-8317-7125-9

Illustrations by George Winnick

Acknowledgments

We wish to express our gratitude to Gloria and Monroe Gott-segen who originally conceived of the format of this book, to Jordan, Rona, and Lyda, who influenced so much of the developmental thinking, and to Bernice who played a part in the conception of both.

Contents

Introduction

We are born into this world a packet of chemicals and chemical processes. These are our links to the physical world. At a higher level, our urge to explore the world and ourselves as well as our ability to learn from our experience link us to the animal world. Still higher, as we encounter the social world—first our mother, then our family, and finally the society at large—we take our place in the human world. All these connections serve to establish our common, generic nature—what we share with other parts of nature. At the same time, we begin at birth to establish, discriminate, and sharpen the sense of uniqueness, our individual indentity. Our behavior and our sense of being in the world is impinged upon by all these spheres—the physical world, our animal nature, the social sphere, and the private and internal sense of who we are.

If we want to understand ourselves, to know why we do things in a certain way and to discover other possible ways, we must look at ourselves as a whole. No single factor can explain how we act or do not act. Throughout this book, we will have occasion to single out and emphasize one single aspect of our total being—e.g., genetics, physiology, culture, child rearing, interpersonal relations or the internal sense of self—but at the same time we will be talking about the whole person. These individual aspects are not separate and discrete, but overlap and mutually affect each other. The primary emphasis of this book is on psychology, but to understand this important aspect and to locate it in the larger context of our total lives, we will refer to other non-psychological factors: nutrition, culture, physical processes. Human beings cannot really be divided up—we are one person—and anything we can say about one aspect of our lives has corresponding relevance to other aspects.

Along with the processes of physical, mental, and emotional development, the totality of factors we have been discussing shape, even determine, our behavior. Our behavior is a set of responses to stimuli from the external and internal world. Some of us, however, for reasons we shall be discussing at length, learn an extremely narrow range of responses, and our behavior becomes restricted and difficult to change. In other words, we become neurotic. Neurosis is limited choice. Psychological adjustment, on the other hand, involves flexibility, a wide range of options, and the exercise of conscious and realistic choice. Every individual, to one degree or another, has this option. We can, if we have some measure of understanding, choose to act and think differently. The reasons for the common restriction of choice and freedom as well as the opportunities for growth, change, and choice are the major themes of this book.

People have always been interested in these problems, and have given thought to how to live as full a life as possible. In the past, philosophy and/or religion have provided the guides for living, and many people still derive guidance from such sources. In this book, however, we will be presenting a psychological approach to the problems in life. This is not the only approach. A psychological approach becomes most useful when it is supplemented by an awareness of other approaches—political, moral, religious, and aesthetic. Again, individual personality is a whole and it is impinged upon by all of these realms. Still, it is really only in this century that we have discovered most of what we know about psychology, and although almost everyone has some general notion of these ideas, the ideas themselves may be relatively new and unfamiliar to many. We will be attempting to give expression to some of them, not because they represent a complete guide to life, but because an acquaintance with them can help us understand our behavior and motivate us to change if we find that our behavior is in some way inadequate or undesirable.

The person who did most to help us understand behavior and attitudes from a psychological point of view was Freud, who began writing around the turn of this century. Of course, three-quarters of a century of thinking and research has modified, expanded, or rejected many of Freud's ideas, but the basic ones, for the most part, have remained intact and form what we have been calling a psychological point of view. Present-day psychology is an enormously eclectic field, but most of the competing schools of thought generally agree about basic principles.

Freud's most important insight, although it was not entirely new with him, was the distinction between conscious life and the unconscious, and the idea that conscious behavior and attitudes are powerfully influenced by unconscious wishes and urges. That is, although we like to think our behavior is determined by our conscious values, ideas, and desires, the basis for what we do and, more importantly, the basis for our inability to do what we would like is a mass of infantile urges and needs of which we are largely unaware. This motivation is unconscious, but as Freud showed, it does reveal itself in certain ways, and if we pay attention to these signs, we can become conscious and aware of it.

The ways in which the unconscious reveals itself are subtle and elusive but follow a consistency and logic of their own. Dreams, according to Freud and most psychologists after him, represent disguised wishes and urges that we do not recognize in our waking lives. Similarly, minor and annoying interferences in our daily behavior, like slips of the tongue or lapses in memory, are also signs of what is unconscious. But most important, the patterns of our everyday behavior, the peculiar ways we go about doing things, and our seeming inability to change them can also be used to understand what lies below the level of our conscious understanding of ourselves. In other words, although neurotic symptoms and neurosis as we have been discussing them are unfortunate hindrances, they are signs that we can learn to read. Implicitly, if we can gain some measure of understanding of our unconscious nature, we shall be better able to understand and choose our way of life. The unconscious is an important part of us, and, as with all aspects of our lives, the greater and more complete our understanding of it is, the richer, fuller, and freer our lives can be.

Freud's other great insight was that although we grow and change, we never entirely leave a previous stage behind us. Instead, we continue to carry all previous stages around inside us. And the most important stage is infancy. That is why we have already characterized the unconscious as infantile. What happens to us in the earliest stages of our lives— our relation to our mother, our experience of early feeding and toilet training, our success or failure at having our earliest needs attended to and satisfied—all this leaves a permanent mark on our personalities. In fact, a strict Freudian would claim that our later personalities are really only developments and elaborations of patterns and tendencies that have been established during the first few years. Later psychologists, like Erikson, put more emphasis on later stages and also stress the importance of the effects of culture and society on the developing personality. Part of a complete understanding of our present, mature behavior, then, involves an awareness of how it relates to our earliest experiences, and this understanding will enable us to have some measure of choice about how we will act and feel for the rest of our lives.

If Freud was right about this, and the preponderance of evidence suggests that he was, early childhood and child rearing practices are enormously important. As adults, we are all responsible for who we are, but the options open to us have been at least partly determined by what happened to us as infants. The burden of responsibility placed on parents is therefore enormous. If we have some comprehension of what effect these early experiences have, we stand a better chance of raising children who are healthy, not neurotic. At least, we may raise children who have a greater degree of choice about what they will do with the rest of their lives.

Parents have, obviously, been raising children for thousands of years without the aid of modern psychology. Parents can trust their instincts and their natural affection and care to guide their actions. It is when a parent is confused, ambivalent, or anxious about what to do, or when a child begins to develop problems, that some acquaintance with psychology can be particularly useful.

Styles of child rearing change—feeding schedules, toilet training, and the handling of sexual and aggressive behavior in children are issues that have provoked different pronouncements from different authorities. Still, it is generally agreed that the attitudes and emotions behind any particular child rearing practice are more significant and have a greater effect than the actual practices themselves. If a child experiences his or her early environment as loving, responsive, consistent, and free of anxiety, that child stands a good chance of growing up fairly well, no matter what the actual procedures of child rearing are—within reasonable limits.

Nevertheless, there are several important guidelines that parents can adopt. Children are different from adults, and they are different from each other. That means that a child's individual temperament and his or her individual rate of development must be respected and taken into account in the parents' expectations and demands. It is not reasonable to demand of a child something of which he or she is physically or mentally incapable. Whether it is a case of when to begin toilet training or whether to expect a child to understand another's point of view, the child's physical and mental abilities must have developed to the degree that he or she is able to fulfill the expectation. What may seem to an impatient parent like uncooperativeness or recalcitrance may really be a simple case of a child's abilities not yet having matured. Similarly, rates of development are different for each child, and one child's achievements should not serve as a model for another's. There are, of course, general developmental patterns and schedules, but they should always be qualified by a sense of individual differences.

The basis for a parent's relation to a child is affection, interest, and caring for the child's best interest. Of course, we all experience moments of irritation, frustration, and exasperation, but the basic conditions of affection, interest, and care are the abiding qualities. Children grow into freer, happier, and more productive adults if they have been deeply convinced of this abiding concern. While discipline and even punishment may be necessary, these are not to be confused with the withdrawal of love. Nor should love be made contingent on a child's performance. Children who do experience such unfortunate conditions grow up feeling that the world is basically an unfriendly place and that they have to earn affection and respect. For such people, intimacy becomes a difficult, if not impossible, achievement.

On the other hand, children do not flourish in an entirely permissive atmosphere. They require structure and consistency as well as affection and responsiveness. They need to learn that the world runs according to some logical and consistent rules and that merely wanting something does not cause that thing to happen. Children are often at their most difficult when they test the rules and limits of their environment. Tantrums and uncooperative behavior more often than not are attempts to elicit firmness and structure from adults. Giving in to unreasonable demands or behavior in a child causes the child to become unreasonable.

All people, especially children, learn from the results of their behavior and tend to repeat behavior that is rewarded and to discard behavior that is punished. This simple scheme gets complicated when someone is simultaneously rewarded and punished for the same behavior. For example, a mother who lectures her son not to be aggressive, and yet is secretly pleased with early displays of tough manliness, confuses him and gives him no reliable guide for conduct. At its extreme, such inconsistency can lead to very serious mental disturbances. Generally speaking, it is almost better to be mistaken in values than to be inconsistent, ambivalent, or contradictory about them.

It is probably almost impossible to avoid punishment in raising children. Nevertheless, it is essential to be very clear about exactly what is being punished and to convey this clearly. Children tend to overgeneralize such lessons, and while parents may think they are punishing specific acts, the children may feel that they are being punished for what they are, not for what they have done. If the children do overgeneralize, they may grow up thinking at a deep level that they are bad or dirty, not that certain actions are to be avoided.

This confusion is rather common when it involves aggression, sexuality, and emotions, especially so-called "bad" ones. When parents attempt to guide their children's behavior, it is important that they are not prohibiting emotions as such, but prohibiting an immoderate or inappropriate expression of emotion. Much of the neurosis we develop stems from a deep, often unconscious, conviction that certain emotions, like aggression, lust, or even tenderness, are bad. We cannot control what we feel—we are responsible only for our actions.

A great deal of maladaptive behavior comes from either the inability to deal with emotions appropriately or from a lack of contact with them. We are over-indulgent or over-controlled. By far, the latter is more common. All too many of us have learned to disown our emotional natures and to live a life devoid of any real pleasure or pain. At some time in our lives, some of us have learned that any or all emotions are ugly, bad, or dirty. Men have learned not to feel tenderness or hurt; women not to be assertive; children not to be spunky or mischievous. These lessons get overlearned, and we grow up feeling little. But the truth of the matter is that emotions in themselves are neither good nor bad. They are part of our biological equipment for responding to the world. The proper lessons to be learned are how to express emotions appropriately, and these are the lessons we do well to teach our children.

If, however, we have learned to deny our emotions, they do not disappear. Instead, they go underground, become strangers to us and make their appearance surreptitiously as neurotic symptoms. We may find ourselves unable to concentrate on a task, or we may labor under a persistent fatigue and exhaustion. We may experience irrational bouts of irritation or tearfulness. We may find we are botching up all sorts of projects and social or personal relations. Or we may become ill. Much of the illness people develop has some relation to their emotional life. In so-called hysterical symptoms— certain failures of bodily functions, blindness, or paralysis— there is no organic, physical basis for the distress whatsoever. In other more ambiguous psychosomatic disorders, chronically denied emotion or the resultant cumulative stress can result in more nearly organic disturbances—headaches, high blood pressure, ulcers, even heart conditions. In such an event, of course, we should consult with a physician to see if there is an organic basis, but the psychological aspects of the disturbance are also important.

More commonly, however, we simply undergo a progressive narrowing of the range of our activities. We do things in the same old, stereotyped, unsuccessful ways and seem unable to change our behavior. We have become neurotic, or more precisely, part of our behavior has become neurotic. Any aspect of our lives can be so affected, from our sexual activities to our business and professional behavior to our relations with other people.

If we suspect that this has happened to us, there are three questions to ask, and if the answer to any of them is Yes, our suspicions may be justified. Are we unable to perform the activity in question in another way, that is, are we bound to repeat the same pattern? Is the activity compulsive, requiring that we engage in it even when we feel it is undesirable; are we stricken with anxiety if we manage to control our impulse and refrain? Does the activity—when we give in to it—lead to anxiety and a nagging frustration? An affirmative answer to any of these questions means that we are no longer entirely free to choose our activities and way of life.

It is at this point that we decide to remain in our unfree condition or to change and again take control of our lives. The preconditions for successful and lasting change are subtle and complex. (We will discuss them at length in a later chapter.)

But generally, change requires a genuine motivation to take risks, undergo pain, uncertainty, and disappointment, and to be the masters of our lives. Implicitly, there must be a willingness to let go of deep, often unconscious, illusions. All of us, to some degree, carry around within us the infantile fantasy of being taken care of, and much of neurotic behavior involves the relinquishing of control over our lives to someone or something other than ourselves. But once we determine to lead our own lives and not to be led, we are well on our way to growth and change.

Every individual has the capacity, more or less, to vary his or her behavior. We do not have the ability to alter another's behavior. We certainly do not have the responsibility to do so—not even for children. We may influence a child's behavior, but by guiding rather than driving, by encouraging rather than enforcing, and by structuring rather than training or disciplining.

Many people are frightened or dismayed by the prospect of change. This in itself is a sign of a neurotic condition, an indication that behavior has become rigid. A free, flexible attitude toward life implies an eagerness to meet changing conditions in our environment and in ourselves with new, fresh responses. While many people derive their sense of potency from material possessions, social status, or control over others, genuine potency is the power we have over our own lives. As adults, unless we are seriously impaired, we always have the power to express our emotions in appropriate ways, to gain knowledge of our nature, and, more generally, to change in ways that are suitable to our individual temperament, abilities, and desires. Often this means the challenging job of declining to follow roles imposed on us by our upbringing and society.

Although a mature attitude involves a willingness to change, it is important to recognize that different stages in our lives pose specific emotional and developmental tasks. The most important ones, as we have said, occur in childhood, when basic issues of trust, autonomy, and self-esteem are paramount. Later stages confront us with such issues as identity, productivity, intimacy, and integrity. Our entire lives are spent discovering who we are; different stages emphasize different aspects of our identity. We must not think, however, that we have done with a stage once we have passed through it. We carry all previous stages around with us, and the way we have resolved one stage affects our chances for success at the next. Each stage carries the seeds of the next.

If we have failed to resolve a certain issue, it will distort and limit our options in the future. In other words, any disruption in our development will be compounded and complicated as time goes on. It is essential, therefore, that we pay attention to what is happening to us in the present and not put off such attention to a future time. Often, the press of business or other responsibilities makes it inconvenient or difficult to cultivate our emotional nature, but most often such reasons are really excuses and rationalizations. Our emotional development cannot be deferred, and, as Jung, the great psychiatrist and psychologist, warns us, "The unlived life will avenge itself."

In addition, problems are most easily ameliorated when they first appear, before they have had a chance to deepen or complicate or to become integrated into larger personality structures. It is important, therefore, to be alert quickly to disturbances in our development or behavior. With children, this can be rather difficult, since individual children develop at different rates. What may seem like a sign of disturbance in a child may simple be a case of slow development. It is therefore important for parents to have some notion of the general stages of development in their children, so that they can recognize truly retarded or disturbed behavior. Similarly, people can be attentive to signs of disruption in their own behavior. Disturbances in such common activities as sleep, eating, and sexual behavior are signs to be heeded. In addition, many activities, like sports or conversation, can become contaminated by other drives that are not being satisfied in more appropriate ways. Again, it is always easier to treat a disturbance when it first appears.

It is generally true that a function that is not exercised will atrophy. This is true for both simple and complex functions. If we do not engage in physical exercise, our muscles lose their tone and become flabby. The same is true for memory, thinking, and sex. As we get older, we can expect a gradual decline in speed, endurance, or resilience. We can help ensure a vital and interesting old age by regularly exercising all our faculties. Much of the common opinion about the deficiencies of old age is misinformation. The vitality of our old age is a function of how active, wise, and attentive we have been in our prime.

There is, in fact, evidence that certain powers increase with age. Specific functions like IQ actually improve in certain of its aspects, and if we have led a full and rich life previously, we can expect to grow in wisdom and experience. We are again beginning to understand how much people who have attained old age have to offer to society and to other, younger people. Certainly, the leisure that many people find in retirement is an opportunity to cultivate and understand the self with an intensity that was, perhaps, not possible earlier. Each stage of life has its own satisfactions and privileges—part of the wisdom of living lies in recognizing and cultivating them.

1
Stages

Most of us have experienced sitting alone on a quiet night watching a cat or dog go about its business. It sleeps, gets up, eats, wants to play, sniffs around the room. Sometimes it is quiet, and then goes into periods of excitement and playfulness only to become quiet again. If we watch long enough, we may feel a kind of envy. Our pet goes through its life unfettered by the concerns that nag at us. It doesn't think about the future or whether it has performed the past day's responsibilities. It doesn't worry about who it is or what it will become. It never asks whether its life has been worthwhile or what it should do to make it so.

Life is not the same for us. We have our pleasures and moments of satisfaction, but much of our time and energy is spent thinking about what we have done and what we must still do. Strangely, we worry about who we are and whether our lives will have been worthwhile. In short, our entire lives are a search for an identity.

You may have heard the term "identity crisis," that event which occurs in adolescence when we first consciously begin to think about who we are and to define ourselves with respect to our families and the society at large. But the search for an identity begins before adolescence and continues long after it. It begins, really, at birth, when we learn our first lessons about trust. We go through other stages in which we confront the problems of autonomy, initiative, industry, integrity, and faith. It is a mistake, however, to think that these stages are separate and distinct. In fact, each is built on the foundations of its predecessor. If we have failed to resolve a previous stage, our success at the next will be shaky; if our resolution has been successful, we have a better chance of coming through the next stage with an enlarged and stable sense of who we are.

The search for an identity, then, is really a life-long task, although it can be seen as a series of stages, each dependent on the previous ones and each with its own set of concerns and dilemmas. If we are successful, we finally come to see who we were, who we are, and how we fit into the infinite network of humanity. We all die, but we can look forward to a final wisdom and faith and a sense that the whole process has been worthwhile and possesses a unique meaning. As we have said, this process begins at birth.

Infancy

You were warm, moist, and secure; you didn't have to scrounge for food or shelter; you didn't even have to think. Then suddenly you were expelled into a cold, discordant world that was overwhelming and terrifying. You were born!

We know that the newly born infant is sensitive to pain, discomfort, fear, and soothing. The procedures during and following delivery that most nearly duplicate the intrauterine environment have benign effects on the infant. Conditions are best when the temperature in the delivery room approximates the intrauterine temperature, when the baby is handled gently (and not slapped, except under unusual circumstances) and is placed in a warm saline solution, and when lights and sounds are kept soft. Rank and Sullivan both thought that the events surrounding delivery were the prototypical antecedents of anxiety.

From the moment we enter the world, we learn to trust or to mistrust. Naked, we must rely on others to keep us warm. We are unable to stand like a new born horse or even to scuttle like an infant turtle. And for the first couple of years, we are absolutely dependent on a breast or its substitute to sustain our lives.

Erikson sees the first demonstrations of social trust in the case of babies' feeding, the depth of their sleep, and the relaxation of their bowels. Infants' first social achievement is their ability to permit their mothers to go out of sight without excessive anxiety or rage. The babies have then learned to trust an inner consistency in themselves and a predictability in the sameness and continuity of their mothers' behavior. These are the lessons they have to learn, and the endlessly engrossing game of peek-a-boo is one of their exercises.

In short, our first task in life—during the first eighteen months or so—is to learn to trust another as well as our own bodies, and to be able to have our urges satisfied. When there is mutuality between mother and child, what is achieved is a basic trust and the ability to get, receive, and accept. Simultaneously, we develop a sense of giving, in the same way that the mother gives. The degree of trust established is not based on the absolute quantity of food or even demonstrations of love, but on the quality of the maternal relationship.

Erikson, on whose notion of stages most of this chapter is based, points out that infants are able to undergo a great deal of frustration if that frustration is followed by an experience of continuity and coherence, and if the infant learns to fit this pattern into a strong conviction of what Erikson calls "belongingness." Parents are able to guide their children alternately by permission and prohibition, but more importantly, they must be able to convey to them the deep belief that what they are doing has a meaning, endurance, and coherence. Neurosis does not come from frustration per se, but from frustration that is felt to be arbitrary and meaningless. Here, as elsewhere, what parents actually do is not as important as the spirit in which things are done. The range of child rearing practices can vary enormously and is affected by both fads and important changes in the society and environment. What children need to learn, however, is the sense that they belong to a family unit and that what they have experienced fits into a larger pattern of familial and social meaning.

The issues surrounding feeding are discussed in the chapter on Eating, but we may emphasize here that it is important to allow babies to develop and retain a pleasure in eating. This is done by creating experiences in which parents and children participate enjoyably. The babies are encouraged to give up the breast or bottle at seven or nine months (perhaps later, if there are significant circumstances prevailing for mother or child), and to feed themselves at ten to fourteen months. When a baby repeatedly spits up, refuses food, or eats very little, it is necessary to check with a pediatrician. If physical allergies or gastrointestinal or nervous defects are not present, then the relationship between child and parent during feeding needs to be examined. As long as the food is nourishing, and the necessary caloric intake is ensured and not exceeded exorbitantly, it really does not matter what is eaten or how much or how often.

The same is true for sleep. Babies not only have different digestive needs, but they vary in their sleeping cycles. (This will be discussed in the chapter on Sleeping.) If there is no physiological disturbance, emotional factors in sleep disturbance need to be explored. But there are really no fixed quantities or prescribed periods of sleep for all babies. What is important is that the well-being of all concerned, baby and the rest of the family, be taken into account. Sensitivity and permissiveness are necessary, but not sufficient without structure. And structure is related to the family system as well as to cultural expectations and requirements.

Babies do need to be held and spoken to. They require response from others. Harry Stack Sullivan believed that if this response is anxiety, the infant will also experience anxiety. As soon as the baby learns to talk—even by learning that the accidental "da" or "ma" gets a significant response from adults—he or she is making the transition into childhood.

In the chapter on Behavior Disturbances, we will discuss childhood schizophrenia and autism. The absence of trust, however, is what is relevant to these conditions even when an organic or physical factor is present.

Early Childhood   During the first half of this period, from eighteen months to three and a half years, the child becomes socialized. He or she becomes human. Erikson sees the second task of life which faces all of us during this time as learning when to let go and when to hold on. This is the first effort to emancipate the self from parents and adults in general. The use and coordination of the muscles has permitted the beginning of autonomy. This is especially true of the sphincter muscle. There is a pressure from within to expel—to let go—and from our parents about how, when, and where. But for the first time in our lives we have something to say about the matter. We can say no, hold on, and know what is me and mine. We have the power to control our bodies, as well as to exert control over others.

It is at this stage that certain tendencies are laid down for later life. How successfully we emerge from this stage will partly determine how cooperative or rebellious we will be in later life, how much we will value our self-expression, or how much we will strive to suppress it. If our first attempts at self-control meet with success and approval, we have achieved our first sense of pride and good feeling about ourselves. If we are unsuccessful, we may grow up prone to doubt and shame.

If the relationship with parents is benign during this period because they themselves have resolved their own issues of autonomy, shame, and doubt, then the pattern of their holding on can become one of caring, of having and holding in a positive sense. If this period is fraught with tension and frustration, the pattern may become one of stubborn withholding and of obsessive conflict over control. Again, the issue is mutual regulation and respect between parent and child. How this pertains to toilet training will be discussed in the chapter on Eating.

Shame is a powerful and common weapon that parents and society use to keep a child in line, although it may have harmful results. It always involves some degree of humiliation and cruelty because it generates guilt and implies inadequacy, smallness, badness, and dirtiness. Even when shame seems to work as a disciplining device, the child's resultant rage and frustration is directed against others or back on the self, often in indirect and destructive ways. A child needs to be encouraged to be independent and to be protected against irrational doubt and shame.

A secure parent will expect the inevitable testing by the child and be circumspect about the process. Testing with bites and "no's" and smearing as well as withholding behavior will reappear, magnified, in adolescence. But much of it will have already been resolved if both parent and child have learned to cooperate at this earlier stage.

Perhaps the most important achievement of early childhood is the acquisition of speech. Without language, children are mentally and emotionally handicapped and will experience grave difficulties in mastering later tasks. Difficulties in learning to read, for example, are often related to language difficulties. There is a clear relation between intelligence and language ability, so that children who have difficulty in expressing themselves and in being able to characterize their experience verbally will suffer difficulties in all sorts of mental and social situations.

Children do not begin to learn real language before eighteen months, but if by two years a child has no words, professional help should be sought. Some famous and prodigiously intelligent people—Einstein and Dr. Samuel Johnson, for example—were delayed in learning to talk, but it is best not to take a chance. Speech therapy is a large field and can treat many speech disorders quite effectively. The range of disorders, however, is quite vast. It extends from problems in voice (pitch and loudness) and articulation (proper pronunciation of sounds) to delayed speech and stuttering. The first two have not been shown to be related to emotional problems, and often disappear by themselves by age seven or eight. The last two can be caused by several factors.

Delayed speech can be due to organic, physiological factors like deafness, mental retardation, or some defect in the brain. It can also be a symptom of a serious mental disorder like infant autism. (See section in Behavior Disturbances.) It is imperative to detect these difficulties early and to enlist the aid of a professional who can help relieve part of the problem.

Delayed acquisition of speech can also be due to emotional or environmental causes. Children should be spoken to. It is known that the size of a child's vocabulary is affected by how often he or she is spoken to. More important, children learn to talk from hearing other people talk and from being responded to when they themselves begin. If a child's experience of adult speech is limited, he or she will very likely have difficulty in learning. Immature or delayed speech can also be due to the parents' need to infantilize their child. If a mother is threatened by her child's maturation, she will discourage or at least fail to encourage such signs of emotional growth as speech. In this case, family therapy may prove effective.

Because a child learns to talk at about the same time he or she is toilet trained, difficulties in language can represent a displacement of difficulties associated with anal functions. Both involve the process of letting go and of presenting a product to other people. Finally, an emotional trauma can cause difficulties in speech. The birth of a brother or sister or some family difficulty can cause the child to feel guilty or ashamed of his or her feelings and consequently to inhibit their expression in language. In this case, speech therapy along with family counseling is recommended.

Stuttering is a rather common speech disorder. Approximately 1% of the population suffers from it, although perhaps

40% of stutterers outgrow it. The first onset of stuttering commonly occurs between four and six years of age. Boys are more likely to develop this problem than girls, and stuttering tends to run in families. There are many theories that try to explain stuttering, but none of them is really convincing. There are, most likely, a number of factors that can result in this difficulty. Although it is not clear that stuttering is caused by emotional disorder, the fact that a child stutters can make him or her feel inferior, incompetent, and different.

Stuttering, unless it is severe, is only an annoyance. Most often it becomes serious only because the child and his or her parents think it so. The best approach to take with a stutterer is patience and understanding. Don't tell children not to stutter. It won't help, and they don't want to do it any more than you want them to. If the child asks about the stuttering, it is honest to admit that you've noticed it, but that it doesn't seem to be that important a difficulty. It is a good idea, however, to think about whether a particular situation provokes or aggravates stuttering. If excitement, fear of punishment, or exhaustion is associated with stuttering, try to eliminate these situations. On the whole, it is a good idea to allow the child to become less self-conscious—about his or her speech and behavior in general. If a household is tense or bound by too many rules, it can't hurt to try relaxing some of them.

Pre-school Years

The second half of the early childhood period—roughly from three and a half to five and a half years of age—has been designated by the Freudians as the phallic stage. Sullivan describes it as the juvenile epoch. These are the pre-school years when children literally run loose, trying out and developing their young muscles. It is here that the process of civilizing, begun in the first half of childhood, actually takes place. The child is now sensing his or her power and can choose between cooperation and competition. He or she is fully ambulatory and full of energy and increased mental powers. What to do with this mobility, energy, and thinking becomes the task of the child as well as of the parents. (The problem of the hyperactive child will be discussed in the chapter on Behavior Disturbances.)

Our society has traditionally encouraged, or at least permitted, aggression in the male child of this age: he may learn to compete and be intrusive. The little girl, on the other hand, has traditionally been taught to be more indirect or inhibited in her competitiveness and therefore to attract and to be endearing. Erikson sees the life task at this stage as learning initiative. If the stage is unsuccessful, the child may be beset with guilt. Consequently, the mores of our society have traditionally engendered considerably more guilt in women, for they have been far less rewarded for showing initiative. This explanation is an oversimplification, of course, since it is often difficult to tell the difference between aggressive competition and initiative, particularly when the rivalry is with older siblings or more powerful adults.

The problem for the child of this age is to acquire the initiative to undertake, plan, and work at a task and to learn a sense of moral responsibility. He or she needs to comprehend the institutions, functions, and roles of the culture which permit the child's active participation. Here he or she gains pleasure in utilizing his or her body, accomplishment in wielding tools and in manipulating toys, and satisfaction in caring for those who are smaller and weaker.

Only too often, however, the child "overlearns" by developing a superego, his or her own internalized parent, that is harsher and more tyrannical than the real ones. He or she becomes over-controlled and over-constricted, filled with repressed hatred and guilt. The literal need to kill off the father and possess the mother for boys, and the literal need for girls to fuse with and take over the mother, now begin to be translated into a symbolic or figurative necessity extending throughout adolescence. If and only if these needs are resolved can children achieve a sense of pleasure and pride in their own identity and sexuality.

Again, as in every stage, what is required is a mutual regulation. In childhood and adolesence, this calls for cooperation between parent and child. Since this task requires resolution of these issues and a sense of security in the parent— not all that frequent an occurrence—the resolution usually extends well into early adulthood and beyond.

One of the most disheartening phenomena is the failure of the parents to resolve their own needs for dependence and autonomy, thus causing a similar failure of resolution in their children. The cycle of neurotic and self-destructive behavior is thus repeated from generation to generation. We are strongly convinced, as a result of our experience, that counseling or psychotherapy in general is extremely helpful for most people at some time in their lives. Often the harsh conflicts that arise in families are appropriate occasions for parents to come to some understanding of their own unresolved needs and conflicts. Societal values and styles of child rearing may be at fault, but the most appropriate place for individuals to begin to gain such understanding is in their own lives.

Having gotten through this stage, the child has pretty much passed through the most important formative years.

His or her success at later stages will, to a large extent, be made possible by what the child has become as he or she leaves early childhood. Although the child's innate temperament has played a part here, by far the greatest influence is the treatment he or she has received at the hands of his or her parents. This places an enormous burden of responsibility on parents, and it is no wonder that, knowing this, some feel overwhelmed with the seriousness of the task of parenting.

Modern parents are blessed or cursed by the proliferation of child rearing experts and the advice they give. Styles of child rearing, however, undergo enormous changes, and one book on how to raise a child may very well contradict another published twenty years earlier. For example, in 1920 almost all published advice recommended rigid feeding schedules for infants, while in 1948, almost all recommended self-demand schedules. There have been similar fads concerning such issues as thumb-sucking and breast feeding. Surely, those at both extremes of each issue cannot be as emphatically correct as they claim.

It must also be recognized that parents have been raising children for thousands of years and that children have been growing up relatively healthy. Barring serious deprivation or real trauma, children can adapt to a wide range of child rearing styles. Within limits, no conclusive relation has been demonstrated between the future personality of the child and any of a number of moderate child rearing practices. The issue is not really such specific decisions as whether or not to breast feed or to encourage infant nudity, but a more general tone and attitude in child rearing. Generally speaking, parents who are anxious and strict about eating habits will be the same about their child's sexuality and aggression. It is this larger, encompassing attitude which affects what course a child's emotional development will take.

Of course, severe deprivation, inconsistency, unreliability, and punitiveness will confuse and stunt a child, but within limits, a moderate range of practices will enable a child to grow up healthy. There are really three factors to consider in this matter: the child's natural temperament, the personality and habits of the parents, and the values and demands of the society. Parents, unless they are under great pressure or are emotionally disturbed themselves, are pretty good judges of these three factors. Parents can rather confidently trust their own instincts, affection, and knowledge of their children. Experts may provide guidelines, but the variety in children, in the family structure, and in the roles into which a child can be expected to grow is great. Parents do best when they do what they and their culture believe is right, and when this is done in a relaxed and anxiety-free manner.

Of course, neurotic parents are more likely to raise neurotic children, and if parents are confused and baffled by their tasks, specific professional advice may be sought. There is no substitute for love, attention, and concern for the child's welfare, coupled with rational, consistent, and considered values.

The School Years

Freud labeled the period from ages five or six to puberty as the latency period. He believed that sexual and aggressive urges are relatively repressed during this time and break out in full force during adolescence. Any alert observer of children this age, however, will note that neither sexuality nor aggression is fully repressed or even suppressed. It is not so much that these drives lie dormant, as that children are more constrained by family, society, and school from manifesting this behavior. Compared to adolescents, children of this age are also less able to act on their drives.

Erikson sees this stage as a most decisive one. Here the child develops a sense of industry and learns to learn, work, and produce. The child learns from people other than his or her parents—from school, peers, older children, and adults. He or she not only appreciates the value of work and productivity, but if encouraged, thrives on it and feels incomplete in its absence.

The "latency" child is open to learning skills, using tools and manipulating his or her environment. It is at this stage that learning disorders begin to show up. It is estimated that perhaps 75% of all child referrals for counseling involve learning disorders. They are more common and appear earlier in boys than in girls. While some boys begin to have difficulty in learning in early elementary school, girls more commonly experience this later, in late elementary school or junior high school. Such difficulties can be caused by a number of factors, from such organic causes as poor nutrition, sleep deprivation, or mental retardation, to more nearly emotional problems that stunt a child's ability to learn. Here, however, we are considering only the latter, which may be characterized by the term "underachievement," the discrepancy between ability and the level of achievement.

Generally speaking, there are several preconditions for successful learning that are part of the child's larger emotional development. A disruption in this development may be symptomized as a slowness or inability to learn. Basically, for a child to learn effectively, his or her early interest in the world must not have been damaged. To a great extent, the quality of this interest depends on the handling the child has received from his or her caretaker, usually the mother, before the age of two. If the world (which for the most part is the mother) is basically friendly, responsive, and predictable, the child will naturally look out to it both to secure gratification and to satisfy natural urges for mastery and comprehension. Deprived, harsh, or inconsistent early experience will, however, stunt these urges. In addition, at about this age, the child makes the transition from passivity to activity, from being acted upon to the sense that he or she can positively affect his or her environment. This is partly accomplished through imitation and identification with those around the child.

At around the age of two, the child becomes curious about the world. Later, he or she begins to ask questions, sometimes unceasingly, about what seem to be unfathomable mysteries—questions about nature, society, sex. This is a natural and healthy development, but if it is met with irritation and embarrassment, the child may learn not only to stop asking questions, but also to stop wondering about the world in general. Also at this stage, intellectual curiosity, along with almost everything else, becomes associated with aggression. Now the child may have a tendency to show off and to engage in a kind of intellectual exhibitionism. The parent is faced with two tasks at this point: to encourage and foster curiosity and intellectual mastery and also to allow the child to develop a sense of self-gratification and self-appreciation. If the child becomes too dependent on parental approval, he or she may have difficulty in developing a sense of initiative and self-evaluation.

Learning disorders, once they develop, are best treated by professionals, often in conjunction with psychological counseling—particularly family therapy. But there are things parents can do to help assure that difficulties do not develop in the first place. A child's inability or refusal to function well in school may be due to difficulty in relating to authority. If discipline in the home has been irrational, punitive, or unnecessarily coercive, the child may respond to any show of authority with resistance and a sullen lack of cooperation. Similarly, academic achievement is an occasion for self-assertion, but if healthy aggression has been punished in the home, the child may avoid learning for fear of his or her own self-assertion. An inability or refusal to learn can also represent a fear of growing up or of the many consequences of competition.

Very frequently, children who do not learn well possess an ego ideal that does not contain the value of academic achievement. There may be cultural reasons behind this. Or the father may have subtle or overt anti-intellectual attitudes.

This has a particularly adverse effect on little girls. In this, the father is a figure at least as important as the mother for both boys and girls. If the father considers himself dull and stupid, and if the mother agrees with that estimate, children may well pick up clues about what is expected of them, or they may experience guilt or anxiety over having defeated their father in this area.

Sullivan called this stage pre-adolescence and saw it as critical from an interpersonal or social point of view. The child of this age can for the first time form real friendships and engage in a meaningful interchange with a peer. The chum, as Sullivan called him or her, permits the child to validate his or her innermost feelings and to form hypotheses about the self, others, and the world. And it is this consensual validation that allows him or her to leave childhood for the child-adult era of adolescence.

Adolescence

Perhaps the most trying and confusing time of our lives is adolescence. We are propelled from childhood into a half-way world that is neither childhood nor adulthood by the revolutionary changes that go on in our bodies, by the expectations of society, and by the very fact of our having entered the turbulent teens. We say propelled, for few of us slide in easily, and many of us are dragged in screaming, kicking, and protesting. It is not unlike being born again.

It is a wild and crazy age. One moment we are fifteen going on thirty-five, expressing the wisdom and sensitivity of a mature adult. The next, we are silly or engaged in the tantrum behavior of a pre-school child. Our moods, our urges, our ideas about ourselves and our world undergo tempestuous and wildly veering changes. We want the car keys, booze, and sex, but we're just as apt to whine, "I'm only a kid." We're excited but frightened by our new sexual powers. Although not taken seriously, we are coolly (or hotly) appraised by our elders for our sexuality and attractiveness. Gawky, pimply, nubile, and sleek all at the same time.

"Grow up already!" We are supposed to know who we are and who we will become. Yet we are not sure of anything—even of our sexual identity. In the past and with primitive people, rites of passage have been celebrated to formalize the transition from childhood into adulthood and to prepare for the passage. We can recognize residues of such rites of passage in gang and group behavior. There are also vestigial signs in Confirmation and Bar and Bas Mitzvah, but these are vestigial indeed. Instead of the proud statement, "Today I am a man," or "Today I am a woman," we hear the joke, "Today I am a fountain pen." Funny, perhaps, because of the popularity of the gift for the fledgling adult. But the pen signifies the expectations for the teen-ager: no more free ride. Study. Prepare yourself for life and for a career.

And study we must, if we are to compete successfully for the good job, the apprenticeship, or for the college slot that will give us a chance to hold our own in the adult world. At the same time, we are struggling to clarify who we are physically, sexually, and socially. In competition with the exhortation to study is the demand from our friends to have a good time. We are pulled by our parents, by our peers. Which way to go? Often, both ways and neither way at the same time.

Schizophrenia was originally called *dementia praecox,* or premature insanity. It occurs most frequently at puberty and in late adolescence at about the time we graduate from school and face the world of work, college, or marriage. Extreme depression in adolescence or withdrawal from the familial or social world are often the signs of such a disturbance and should be looked into. (See the discussion of schizophrenia in the chapter on Behavior Disturbances.)

As of 1975, suicide was the second leading cause of death among those aged fifteen to twenty-five. Its rate has almost doubled in the last decade, and is increasing at a faster rate for adolescents than for any other age group. In adults, suicide has been directly linked to the earlier experience of depression and hopelessness. It has been suggested that the rise in teen-age pregnancies and juvenile delinquency may be other indices of serious depression. (See the discussion of depression in the chapter on Behavior Disturbances.)

As Erikson sees this stage, the adolescent faces the task of connecting the roles and skills cultivated earlier with the requirements of adulthood—particularly occupational demands. In their continued search for continuity and sameness, adolescents have to again wage many of the struggles of earlier years. Now is the time for consolidation, just as late adulthood is the time for integration. The struggle is particularly keen, as Freud first pointed out, because of the new, exciting, perplexing, and terrifying genital role. This is the time of the identity crisis. If it is not resolved—and often the resolution is very delayed or incomplete—then role confusion follows.

Because the quest for identity is so urgent, adolescents strive mightily to identify with their peers. Sullivan's point that consensual validation is what keeps us sane is particularly true in this age. Sameness is so important that identification with the group—their language, tastes, dress, manner, behavior (no matter how erratic or bizarre)—becomes all-important. Those who are different in appearance, thinking, and behavior are distrusted and even hated. The older generation can be particular threats. At the same time, anyone with an ideology, a cause, or even a charismatic style can be idolized. The adolescent mind, Erikson points out, has not yet attained the ethics of adulthood; the means or even the style seems to justify the end. Adolescence can be a very dangerous time for the young person, as well as for society.

| Juvenile Delinquency | Adolescence also gives rise to the baffling problem of juvenile delinquency. We are all aware of how pervasive this problem is becoming. Once thought to be confined to lower socio-economic groups in cities, it now includes some of the most privileged young people in the wealthiest of suburbs. Statistics on the subject are unreliable, since they depend to a great extent on police enforcement and reporting, which in turn is determined by local community customs. Still, rates are probably increasing, and the violence of some delinquent actions is horrifying. Juvenile delinquency is not a psychological or medical term, but a legal one, and it includes an enormous range of infractions, from truancy and chronic disobedience to torture and murder. It is the authors' opinion that although psychology can bring many insights to bear on this problem, juvenile delinquency is primarily a social problem. Many, perhaps all, delinquents can be treated, but the causes for their anti-social behavior—the unreasonable lack of opportunity or the lack of a cohesive family—are the real problems to be solved. |

In trying to understand juvenile delinquency, we can still employ a three-fold classification made over thirty years ago. The first type of juvenile delinquents are the "socially delinquent." These are young people whose delinquency is in some ways socially adaptive and calculated to achieve a desired goal. Typical of poor, inner city delinquents, it stems from the inability of these young people to take advantage of the usual ways society offers to attain money, prestige, and success. Values of hard work, thrift, and discipline do not pay off in such sub-cultures, so there is no reason to act under their guidance. Instead, theft, and aggression are the most visible ways of getting what everyone needs. Such behavior is not so much anti-social as determined by the values and opportunities of a particular sub-culture. There are, of course, psychological aspects of this phenomenon, but the primary issues are social, economic, and political.

The second type are the "emotionally disturbed." These are young people who resort to crime as a way of fulfilling basically neurotic needs. Certain kinds of anti-social behavior that seem highly symbolic, like setting fires (pyromania), rape, or compulsive theft (kleptomania), serve to satisfy needs that are embedded deeply in the delinquent's personality. Frequently, such crime is committed for the primary purpose of being caught and punished. Deep-seated and infantile guilt seems to be the basis of such behavior, and although violence seems directed at society at large, it is really used to punish the self. It may also be a way of getting at parental figures, either to hurt them or to gain some measure of attention.

The third type of juvenile delinquents are the "unsocialized aggressive." These are delinquents who commit crimes for no symbolic purpose, but who are simply unable to control their impulses when they are frustrated. The normal inner controls most of us have developed are lacking or defective in these young people. Often they experience large amounts of aggression and instinctively turn it outward onto the society as a whole, experiencing relatively low levels of anxiety and guilt. Therapy with these young people is consequently difficult.

In addition, in their early development these delinquents have not formed strong identifications with adequate ego ideals. Often fathers were not reliably present in childhood. Instead, they tended to form strong attachments with gang members who display what seem to be admirable toughness and savvy. Such delinquents do not feel much empathy with victims, but identify with brutalizers. Their attacks are frequently against members of their own sub-culture. Their conscience, or superego, is defective, and they are unable to reward themselves for discipline, control, and hard work, and, as we have already said, have not incorporated adequate ego ideals. They are unable to tolerate even minimal levels of frustration and anxiety and cannot delay gratification. All these characteristics mutually affect each other and increase the urgency to engage in criminal and anti-social behavior.

In certain ways, we can say that for many of these young people, the world, with its values and ways of doing things, simply does not make sense. This can be true for deprived young people who have never experienced reward for discipline and hard work, as well as for indulged youngsters who have experienced indiscriminate reward. For both, there is no reason for self-control and discipline. Finally, some delinquents engage in criminal activity as a way of acting out their parents' own vicarious needs and fantasies. Parents of such children may on the surface disapprove of such behavior and even seem to be shocked at it, but unconsciously approve of and are deeply gratified by the lawlessness of their children. In such cases, psychological treatment would necessarily include family therapy.

Adolescence is an enormously trying time for parents and teen-agers. Both want to hold on and to let go. Mutual regulation is as important at this age as at any other. When children are about to leave home, the task for the adolescents is to consolidate their own individual identities and to establish their own families, what Gail Sheehy calls the "uprooting passage." The corresponding task for the parents is to allow this to happen—to encourage it, in fact. If parents handle this poorly, the adolescents become blocked in their development. And if this crisis is handled poorly, the parents themselves may be blocked in handling their own mid-adult phase.

Teen-age behavior can be so extreme that at times it is difficult to distinguish it from psychotic behavior. The need to test the self, parents, and society is very strong. Support and validation from peer groups are essential. What is needed is understanding and communication with adults—not necessarily approval. In fact, the teen-ager can tolerate and even seek boundaries, limitations, and mores, provided they are rational, sincere, and direct. What is not tolerated by adolescents is hypocrisy and arbitrary restrictions.

Positive peer relationships, social and physical activity have been identified as essential to adolescent competency. The mutual task of adolescent and parent, as well as of society, is to foster identity and roles with clear steps to attain this goal. Unfortunately, because the next task of development—intimacy—is so difficult in our society, many if not most people remain fixated at an adolescent level. If, however, adolescents can be helped by their prior developmental tasks, they have a considerable amount going for them. That is to say, the adolescent needs to feel nourished and nourishing, to be permitted and encouraged to have a sense of autonomy, and to be given opportunities for initiative and a chance to exercise industry.

Much of this, unfortunately, is restricted for teen-agers. Ghetto youths and, perhaps, affluent adolescents, suffer a dearth of such opportunities. No wonder then that so much of delinquency occurs among this jobless group when goals are missing. But it is this very same age group that is filled with energy and vitality. Adolescents crave to fit in and belong. They can exercise a fierce loyalty and an intense idealism. It is, therefore, the role of family, institutions, and society to provide them with suitable ideals, roles, and opportunities.

Late, Late Adolescence

The period from the late teens into the early twenties is really, for most, an extension of adolescence. For some it ends early, and the demands of an early marriage, parenthood, and a career may hasten it, but for many, the nature of our institutions prolongs adolescence. The umbilical cord has been stretched but has not been severed. There may be a physical but no psychological separation. In this period, we are faced with making decisions or with coping with those made for us. The pattern is not so clearly fixed. We have graduated from school or have left it. Job, training, college, our own place to live, marriage—all these choices face us.

Sheehy sees this time as one of conflict between seeking ourselves and merging with others for strength, support, and a substitute for the family. But this stage can be looked at as a struggle between independence and commitment. The prior struggles of letting go and holding on are pertinent here, but in a way that implies social and personal responsibilities and obligations never before encountered. Up to this time, autonomy meant a relationship within the family complex or rebellion against it. Now it means true independence in the sense of fending for oneself in the larger world.

Commitment is a voluntary personal involvement with another person or thing. We are willing to enter into a contract over a long period of time in which we promise to deliver and expect to receive. This may be a relationship, a job, a study, a life style, and so on. Many of us are afraid of commitment because we fear losing our freedom. We really are afraid of losing our childhood. We may like to keep "doing our thing" without having to feel responsible. When one chooses to be taken care of by escaping into a marriage, by espousing the security of an ideology or cult, or by picking a strong man as in a totalitarian philosophy or government (what Fromm called the "escape from freedom"), we are really shirking commitment—a mutual contract—for a way out.

Many relationships, careers, and allegiances are only temporary arrangements. They frequently survive out of convenience, denial, or our belief that we are incapable of durable, stable commitment. Such a lack of belief in ourselves most often comes from our previous failure to resolve the dilemma of getting and giving, of taking and sharing—all of which are essential to a secure sense of identity. But if we have not resolved these issues, or if the resolution is incomplete, we are unable to cope adequately with adulthood and true intimacy. The failure of our cooperative family enterprise is thus recapitulated in the next generation.

Many people never resolve these issues, and indeed society at large seems to tolerate such a situation and even to encourage it. Often, therefore, it takes a serious crisis to convince us that we need help. But even if we manage to evade such a state of affairs, a sense of frustration in our adult roles or a feeling of superficiality in our relations may indicate that we might profit from psychotherapy or a guided encounter group. (See the chapter on Change.)

Adulthood — The Twenties

Erikson sees early adulthood as the stage when we wrestle with the issues of intimacy and isolation. A young adult, if he or she has successfully resolved the crisis of his or her own identity, is now eager to fuse it with others. This is the need for intimacy, which involves the ability to commit oneself to relationships. To do this, one must be able to develop the personal strength and ethical sense to abide by these commitments, to be willing to undergo appropriate sacrifices, and to accept less than perfect situations. If, however, the young adult has not previously developed a sufficiently strong sense of his or her own identity, commitment may be avoided, and this can lead to a life of isolation, loneliness, and self-absorption.

The eagerness of fusion with others may be there, but the fear of ego loss, of our identity being blurred or swallowed up, is one of the greatest terrors. The resolution of identity is hardly ever achieved in adolescence. In fact, the increasingly complex quest for identity is a life-long search. When it dies down or disappears, we have conceded the struggle. We are more dying than living—we have become old.

If we have had fortuitous, mutually respectful experiences during the first stages of our lives, or if we have been fortunate enough to resolve the interpersonal and psychosexual issues during adolescence, we are ready to accept intimacy. Quite a small word, that "if," but quite a big proposition indeed. Yet when we are ready to relate intimately, we are said to be mature.

Sheehy writes of the two impulses that are at work during the twenties: the need to merge and the need to explore and experiment. But we do not see these as being in necessary conflict. It is only when they are at odds that the intimacy—isolation dilemma becomes crucial. Affiliating with another, whether it be with a lover, spouse, mentor, or company, may, however, be less a matter of an intimate merger than a masking of the desire for self-centered seeking or the fear of it. Instead of painstakingly seeking an adequate resolution to this dilemma, we throw ourselves into a search for the absolute truth, the final security.

We are in such a quandary because we have not distinguished between what is rationally selfish and what is irrationally self-centered. The first is a willingness and a courage to identify what our needs are and how they relate to those of our intimates and our society—an ability to pursue them with persistent and committed energy. The second is a narcissistic, tenacious grasping at our childhood illusions.

It is not easy to discriminate between what appears to be a necessary preparation for the rest of life and an avoidance of intimate commitment. It would seem to make eminent sense to lay a foundation for career and financial solvency, to get established, to make our mark, and to set our dreams. And it would seem to make sense for us to explore and experiment, sample and taste, before we settle down. Even when either approach is not an avoidance orientation, it can become set and a self-perpetuating, limiting syndrome. It is in the twenties that the character disorders assume a prominence and can become a life style, although they are often disguised by seeming to be rational for that particular time. (See the discussion on character disorders in the chapter on Behavior Disturbances.)

A typical dream is to work extremely hard, go to church on Sundays, establish a niche, buy a home in the suburbs, have 2.5 children, and live happily ever after. In the process, the possibilities for intimacy and self-actualization have been lost. Only later do we perceive our lives as stagnant and ourselves as despairing. The struggle is so vigorous that even the isolation accompanying it is not fully noticed. There is no time (and it is too scary) to stop and think. Another typical pursuit is the restless search for thrills and experience, only to discover with a rude shock in the thirties that we have had little or no preparation to live our lives with intimacy and integrity from then on.

But if the industry, mergers, mentors, and seeking of the twenties are viewed and experienced as committed, intimate interactions—a cooperative enterprise—the intimacy–isolation trap need not be set. We then will have a flexibility to reorient, if not renew, our commitments later on. Rather than a resentful feeling of being trapped in a job, marriage, or life style, the alternatives may be rationally considered and acted upon. As Sheehy puts it, we tend to overemphasize the "should's" of the twenties—the necessities required by job, relationship, responsibilities, and experimentation. Nothing is more important at this period than determining what we want and what we can accomplish. And this does not mean letting the devil take the hindmost. What we want and can have has everything to do with an intimate, sharing interaction with others.

The Thirties

What we are calling the thirties, the "seasoning" era, can really extend from the twenties into the early forties. Numbers, however, have a symbolic significance—even a magic—for us.

Thirty, the big "three-oh," signifies to many that we are no longer young, certainly not kids anymore. We can no longer get by so easily on charm, youth, ability, and dreams. The recognition is inescapable that we are mortal, that we have only a certain number of years to live, and that our energy and opportunities are not unlimited. All around us are younger, more energetic and optimistic people. We feel we have got to carve out a career or vocation, build a family and social network, and establish ourselves in the community.

Sheehy sees this age as a building phase, a time to put down roots and send out new shoots. Now is the time we make the major investment in the home, plan the children's education, and commit ourselves to our work. Maybe. It is also a time for reappraisal. Just what have we accomplished so far? We may have thought we would have earned our first million by now, or written that book, broken seventy on the golf links, figured out the solution to a happy life with family and friends, or worked out the perfect marriage. Instead, we now may suffer a vague or acute malaise about any or all of our attainments. It is a time when we may rush for a second chance, change our jobs, and leave our marriage. Or we may get married and quickly start having children. It is often a time when we sink into a depression or when the hidden life-long depression catches up with us. External reality is now too discrepant with our cherished illusions.

Thousands of thirty, fifty, and seventy year old people were asked what factors they perceived as affecting the quality of their lives. Almost all reported that their needs should be well met. More than 95% stated that health and personal safety were very important. The other two factors that more than 80% of each age group reported as important were having and raising children and understanding themselves. Additionally, two other important factors were a close relationship with a spouse and marital comfort. Work was important to 90% of the men and 85% of the thirty year old women. Seventy percent of the men and 80% of the women of all three ages stated that close friends were important to the quality of their life.

Erikson sees this stage as the one concerned with generativity and stagnation. That is to say, the mature individual needs to be needed, as well as to provide care, encouragement, and guidance to others. Maturity may specifically signify procreating the species, thereby satisfying our need to be productive and creative, to leave our mark, to pass something of ourselves on to others. Or it may more generally be expressed in any of the creative products of our teaching or training. It may be the proud result of our thinking, labor, or evolution of our artistic abilities.

There are those of us, however, who see ourselves as our own children. We focus, at first languorously and then frenetically, but always indulgently, on ourselves. We may do this even when we appear to be generative or productive by having children or producing an endless stream of products or accomplishments. But this is being prolific rather than generative. We have not separated the production from ourselves, and so we want to hold on to it and not let go. We are really not that different from the babies who cherish and want to hold on to their feces. But even babies, in sudden bursts of generosity and maturity, may present them to us as a gift. So too, generativity requires the generosity and maturity of giving to others in a non-usurious fashion.

Otherwise we stagnate. The thirties, and even the twenties for many, present us with existential issues: what is life all about? Is everything futile? Could I have been someone—at least a contender? Do I make a difference in this world? For most, the answer to this life-long quest for uniqueness is in our relationship with others. The antidote to a sense of stagnation is generativity, productivity, and creativity in any or all of their senses: to give and to get, to take and to let go, to make and to share.

The Forties

Insofar as biological and institutional factors are concerned, middle age begins in the mid- and late thirties. But here too there is a magic to numbers. Whereas the big three-oh connotes to us that we are no longer young, the big four-oh tells the whole world the news. We are officially middle-aged, no matter how we fight and kick to deny it, no matter what fashion we adopt, no matter what bleaches, preparations, and antics we pursue. Jack Benny (and legions of others) have tried to stop the clock psychologically at thirty-nine. We valiantly rationalize that life begins at forty. So we shall discuss the forties as the middle age for purposes of concreteness, while agreeing that the first half of middle age extends from the late thirties through the early fifties.

We are now likely to be parents—maybe even grandparents—and all but a few of us have withdrawn gracefully or otherwise from frenetically competing in sports, recreation, dress, and career. We have made it or we haven't. Even if we still push to make it, it is with focused goals, rather than with the vague, grandiose sense that the world is our oyster. Anatomically as well as psychologically we are lagging, sagging, and bagging. If we haven't done our reappraisal, we now plunge in with a vengeance. If we are ever going to start our own business or have our affair, now is the time. Of course, if our children are still young, if success is still tugging at us, if there are still bills to be paid, and if we haven't resolved the generativity–stagnation issue, we may delay the last fling or miss the boat entirely.

If we have done our personal and interpersonal work relatively successfully by now, we settle down into a mellow period of enjoying life while still taking satisfaction in our vigor, relatively youthful attractiveness, and hard-earned status, money, and power.

The forties, early mid-life, is a period of both integration and transition. We are integrating the spiritual and philosophical meaning of our work, possessions, and position. Yet two forces tug at us. The first is what we have left undone and still need to complete. These are projects posed by our children, literal or figurative attainment of maturity, the goals of our ambitions and dreams, and the expectations of our families and society. The second force is the recognition of what life is all about—at least of what some of it has to offer. We are impatient to pluck and take a big appetizing bite out of it.

At early mid-age, therefore, we have reached the penultimate stage of maturity. We almost have a sense of our identity. Of course, we never complete that project until we resolve our integrity and what it means to be alive, and finally to die. In early middle age, lack of resolution often results in fear, indecisiveness, withdrawal, or impetuous acting out, usually against the self. There is no more propitious time to evaluate and take advantage of the kind of self-exploration that a therapist or peer group can offer. In both situations, but especially the latter, the forty-year-old usually has as much to offer as to receive. And this, in itself, is an integrating experience.

The Fifties

Later middle age, roughly the late forties through the fifties and even early sixties, is the period, as Gail Sheehy puts it, when we have gained our maximum influence. The average age of men in the upper echelons of business is fifty-four, and although forty to sixty-five year old Americans account for only one-quarter of the population, they earn more than half of the nation's income. At this age, we strive to hold on with our teeth and nails, to conserve or even begin to prematurely yearn for the good old days. If we have resolved, at least in part, our prior life tasks—our children have grown up and away, our jobs have been mastered and the challenges met or put aside, and we have accepted our biology and roots—we are ready for renewal, for new interests, or for attention to those we have neglected.

We have the choice of dwelling on the aches, pains, and disappointments of our bodies by thinking and acting old. We do this by emphasizing somatic illness and aggravating psychosomatic disorders. In reality, we are complaining, whining, and rebelling at the loss of the youth we never appreciated or used. We now refuse to accept it as passed. Or we have the choice of realizing what we will continue to have, including our sexuality, and using it wisely and meaningfully. An informed, interested, active person of this age does not decline significantly in most abilities, except for those requiring considerable strength, competition, and endurance. Now is the time for us to deploy our skills, talents, and knowledge differently. We can now act with greater subtlety, calmness, and even wisdom. It is a time to learn and relearn.

In short, later middle age provides an opportunity to taste the vintage years of life. If it is sour, if all that is available are the dregs of a dreary existence, then one has not accepted or coped with what has gone before. The consequent melancholy is tinged with despair. For this is the time when we either have begun to come to terms with our integrity or we begin to despair that existence has any meaning. We either proceed to our full maturity or surrender in an aged, enfeebled protest.

Late Adulthood — The Sixties and Beyond

When the actress Maureen Stapleton was being courted by the director-playwright George Abbot, who was in his eighties at the time, she rhapsodized about his prowess as a lover. Her older friend, Norma Crane, the silent movie star, wistfully inquired, "Does he have an older brother?" Aging is a state of mind.

We do get older. The 1970 census reported that 10% of the American population—or 20 million people—were over the age of sixty-five. The percentage had more than doubled since 1900, when it was only 4%. It is estimated that there will be more than 30 million in this age group by the year 2000. A child born in 1975 has a life expectancy of 72.4 years. Most adults who are in reasonably good health can expect to live into their eighties.

Unlike the vigorous octogenarian, George Abbot, older adults most often are neither seen nor see themselves in favorable terms. The stereotype has it that old age is a second childhood, old people are always sick, old people are rigid and fixed in their ideas, old people are helpless and hapless. This is untrue for most older people, but many do experience a decrease in visual and auditory acuity and in strength and vigor. But such physiological impairment is aggravated by society's lower evaluation, as well as by the real loss of loved ones, possessions, and roles.

Whenever the individual is unwilling or unable to use his or her intellectual and physical abilities in appropriate ways because of prejudice toward older people, retirement, serious illness, or loss of intimates, deterioration and "vegetation" are hastened. Somatization is thereby fostered and often becomes the primary way of relating to the self as well as to an interested other—in this case, a physician or nurse. Many older people exhibit a pronounced tendency to disengage, to reduce their levels of activity and involvement. While this may merely be an expression of entering another developmental phase, it often appears to be exaggerated in withdrawal phenomena. It is not surprising, therefore, that depression is common among older adults, often masked by physical symptoms. The suicide rate for elderly white males is four times that of the national average. The group over sixty-five constitutes 10% of the general population but 28% of mental hospital admissions.

Yet only 4% of the age group is placed in nursing homes. And many people who are in these homes do not have to be there. Rehabilitation programs set up to counteract the neglect, inactivity, and isolation of life in many of these homes produced striking results. Seventy-five percent achieved higher levels of independence and self-sufficiency, 14% achieved a measure of self-maintenance and self-employment, and 30% moved into the community under supervision and assistance. The concept of using small group residences has been tested and proved promising. This includes adequate food and shelter, medical care when needed, involvement with people of similar age and situation, a relatively independent style of living, continual intellectual and emotional stimulation, a sense of purpose, participatory activity in maintaining group living, and helping as well as being helped. Moreover, participation in groups containing young and old members in which both have something to give and to get, as in the extended families of prior times, seems to have positive results.

In old age it is more appropriate to emphasize self-actualization than productivity per se. Erikson sees the last developmental phase as the task of ego integrity versus despair. Only those who have taken care of things and other people and have adapted to the triumphs and disappointments of life can face this last stage. In the end, the task is to accept what one has been and where one has come from—one's parents and roots—to accept that one has had a meaningful effect on others as they have had on us. One's existence, then, seems not to have been meaningless. We can see ourselves as part of a continuity of what has gone before and will go on after us, and this recognition gives us some measure of integrity and the courage and strength to avoid despair. This final stage is the culmination of the process that begins in trust and ends in the faith that we each have meant something. And that is what our identity is finally all about.

Summary

Our entire life is a search for who we are. Lives pass through different stages, but the search for self is continuous. Although different aspects of our identities become problematic at various times, we are always dealing with ourselves and our relation to other people, to society, and finally to the world at large. The success of each stage is predicated on the completion of a previous one. If we fail to resolve one dilemma, our success at the next will be shakier. We never really finish with a stage. Its associated tasks and dilemmas keep reappearing in different forms throughout our lives.

The most important stage, primarily because it is the first and the one on which all the others are based, is infancy, where we learn the basic lesson of trust or mistrust. This issue primarily involves the process of eating—or taking in—with confidence, although other basic processes are also involved. Somewhat later in early childhood we have our first experience of socialization, which centers around the process of toilet training. Here we learn the reciprocal functions of holding in and letting go, cooperation and rebellion. Generally, we confront the stage of autonomy versus shame and doubt. In late childhood, we learn to solve the issue of initiative versus guilt. We become convinced at a very deep level of our basic competence and of whether or not we can balance our need for self-assertion with a concern for the feelings of others. In the school years, the issue is industry versus inferiority. We experience here the value of work and the satisfactions attached to it. We learn to master skills and learning.

With the onset of puberty, we enter that most turbulent and confusing age of adolescence, and the problem of identity becomes most urgent. Here we begin to think consciously about our person—self and how it fits into the family and the society at large. All the old issues of autonomy, industry, and the others reappear. If we are successful, we develop a deep and stable sense of identity. If we fail, we suffer for the rest of our lives from a nagging sense of role confusion. Late adolescence is a relatively new stage in terms of history and relates to the prolonged period before we truly enter adult life with all its responsibilities. Here we attempt to work out some kind of coordination between the dual needs for independence and for merging with another. Only if our identity is strong can we risk fusing it with another.

In early adulthood, we feel a need both to merge with another, to commit ourselves to a person or a career, and to experiment—to keep our options open. We can at this stage first experience a real intimacy, but we also face the possibility of a frightening isolation. In the thirties, we begin to consolidate our achievements and to look for new sources of satisfaction. We have set down our roots and we become interested in sending out new shoots. We have a sense of being adult and of our lives being finite in possibility. Having children becomes important at this stage, although this alternative can take a symbolic form for teachers and other creative people. The outcome of this stage is a sense of either generativity or stagnation.

By the forties, we and those around us are convinced that the first half of life is over. Those younger and more energetic are beginning to make their presence felt. We begin at this point to think about a transition to a different style of life. Now is the time to begin to take pleasure and satisfaction in our achievements and to look for alternative ways of using our energy. This process is continued into the fifties, when we begin to mellow and to savor our lives, to see the fruits of our labor mature, and to confront the problem of our mortality.

In late adulthood—from the sixties onward—when many of the previous possibilities that concerned us are no longer available, we turn inward and can pay attention to the project of self-actualization, of realizing our deepest sense of self in private and enduring satisfaction. Death is now something we must face, and we look back on our lives. If our lives have been good, if we have not squandered our possibilities or neglected them, we develop a profound sense of ego integrity. If our lives have been a disappointment, we suffer despair.

The preceding outline is a rough sketch. The stages we have discussed can be passed through quickly or they can be prolonged, but their order is fairly regular. The success of one stage depends on the previous one, and our energy and hopefulness come from having achieved a satisfactory resolution to the earlier stages. But all of it is part of the great stream of humanity of which we are a part. Our deep sense of our own humanity comes from our recognizing this fact.

2
Eating

Our nourishment begins before we are born—in a certain sense, even before we are conceived. Well nourished women have a much better chance of conceiving, carrying through term, and delivering healthy babies. The mother's eating habits during pregnancy are vital to the health of the fetus. We know that pregnant women who smoke cigarettes are much more likely to abort than those who do not. Even more tragic, women who are addicted to drugs often give birth to addicted babies. Less dramatic, but just as significant, is the pregnant woman's need for well-balanced meals, which may require vitamin and mineral supplements. The prospective mother is not only feeding herself, but another living organism as well. The hormonal and glandular changes that take place during pregnancy make appropriate nourishment crucial.

Cravings for strange foods such as pickles and ice cream in the middle of the night can be understood in the context of the nutritional flux that is taking place in the pregnant woman's body. She should therefore be supported and encouraged to know that she is not being hysterical but is responding to cues from her body. The actual choice of food to satisfy these bodily cues is, however, less physiologically than psychologically determined. Salt, iron, or carbohydrates may be a woman's immediate nutritional need, but since pregnant women are "supposed" to crave pickles and ice cream, that's often what they want. Cravings may be cues of nutritional deficiencies and ought to be discussed with the obstetrician. It is just as important, however, for the woman to experience the humor and excitement of all aspects of her pregnancy. If pickles and ice cream reinforce her sense of being special and of needing to be cared for and nourished—something to laugh over with her husband and friends—she is welcome to eat pickles and ice cream.

As a fetus, you were nourished entirely by the fluids and substances inside your mother's womb. The instant you were delivered into the world, you became a more active participant in nourishing yourself. Your tastes, your reactions to substances placed in your mouth, and your general physical and mental status determined, in part, what your food intake would be. Breast milk or formula was the first—and an extremely significant—determinant of your future food choices.

Breast Feeding

Breast milk contains all of and only those nutrients necessary for the baby. It also contains ingredients that promote digestion and immunity to disease. Nursing itself initiates the infant's first interaction with another person. At best, it establishes the model for all mutually gratifying relationships—gratifying physically as well as psychologically. Two beings, mother and child, are deeply engaged in a symbiotic, interdependent, pleasurable relationship. If the mother, for psychological or physical reasons, is averse to nursing, or if the infant is physiologically disinclined toward it, a negative model for taking in nourishment or, even more significantly, relating independently, may be established. We previously noted that the earliest feeding relationship with the mother may influence later attitudes toward taking everything, including love and affection, from others.

Cow's milk does cause some problems. A large portion of the child population cannot fully digest this fluid and may even have allergic reactions to it. Some people go so far as to argue that cow's milk is appropriate only for a calf, which has a different digestive system, body weight, and body composition than a child. Therefore, they argue, cow's milk is inappropriate for children. Whatever the truth of the matter, attitudes about mothering, milk, and feeding are so inextricably bound together that the source and quality of nourishment, as well as the rituals surrounding it, are an extremely important though often subjective choice.

Bottle milk or formula provides a different, artificial nutrient base, and it may contain ingredients that are not fully digestible. In addition, this feeding method is by nature a more mechanical and less humanizing activity. In 1978, the American Academy of Pediatrics formally recommended breast feeding as the preferred procedure. That is not to say that babies nursed on bottles will be less healthy. Millions of healthy children have been raised on the bottle.

The general rule for many such decisions about child rearing is that the actual procedure is less important than the attitude of the people involved. If a mother is nervous or resentful about breast feeding and feels better about bottle feeding, she should opt for the latter. A reluctant breast is certainly less desirable than a wholesome formula prescribed by a pediatrician. Much more important is the psychological status of the mother. A mother who is free to pursue activities of her choice may be more loving than another who chooses to breast feed but feels tied down by the feeding schedule. And a loving mother is the most important experience in a person's life. But, all things being equal, breast feeding is preferred.

The more critical issue, however, is that babies must be held, touched, and cradled to develop normally. If they are not, they may literally wither. The most acute and very rare form of this condition is called marasmus, from which a baby may die. Another extreme and unusual consequence may be infantile autism, although its precise causes are unclear. (See the discussion of autism and childhood schizophrenia in the chapter on Behavior Disturbances.)

Erikson theorized how the foundations for future trust or mistrust are laid down during early feeding. If we learn to take in with pleasure, we learn to trust. If we experience discomfort in how we are fed—we do not so easily take, we spit out—we become distrustful. Freud saw the entire adult personality as determined to a great extent by the child's first eating habits—the "oral" stage. There are various forms of orality, including smoking, chewing, and talking. More subtle but pervasive is dependence on others for literal or psychological nurturance. (See the discussion of infancy in the chapter on Stages.)

If a child has had a satisfying experience of early nourishment, he or she stands a good chance of avoiding later problems with eating. It has been estimated that fully 75% of eating problems in pre-school children begin during the first year of life. Generally speaking, the patterns and success of such later stages and crises as toilet training and discipline are strongly influenced by how successful and gratifying the child's first year of taking in nourishment has been.

Thumb Sucking

There is no clear evidence about the relationship between thumb sucking and the style or length of feeding. Thumb sucking is a frequent, even normal, phase of development which may provide real relaxation and peace to the child. There is no substantial evidence that it is a neurotic symptom or that it has a permanent effect on teeth and jaw development. It is also difficult to say at what age thumb sucking becomes abnormal, partly because the amount of sucking is also important. If it is abnormal, it is almost invariably part of a larger personality disturbance. The issue is not thumb sucking in itself, but such larger issues as immaturity and deprivation.

Colic

A common disturbance associated with early feeding is colic. Although it may be caused by a variety of factors, it can be defined simply as excessive crying. A frequent cause may be some gastric disturbance. Colic, however, has frequently been found to be a consequence of a disturbance in the mother—child relationship.

Mothers of colicky children were compared to mothers of babies without this symptom. The former, more significantly than the latter, had experienced poor parent—child relationships with their own mothers, had conflicts about their value as mothers and women, and were generally pessimistic. They had stopped working earlier in their pregnancies, stopped intercourse sooner, manifested emotional symptoms before and during pregnancy, described themselves more frequently as tense and nervous, and more frequently asked their own mothers to help them with their infants. Babies' diets, birth weights, specific types of feeding, lengths of labor, allergy histories, etc. were not found to differentiate colicky from other babies.

Of course, the fact that babies cry chronically does not necessarily imply that their mothers are relating poorly to them, but it may signal this as a possibility. In fact, a mother's anxiety about her relationship to her infant may be a consequence of the chronic irritability of her baby. Such mothers may, however, want to explore supportive counseling if the problem becomes anything more than a nuisance. Short of this, they may try holding the baby more and spending more time with the infant.

Nutrition

Eating is imbued with strong emotional undercurrents from the very beginning of life. When the baby swallows its food, the mother rewards him or her with smiles, kisses, and encouragements. Like most mammals, infants are more prone to accept sweet substances and to reject sour or tart food. The food industry has collaborated with mothers to add sugar liberally to food for babies and children. In this way, children learn to expect and want sweets. If they behave, they are rewarded with candy and are told that they themselves are sweet. If they misbehave, they are told they have sour dispositions. Being loved is too often equated with getting something sweet.

Later we will discuss how this conditioning may contribute to psychological disorders related to eating. It is important now to note that many people develop an inordinate need to eat a great deal of sugar—to sweeten almost everything they eat. Not only does sugar often cause unnecessary weight gain, but it contains relatively little nutrition, and, most important, displaces foods that are nutritious. Furthermore, there is increasing evidence to suggest that for many sugar may contribute to cardiovascular and other physical difficulties. Addiction to sweets may be as physiologically real as addiction to certain drugs, and in this sense must be recognized and treated as such. It is best to prevent addiction to sugar before it can be developed. And the best of all approaches is to eat food naturally, perhaps modestly spiced.

In the last several decades, our food habits have changed dramatically. Our foods are not only sweetened but processed, frozen, dehydrated, added to and subtracted from. Literally hundreds of chemical additives are consumed in the average person's daily meals. There is good reason to believe that hyperactivity in some children is often associated with the intake of food additives. Some hyperactive children who have been given food without such additives have improved dramatically. (See discussion of hyperactivity in the chapter on Behavior Disturbances.)

Our very moods and psychological reactions may be determined by the food we eat. For example, over thirty-five years ago, a group of women were restricted to a daily intake of .45 mg of thiamin (vitamin B). This amount varies little from the average American diet. In six to eight weeks, these women manifested emotional instability, irritability, moodiness, quarrelsome behavior, lack of cooperation, vague fears, agitation, and depression. Hyper- and hypoglycemia, or irregular blood sugar levels, involve symptoms that overlap with those usually diagnosed as psychological. Yet the management of this disorder, rather than requiring long and extensive psychotherapy, may often simply call for restriction of sugar and carbohydrate intake. Similar disorders may be related to other vitamin and trace mineral (e.g., copper, zinc, iron, and potassium) imbalances. The relatively new specialties of holistic health and orthomolecular medicine are addressing themselves to these phenomena. (Magazines, such as *Prevention*, discuss research in these areas.) A conservative stance for the reader to take would be to ensure a well-balanced diet supplemented by vitamins and minerals. This is particularly important for women suffering menstrual and menopausal difficulties.

Eating and Emotion

Since eating is related to love, security, pleasure, and communication, the conditions under which a family partakes of its meals are very important and establish patterns for the rest of life. It is important to have a leisurely, relaxed environment where there is both structure (everybody does not receive a separate menu) and flexibility (some choice should be available, especially in the size of portions). Conversation and humor are to be encouraged, and tension, conflict, and quarreling avoided. A family that has fun and gratification in eating together is enabling, to a significant degree, a child to grow up with good prospects of loving, relating, communicating, and being able to derive enjoyment from life.

Eating, like a bodily function, can be eroticized or sexualized. From birth, orality, together with eliminating waste, results in an organismic—an over-all bodily— gratification, and this gratification intimately involves another human being. Watching babies sucking contentedly at the breast or bottle, you will note that they are playing with a finger, toe, strand of hair, or their genitals. Freud's theory of psychoanalysis stresses the sexualization of bodily functions—particularly oral ones. The association of erotic and oral stimulation persists throughout life.

At least half of all middle-aged people in the United States are overweight. Studies have shown that overweight executives earn less than their thinner colleagues, while obese women have about one-third the chance of getting into a prestige college, the college of their choice, or any college at all compared to their normal-weight peers.

There are many factors that contribute to obesity or overweight. A genetic and environmental interaction is suggested by the fact that obese parents tend to have obese children. The psychological factors, however, are paramount. Compulsive eating is often an attempt to cope with frustration or to allay anxiety. In common parlance, we say that a certain problem is "eating us up," or, when we try to frustrate people, we tell them to "eat their hearts out." If eating becomes compulsive, the gratification it brings can only be elusive or transient, for then, a person can never eat enough to be fully satisfied.

Another motive for overeating is to fill a void or nagging psychological hunger. The emptiness experienced inside is not so much physical as emotional. Love and comfort are lacking and may have always been lacking. So we eat to feel nourished, comforted, loved. Sexual frustration, especially, can lead to compulsive eating. Since obesity often results in a poor self-image, the fat person despairs of love and eats frantically to compensate for sexual hunger. This distorts his or her body image even further and thereby establishes a vicious cycle.

A person with low self-esteem that is compounded by anxiety over sex may use obesity to keep the other sex at a distance. Alternatively, obesity may give the person a sense of power. A typical case is someone who feels powerful and has a sense of presence when he or she is very heavy, but feels small and insignificant otherwise. Such a person may lose and gain enormous amounts of weight without understanding why.

In a similar vein, overeating (as well as undereating) can be an expression of hostility. We use such expressions as "a biting tongue," "chew you out," "I can't stomach you," "I've had a bellyful," and so on. Instead of venting our anger directly, we may displace it onto compulsive eating. We may push people away with our excessive weight, thus showing our hostility and avoiding the risk of their rejecting us. Or we may be expressing resentment toward our parents (as they are or as we fantasize them): "You wanted me to eat—I'll kill myself eating!"

Whether we see ourselves as fat or thin can influence our self-esteem and consequently our behavior with other people. If our culture puts a premium on being skinny and we are plump, we may be constantly beset with nagging doubts about our appearance as well as our worth. We may then involve ourselves in endless campaigns of dieting, a project doomed to frustration, psychological issues aside, if our body type can never conform to some svelte prototype. The consequence is that we feel ourselves to be a failure—a fat slob.

Many a woman believes that to be a good mother she must fatten her children. A fat baby, she has been led to believe, is a healthy baby. This unfortunate syndrome may continue into adulthood: the mother demonstrates her love by feeding and stuffing; the child-adult accepts love by eating it all up and being stuffed. Of course, a mixed bag of love–hate feelings is often the consequence. What is more important, forced feeding, forced love, or parenting that is excessively supportive can be infantilizing.

The real problem with fat babies is that almost 85% of them grow up to be fat adults. Apparently, our very cellular structure can develop a norm for being fat. It is thought that obese people have as many as three times the number of fat cells as normal individuals. Dieting can only change the size, not the number of these cells. Weight loss, therefore, can only be temporary. The cells can be deflated; they cannot be made to disappear. Growth of these fat cells can be stimulated most dramatically during the fetal stage, at nine months, at six to eight years of age, and during late adolescence. It is during these periods that proper and disciplined eating is the most important.

Most people get fat through a slow, inexorable accumulation of calories that mark the creeping obesity common to middle age. The average American is twenty to fifty pounds heavier at fifty years of age than he or she was at twenty-one. The fact that most human beings maintain a constant weight is more remarkable than the fact that many tend to gain weight. It is not uncommon for the weight of an active young adult to vary less than three pounds over the course of a year, even though the amount of food and physical work may vary widely from day to day. If such a person were to consume each day only 100 calories more than he or she needed (for example, by eating one extra ounce of cheese or neglecting to walk for twenty minutes), in one year that person would accumulate ten pounds of extra fat. In five years, he or she would be fifty pounds overweight. So it is rather mysterious why some people do gain weight and others don't. Simple gluttony is not the reason. Inactivity or lack of exercise is a significant contributor.

Studies have demonstrated that obese people, in general, are more influenced by external rather than internal cues. Other people eat when they are hungry, when internal cues signal this state. Obese people pay attention less to hunger and more to whether something looks good or smells palatable. They associate eating with social factors and with such psychological conditions as tension and excitement. When given drab food in a drab environment, their eating decreases in comparison to normal—and they lose weight.

Dieting to lose weight is a complicated business. A person who has been overweight for his or her entire life may diet down to normal proportions, but does so at the price of perhaps being chronically hungry. An individual's "set-point," as determined by his or her body's chemistry and number of fat cells, may be higher than prevailing social norms. It seems likely, however, that one's weight is at least partly the result of an interaction between caloric intake and exercise. Any diet, then, will be most effective if it is coupled with a sustained pattern of exercise.

In addition to a well-balanced, low caloric diet, sustained motivation and psychological support are required. That is why groups such as Weight Watchers are so successful. The structured programs provide support from others and reinforcement for dieting and exercising—in other words, love and understanding in place of compulsive eating. Very important also is the fact that our eating habits, good and bad, are learned. Therefore, they can be unlearned or relearned. Such new learning requires organized, planned, and sustained effort, perhaps even behavior modification.

Undereating

Though less conspicuous, a significant portion of the population suffers from undereating. Since thinness has an aesthetic and sexual premium in our society, problems are not noted unless they become extreme. Very often, a weak appetite may involve a multiplicity of food phobias or fetishes. These may be so mild that they appear to be mere fussiness about food, but they are habits learned in childhood—often because of unpleasant experiences associated with family patterns of eating and relating.

Loss of appetite (and sometimes compulsive eating) may be a sign of depression. This condition is even more likely if it is accompanied by weight loss, constipation, difficulty in sleeping, restlessness, boredom, apathy, and feelings of worthlessness. Depression will be discussed in the Behavior Disturbances section, but at this point we may say that depression more often than not involves an interaction of psychological as well as physical factors. Really, there is no separating the two—both the body and mind must be considered.

Many people undereat because they are fearful of not looking attractive. This seems to be more prevalent for women who also at some level of consciousness fear growing up and wish to remain and look like little girls. The most dramatic example of such a syndrome is anorexia nervosa. This condition is nine times more common in females than in males. Such people literally starve themselves—sometimes to death. In acute cases, they must be fed intravenously. The typical anorexic has starved herself to underweight, has menstrual difficulties, and is markedly depressed. She has a very distorted body image and may not recognize or admit that she has an emaciated body. Instead, she believes she is beautiful. Often, psychotherapy reveals that anorexic women confuse weight gain with pregnancy. Such conditions can often be treated by behavior modification programs, but since anorexia nervosa is such an extreme condition, deep psychological disturbances are very likely.

Some anorexics are restrained eaters and others are bingers. The restrainers do get hungry, but don't want to eat because they wish to stay slim and they enjoy controlling their diet. The bingers, on the other hand, alternately binge (eat prodigious amounts) and either vomit, starve, exercise, or abuse laxatives; they feel compelled both to eat and to diet, often as a compensation for having eaten so much. Unlike the restrainers, the bingers feel their eating is out of control. Therefore, behavior modification and restriction of diet for these people often miss the sharp conflicts, and the anorexia may resume when a particular program or hospitalization is terminated.

Anorexic people are frequently found to share certain characteristics. Often they come from families where food has had unusual importance, especially for the parents. Indeed, often food was the basis of power struggles among members of the family. In addition, anorexics often harbor deep resentments about their own sexuality, and have used self-starvation as a way of suppressing secondary sexual characteristics—hips, buttocks, and breasts. Many anorexics, though possessing high IQs, often use emotional regression as a way of responding to difficult situations.

These conditions are very extreme and rare, but more moderate forms are common. Many women who rationalize that they are striving for a size three are mildly anorexic. A woman of 5 feet 3 inches who has bone structure that is not particularly petite and who weighs less than 105 pounds may be suffering from some psychological disorder.

Just as feeding influences our character, early in our development, with respect to loving, relating, and depending, and just as eating disturbances denote problems in these areas, toilet training similarly influences our character with respect to self-discipline, conformity, and rebellion. Moreover, both eating and toilet habits and their effects seem inextricably bound up with our attitudes toward sex. (See the discussion on infancy in the chapter on Stages.)

A study found that middle-class mothers could not keep their own attitudes toward sex separate from toilet training. This is often the reason for severity in toilet training, with frequent consequences resulting in emotional disturbance. Such consequences are manifested in hostility and fear toward the trainer—usually the mother—anxiety over sexual thoughts and behavior, anxiety over dirt and messiness, thinking of the self as "dirty" and "bad," and inhibition of spontaneous expression.

Toilet training ought to be delayed until children have fairly complete postural control, voluntary control over the sphincters, and can signal the need to vacuate. Indeed, the part of the nervous system that controls the sphincters is not fully mature until after the first year. Training ought to be delayed until the children are motorically and conceptually prepared for it. They should be able to sit up comfortably by themselves and to understand simple communications about the task required of them. This is usually not possible until well into the second year. Yet in 1957, the majority of mothers initiated training between nine and fourteen months and completed it at one and a half years. Mothers who began training later in the second year trained children more efficiently in less time. The most ease seemed to result after twenty months. The point is that children should be led rather than driven in this training.

Eneuresis, or bed-wetting, is the inability to contain urine during sleep. It is twice as common among boys as girls. Psychodynamically-oriented psychologists have long believed that bed-wetting is an expression of resentment or hostility. While this may be true in many cases, eneuresis can persist long after the original disturbance has been mitigated. The secondary consequences, feelings of inadequacy, dirtiness, and familial frustration, aggravate and reinforce this condition.

Psychodynamicists have argued that if this symptom is removed, others that are even more troublesome will take its place. Evidence exists, however, which suggests that this is not the case. As early as 1938, a device was used that rang a

Eneuresis

bell when the bed was wet. In 1960, several such experiments were reviewed: there were 76% cures. There were no reports of symptom substitution, but rather, evidence of positive changes in successful cases.

Irrespective of whether or not a mechanical arrangement is decided upon, it behooves parents to explore with their children the youngsters' feelings about themselves, the family environment, and the bed-wetting behavior. Here children and parents are engaged in a collaborative endeavor to eliminate a condition that must be a nuisance (notwithstanding its underlying motives) to the children.

Common sense dictates doing without liquids well before retiring and a night light in the bathroom, which should be well heated. When children are successfully dry, appropriate rewards are indicated (mostly of pleasure and approval), and when there is not success, there should be understanding and commiseration and the sense that all have to collaborate more effectively and imaginatively. Bed-wetting may be looked upon as a prototypical example of a wide variety of indicators, such as headaches, tantrums, school failures, stomach upsets, nightmares, and so on, of a problem in the family.

There are generally two kinds of bed-wetting: persistent and acquired. In the first, the child has never learned to contain his or her urine while sleeping. The persistence of bed-wetting into the third year indicates a problem, but this type is relatively easy to treat. Acquired bed-wetting, on the other hand, occurs after the child has learned to contain his or her urine. A relapse generally indicates some important disturbance in family relations, and the psychological causes of this condition should be inquired into. In all cases, punishment is not the solution. Instead, family exploration, understanding, and collaboration, as difficult and taxing as these can be, are necessary.

Encopresis, the inability to control the bowels, is a more serious condition. If it persists or occurs with regularity, professional help should be sought without shame or undue delay.

The two primary purposes of eating are nourishment and gratification. We are not only what we eat, but how we eat. From conception through birth, childhood, and into adulthood, our mental and physical health, how we think of ourselves, and the way we relate to others are all influenced strongly by eating—by all of the rituals, customs, activities, and emotions that surround it. Adult patterns of eating are established early in childhood, and the infant's experience at the breast or with the bottle are perhaps the most important influences in forming later personality patterns.

Mother's milk is an ideal food and breast feeding the most desirable mode of feeding. But generally, the attitudes and emotions surrounding infant feeding are more important than the actual choice of procedure. Because of early associations of sweetness and affection, many people become addicted to sugar and food additives in their food. Besides replacing truly nutritious substances, such additives can have harmful psychological and physiological effects.

Overweight most often is caused by an imbalance between caloric intake and energy expenditure. Many people overeat to fill some psychological need and to fulfill a need to be nourished and taken care of. The resultant obesity and poor self-image only increase the sense of deprivation. Other people may become overweight as a way of keeping people and the world at a distance. Finally, some people are overweight because they have been brought up that way as children. This situation is particularly unfortunate, since the number of fat cells may be permanently established by the end of adolescence. Dieting may therefore be only a process of chronic hunger, since the cells can only be deflated, not eliminated. Successful dieting involves a long-term commitment to limiting food intake and to regular, exercise.

Undereating, although less conspicuous, is quite common and can be due to food phobias or depression. In its most extreme form, anorexia nervosa, people literally starve themselves—sometimes to death. The psychological roots of this condition, which occurs most commonly in women, are very deep and probably involve a fear of physicality and sexuality and an attempt to withdraw from the family.

Toilet training also has an extremely important influence on our later character with respect to cooperation, rebellion, and sexuality. Children should be toilet trained only when they are mentally and physically capable of succeeding at this task. It is most desirable to lead children in this task, rather than to drive them. Bed-wetting, for the most part, can be treated by a number of methods, although parents should attend to its psychological causes.

Summary

3
Sleeping

One third of our lives is spent sleeping. Few activities come even close to taking up that much of our time. Yet the function of sleep and of that perennial mystery, dreams, is still largely unknown. What is clear, however, is that sleep, like all important activities of our lives, is influenced by physiological and psychological factors and in turn influences our waking lives. Each individual has his or her own pattern of sleeping, and to understand these patterns, whether or not they are disturbed, we must consider the whole individual.

Patterns of Sleep

Although each person has his or her own sleep habits, certain characteristics and sequences seem pretty uniform for all people. We know this from laboratory investigations undertaken in the past few decades. Electrodes are attached to the scalps of sleeping people, and the record of electrical activity in the brain—the electroencephalogram or EEG—is examined for recurrent patterns.

It seems that there are four stages of sleep, each with its own kind of brain waves. When we fall asleep, we enter the first stage, a period of light sleep with no dreaming and rapid brain waves. After a few minutes, we enter stage two, a period of deeper sleep. Brain waves are slower, and fragmentary dreams and images appear. After about twenty minutes, we go into stage three for a few minutes. Here, brain waves are slow and larger. Finally, we go to stage four, the period of deep sleep, for about twenty minutes. Then the entire cycle reverses itself, and we return to stages three, two, and one in that order. The entire cycle takes about ninety minutes and then repeats itself throughout the night. Although time spent in each stage may vary during the night, the sequence of stages is always the same.

Almost three-quarters of stage four, or deep sleep, occurs early in the night. Interestingly enough, the amount of time we spend at this stage begins to decrease by the age of thirty, and old people have very little of this kind of sleep. This seems to indicate that the different stages of sleep fulfill different functions, and that whatever it is that stage four does, it probably has something to do with a maturing body.

The most interesting things happen at stage one, where many of the physiological characteristics of the other three stages—decreased blood pressure, body temperature, heart rate, and respiration—are reversed. Stage one is hardly a time of rest. It is, in fact, known as "paradoxical sleep"; that is, its physical signs bear more resemblance to waking than they do to the other stages of sleeping. Yet it is most difficult to wake the sleeper during this stage.

We know a lot about this stage, primarily because of the discovery of rapid eye movements, or REMs. Sleep investigators observed that sleepers in stage one often twitched their eyelids and moved their eyeballs. When awakened, they reported that they had been dreaming. Apparently, they had been visualizing the dream scene and action. Insofar as sleep fulfills a psychological function, it seems to do so at this stage. If laboratory volunteers are artificially deprived of sleep, they will try to make up for lost stage one sleep the following night. If they are prevented from doing so, they begin to show bizarre signs during their waking hours and may even become psychotic.

From these REM investigations we have learned several interesting facts about dreaming. First of all, all people dream. Although they may forget their dreams, they dream from four to six times each night. Dreams are not instantaneous, but usually last from ten to twenty minutes each. Dreams early in the night tend to be light and trivial, while the later ones are more involved and strange. In an interesting experiment, when electrodes were attached to the throats of sleeping people who were blind from birth, the results indicated sub-vocal sounds. When the blind subjects were awakened, they reported having been dreaming. Apparently, the blind vocalize their dreams, while the sighted visualize theirs.

Rapid Eye Movement

Lack of sleep or insufficient sleep—and this varies for people of the same age and for people of different ages—often results in irritability, fatigue, emotional outbursts, and an impaired physical state. Young children and older people require more sleep (either at a regular daily period or supplemented by naps). From the teens through the fifties, the range of sleep is considerable, but the average is six to nine hours.

The physiological correlates of sleeping continue to occur at the individual's usual time for sleeping, even if he or she does not sleep. And patterns typical of the aroused waking state appear during the usual waking period even if the individual has not slept that night. Almost everyone who has crossed time zones has experienced jet lag—a drowsiness or weariness during waking hours that were usually sleep time. People who have work shift changes or who are kept awake by crises or unusual pressures may suffer similar effects. While psychological factors may play a part, there seem to be bodily rhythms that need to be attended to.

It has been theorized that sleep is necessary to give the body, particularly the heart, an opportunity to rest and to

Physiology of Sleep

eliminate metabolic wastes, but this has never been proven conclusively. Many individuals, including some very successful people, do with very little sleep. Many so-called "non-sleepers," however, are very fond of cat naps. Some theorize that a major purpose of sleeping is to provide an opportunity to dream (more on this later), rather than to fulfill other functions. The fact that animals sleep or enter into comatose states raises questions about this theory, although, for all we know, there may be bird dreams and dog dreams. Watch your pet dog sleeping, and you will see behavior that strongly suggests that it is dreaming and even "talking" in its sleep.

There is no doubt that many of our sleep patterns are learned. When we have a lot to do, we sleep less. When we are bored or depressed (but not agitated), we sleep more. Many people learn to grow sleepy when they are faced with tasks and situations which they wish to avoid. The syndrome of cramming for an exam or report that gets interrupted by frequent bouts of drowsiness is familiar to many.

We also learn to sleep at specific periods—at certain hours of the night, after the eleven o'clock news, after sex. Most of us adopt, from earliest life, a routine schedule before going to sleep. We may wash up, brush our teeth, say prayers, fantasize or review the day's events before dropping off to sleep. In reviewing the day, if we focus on knotty or troublesome issues, we may obsess, ruminate, and have thoughts racing through our minds—all of which preclude sleep. But less pressured rituals, particularly fantasizing, seem to serve an autohypnotic function that triggers sleep.

Sleep, as we suggested before, does not mean an absolute suspension of consciousness. Often we solve problems while asleep. Some of the world's great discoveries were made in sleep. The famous chemist, Kuekule, solved the problem of the benzine ring in his sleep. The poet Coleridge claimed to have dreamt one of his greatest poems, "Kubla Khan," in his slumbers.

There is a small area on the hypothalamus, a part of the brain, which, if injured, results in chronic somnolence. This area, responsible for wakefulness, is called the waking center. Another area is the sleeping center. As an infant matures, his or her cortex, the crust of the brain and the seat of higher functions, gains control over these centers, and the infant progresses from many naps a day to the adult pattern in which sleep is postponed until one long daily stretch.

What, then, is sleep? It is a complex sequence of stages, during most of which the higher functions of the cerebral cortex are relatively inactive. Certain pathways from the brain to the nervous system shut down, particularly those involving large muscle groups. That is why we do not usually engage in gross physical movements even when dreaming, although twitching of the fingers and face are common. Sleepwalking seems to be an exception to this rule, although the reasons for this phenomenon are not as yet understood.

Sleep is at least partly caused by the fatigue of the neuromuscular mechanism concerned with maintaining muscle tonus. In the absence of such fatigue, sleep may result from complete muscle relaxation, intentional or unintentional. The daily alternation of wakefulness and sleep is a learned or conditioned phenomenon.

All individuals are different, even at birth. One of the first signs of these differences is the infant's sleeping pattern. Indeed, individual cycles of sleep and "wakefulness" can be observed even while the fetus is still in the womb. By birth these differences are well established. Some infants sleep the night through; some are up every few hours. Digestive disturbances, such as colitis, can keep babies awake, as can other physical upsets. Temperament also plays an important part. In the hospital nursery, one may note placid infants sleeping frequently and quietly, while energetic, tense babies sleep fitfully and for shorter periods.

Individual Variation

Later in life, significant numbers of people can be categorized as day people and night people. While body rhythms and temperament may play a part, this behavior seems to be largely learned. If the activities these people are interested in or wish to avoid are examined, at least part of the explanation for their diurnal habits is found. This is especially true when we find a couple with contrary sleeping cycles. They may, unwittingly, be avoiding each other.

Children often use problems with sleep to gain attention. This may be because they are not receiving sufficient attention or because they simply are testing the structure of the relation to their parents. The child who repeatedly requests a glass of water after he or she is in bed and the infant who cries at night are similar cases in point. After it is determined that there is no illness or other disturbing condition present, parents require motivation and firmness to terminate such behavior, particularly if it is chronic. A wailing baby is biologically equipped to trigger a response in a parent. The wail has more effect on the mother than an ambulance siren, a fire alarm, and a police beeper combined. Nevertheless, the courage to allow the baby to cry several nights without fussing over it usually results in the termination of such crying. The parents sleep more, are more relaxed, and the child gets more undisturbed sleep. Most important, the child learns that he or she is not omnipotent, that a shriek does not get instant gratification, and that the realities of the world must be recognized and adapted to.

On the other hand, some sleep disturbances are not due simply to willfulness and the attempt to gain the attention of the parents. There may be genuine and serious difficulties—physiological or psychological—in falling asleep or in maintaining sleep. The child may also experience a genuine fear of falling asleep. In such cases, firmness and discipline are ineffective and may even aggravate the problem. When sleep difficulties persist, a psychological and pediatric consultation is indicated.

The reluctance to go to sleep and the habit of waking up at night are characteristic of the fifteen to thirty month old child. Often the child is fearful of being left alone, and separation from the parent, even for sleeping, is experienced as a separation anxiety. This is especially true, as with the two-year-old, when there is concurrently tension over toilet training and pressure to control aggressive and asocial behavior. Sleep may connote to the child a loss of control, and loss of control can mean soiling or wetting. (See discussion of eneuresis and encopresis in chapter on Eating.)

While comforting a child is important, sleeping with the child may establish a pattern involving more problems and complications than solutions. For one thing, the child learns that resolution of fear and anxiety involves instant comfort and dependency, rather than a recognition that problems are dealt with in a gradual, often imperfect and realistic way. Night lights may be left on, toys and stuffed animals—if the child suggest this—slept with as companions, and the bedroom door left ajar.

It is important to arrange for bedtime to be a pleasant, calm time accompanied by affection—kissing, hugging, and story telling. The child must also know that his or her parents or the sitter are accessible, within earshot, if really needed. Incidentally, unless the child sees the baby sitter as a parent-surrogate or liaison with the parent, all sorts of difficulties can arise. It is important, therefore, to introduce the sitter properly. He or she is a person who cares for the child, will help if needed, is invested with parental authority (especially if the sitter is a young teen-ager), and can summon the parents if necessary. It is important to determine that the sitter and the child have a rapport. Not everyone gets along, even adults. Of course, some children will reject almost any sitter because they are contesting their power and control, or because the parents somehow have conveyed to their child the feeling that they are abandoning or escaping him or her.

It is extremely important not to confuse sleeping with punishment. Don't say, "You've been bad—go to sleep!" It is never a good idea to confuse punishment with any meaningful behavior, particularly such major activities as eating, playing, and loving. The child may well generalize "badness" to such necessary and ordinarily gratifying pursuits. Perhaps there is no way to avoid restricting the child to his or her room as a means of discipline, but even then, it is imperative to embue that room with pleasantness (cheerfulness, toys, etc.) and love. Sleep disturbances are often transitory, especially when both love and firmness are demonstrated by the parents.

Another peak in sleep disturbances occurs between the ages of four and six. Twenty percent of students in elementary grades report sleep disturbances. Often a competitor, a younger brother or sister, has arrived to vie for the parents' attention. This is a time when masturbatory and aggressive impulses are both strong and fearful for the child. Bed-wetting and sleepwalking may occur during this period.

Dread of sleep may also be associated with fear of dying. Very young children cannot always discriminate between the two, and may fear that either they or their parents will die during the night. There are also adults who suffer from thanatophobia and are therefore afraid of going to sleep. The very common nighttime prayer, "If I die before I wake, I pray the Lord my soul to take," has instilled in some children the distinct possibility that sleeping may result in death. So it is imperative to determine with a child what sleep means, and to allay irrational anxieties with reassurances and pleasurable associations.

Some people love to sleep and use every possible opportunity to engage in it. Some of this is learned and some of it is due to peculiarities in energy level, which may be caused by improper diet, exercise, and stress management. If you feel you are sleeping too much, it is a good idea to inquire into your general life style. Your waking life may be so impoverished or stressful that the only relief from it is in sleep. Conversely, such sluggishness may result from inadequate mental or physical stimulation and exercise. Often, serious problems in life show up first as disturbances in sleep. It is always wise to pay attention to these early warning signals and to use the occasion to examine the ways you spend your waking hours.

Twelve to twenty-five percent of adolescents who were surveyed reported serious sleep disturbances. One study found that 13% of emotionally disturbed adolescents were referred to therapy because of sleep disturbances. More girls than boys reported sleep problems. Poor sleepers were more anxious, depressed, and tense than good sleepers. Chronic poor sleepers experienced a greater variety of sleep problems for a longer period of time than occasional poor sleepers. Half of the chronic poor sleepers complained of frequent awakenings during the night and experienced difficulty in returning to sleep once awakened.

This pattern of extended nighttime awakening was once thought to be typical of older people. Although most of this disturbance disappears with age, some of it lasts well into maturity. Indeed, there is evidence to suggest that adult patterns of sleep disturbances are established early in childhood. It is always easier to treat disturbances when they first appear than when they have become chronic and a stable part of the larger personality.

As people grow older—in the middle years and particularly in the sixties and seventies—their sleep patterns often change. Cat napping may become a daily occurrence. Getting up in the middle of the night or rising with the first light of dawn is not unusual. It is not clear what the reasons for this are. There may well be changes in the neuromuscular system, as well as metabolic changes. For many, it is as simple a fact as the bladder's inability to retain as much urine as it did previously. This is especially true of men whose prostate gland has become swollen with age and now intrudes into the bladder space, or for women who have had pregnancies. For many others, muscles have stiffened and joints tightened, and they may suffer from mild or severe arthritic and bursitic conditions.

To ensure relaxing sleep, it would help to retire in a relaxed, rather than tense, state of mind; to forego fluids, especially coffee, tea, and alcohol, several hours before going to bed; to use a firm mattress (possibly with a bedboard as well); and to adopt a body position that does not cramp the arms and legs or impede breathing.

Insomnia

Sometimes we can't seem to fall asleep. In the isolated instance, there may be little or nothing amiss, or the difficulty may be due to a digestive disturbance or some infectious condition. If, however, the insomnia becomes chronic, there may be psychological factors and faulty habits at work. When such sleeplessness persists, it is wise to check with a physician.

About one-third of adult Americans claim to have sleeping problems. Although there are many reasons for this disturbance, many people avail themselves of sleeping pills. More than two million take such drugs every night for two consecutive months or more, and about 8.5 million took sleeping pills at least once in 1977. This is an extremely dangerous trend, primarily because of the serious side effects involved. Especially with barbiturates, but also with the more popular benzodiazepines (e.g. Dalmane), there is a danger of adverse drug reactions in older people and those with kidney problems. Such drugs tend to leave residues in the body long after their use is discontinued, and they can interfere with the ability to drive or operate machinery. All these effects are aggravated by the use of alcohol.

It is important to recognize that sleeping pills are effective only for a few nights and have few, if any, positive effects over a long period. To rely on these drugs for long-term alleviation of insomnia is therefore to court only negative side effects. In any case, the use of drugs only allows the sufferer to avoid facing the factors that are causing insomnia in the first place. If insomnia persists, a physician should be consulted and drugs used only for temporary relief.

There are other, safe methods of ensuring sleep. Meditation seems to work for many. A warm bath before retiring may also promote relaxation for some. Certain kinds of protein are also helpful—which is why warm milk may be beneficial. There are also behavior modification tapes that have proven helpful for many.

For almost everyone, insomnia implies psychological or physical tension, preoccupation with worries, obsession with decisions, and ruminations about failures, defeats, and rejections. Chronic poor sleepers are more likely to report repetitious dreams, faulty sleep patterns, and a preference for staying up later than good sleepers or occasional poor sleepers. Sometimes, insomnia signifies fear of death or of relinquishing control. We saw earlier that the young child may fear sleep because his or her control over forbidden aggressive and sexual impulses may be lost. It is not uncommon for adults under pressure to regress to this state. If the insomnia persists, counseling or psychotherapy is indicated.

Roosevelt said that all we have to fear is fear itself. We may worry so much about sleeping that we force ourselves awake. It is not a good idea to fight sleeplessness. The worst that can happen is that we won't sleep that night. More often than not, the truth of the matter is that the insomniac will go through periods of dozing, which he or she forgets or chooses to ignore. No harm will be done. All the evidence suggests that impairment due to sleeplessness is induced by forced wakefulness. The irritability and fatigue occasioned by struggling against sleeplessness is probably more severe than staying awake with a relaxing chore, reading, or watching the late, late, late show. So don't fight it. Try to relax. Sleep can only be induced when there is relaxation and the mind is at rest. Even if sleep does not follow, the restful state is desirable and wholesome.

Dreams

Freud thought that the major function of dreams was to preserve sleep. If the forbidden wishes and impulses we all have were to appear in their naked form, we would awake in horror. The dream allows us to sleep by disguising the wish so that it can slip by our moral censor, the superego, which is awake even when we are asleep. If the disguise fails, wholly or in part, we awake suddenly from a troubling dream, have an anxiety dream, or have a nightmare. Children, because they have fewer and weaker ways of handling forbidden impulses, suffer more frequently from nightmares than adults do. This is particularly common between the ages of four and six, when children are learning right from wrong and have not yet developed adequate and efficient moral and intellectual controls.

Nightmares may reappear in adult life when we are under psychological pressure or are experiencing unusual conflict or anxiety about some decision or situation. Old people also report difficulty with troublesome dreams. This may be due to disturbances in higher, cortical levels of brain functions, as well as to objective physical and psychological problems. Certainly, for many older people, dealing with reality—physical, social, and emotional—becomes more problematic.

Recent laboratory research has tended to confirm Freud's idea that dreams serve to protect and preserve sleep. When volunteers are awakened during REMs, and are thereby prevented from dreaming, they manifest in the waking state a variety of emotional disturbances. Similarly, people kept awake have developed such symptoms. Dreaming is absolutely necessary to our emotional well-being, and just as dreaming preserves sleep, we may also say that sleeping exists partly to allow us to dream. Disturbed sleep, then, can have very serious consequences to our emotional lives. Thus people who live in noisy and disturbing surroundings, such as in the flight paths of airports, may suffer neurotic consequences. The same may be true for those who must sleep in noisy apartments, assaulted by loud music, blaring TV sets, or the roar of traffic.

Interpreting Dreams

The language and content of dreams conforms largely to what Freud called primary process. That is, in dreams there is no apparent logic or conformity to the limitations and constraints of reality. Time can extend or jump forward or backward, causality can be reversed; the dead can appear living and the living dead; love and hate, attraction and disgust can occur at the same time. Incongruity and paradox are the rule: animals may have human features and behavior, and vice versa; feelings of helplessness and inferiority coexist with those of omnipotence; excitement and dread, curiosity and embarrassment are strong and unaccountable. This process, in short, seems to be non-verbal and to go back to the "thinking" of earliest infancy before language developed. That is partly why dreams may seem so difficult to remember, or, if they are recalled, why it is so hard to describe them. Often they resemble the states we experience when we are under the influence of drugs, trauma, or fever.

Dream analysts have been in business for thousands of years. Joseph's skill at dream interpretation was what made him so successful with the Pharaoh. But it was Freud who provided a coherent and useful theory of the function and meaning of dreams. His ideas are subtle and complex, but his basic view was that all dreams represent the fulfillment of wishes or desires. Often these wishes involve forbidden or "bad" impulses, so the dreamers are in conflict and must hide their evil intentions even from themselves. To do this, the dreams disguise or "code" their meanings. If the wish is un-objectionable, the dream is pleasant, and we experience the fulfillment of our wish for food, sex, or power. But if the wish violates our conscious values and ideas, the dream will appear confused, inexplicable, and mysterious. In some cases, the wish is so horrible to us that we have an anxiety dream or a nightmare.

I am sitting in an airplane. I strap myself in, nod to the headless man beside me, and look out the window as the plane takes off.

Freud distinguished between two levels of meaning in dreams: the manifest and the latent contents. The manifest content is what the dream in itself says it is, the summary given above. The latent content is the meaning that has been disguised into the manifest content. Freudians are among those who are very interested in dreams, and Freud himself called them the "royal road to the unconscious." This is because dreams can tell us things about ourselves that we, because of our training and the way we have grown to think about ourselves, are ignorant of—especially unconscious, repressed thoughts and wishes. A Freudian analyst would therefore pay attention to the personal significance of the headless passenger, the act of strapping myself in, and the flight itself. To do this, he or she would encourage me to associate freely with elements of the dream: what comes to mind when I think about strapping myself in, for example. Often these symbols have a sexual significance (i.e., an elongated object often means a penis; a receptacle, a vagina) because sexual desires are frequently repressed, although other meanings are just as likely. The analyst will also try to relate the dream to the previous day's events and to thoughts that dreamers have when they awaken or when they report their dreams.

Jung's view of dreams differed from Freud's in several important respects. Although most of our dreams concern our personal experiences and difficulties, some of them, Jung thought, deal with age-old, perennial problems that go back to the pre-history of the race. The imagery and contents of these dreams are inherited from our ancestors, and the reservoir of such imagery and content Jung called the collective unconscious, which informs not only dreams but fantasies, fairy tales, and myths as well. Particular symbols, called archetypes—such as the Great Mother or the Wise Old Man—occur in all times and societies and bear a striking resemblance to their counterparts in such remote and diverse cultures as the Chinese, American Indian, European, and African.

Although Jung recognized the function of dreams to express conflict and wish fulfillment, he also thought that dreams serve another important function: to alert the conscious personality to its neglected aspects and to point the way to future development. Thus, if I dream that I am beset by enemies on three sides, but I escape by sea, the Jungian interpretation might suggest that although I feel overwhelmed by problems, I sense the possibility of a way out — perhaps a dramatic change in the way I lead my life.

Jungians interpret dreams literally as well as symbolically. The dream represents in every way the dreamer's personality. A weak father in the dream also means the dreamer's weakness. The end of the dream always points to the dream's conclusions, negative or positive, about the events or situation that provoked it.

Followers of Wilhelm Reich, the psychoanalyst who discussed the development of character and the defenses against psychological pain, see the dream as another example of our character style. The dream and the way we report it is our characteristic mode of dealing with non-verbal and unconscious material. The expressive style of our dreams is at least as important as the content. For example, a man might glibly report a dream of cutting down wheat stalks. Although he may be having a castration dream, it is the glibness that is most important to the Reichian analyst.

The Gestalt school believes that dreams are projections of unwanted or conflicting parts of the dreamer's self. Ideas, feelings, and actions not expressed in waking life are reflected back to the dreamer in symbols that represent that individual. Something a person didn't say or do the day before gets enacted or portrayed in his or her dreams. The dream is a message from the dreamer to the self, and every aspect of the dream—even inanimate objects—is a creation of a part or facet of the dreamer. So for a person to understand a dream, he or she needs, in Gestalt terms, to play every part of that dream—humans, animals, and objects.

If I dream that I am pushing a baby carriage with my aged father in it, and the carriage gets out of control and hurtles toward the highway, I need to imagine myself as the carriage pusher, the aged father, the carriage, and the highway. For example, as the carriage pusher, I say: "I feel I have to do all the work, take care of my elderly father, my family, everyone; sometimes I would like to push everyone away." As the elderly father: "I feel dependent; I wish someone would take care of me; sometimes I feel hopeless and would like to end it all." As the carriage: "I am afraid of going out of control—then what would happen to me?" As the highway: "I can go in either direction, but making a decision leaves me vulnerable to destructive forces—perhaps to the rage that is swirling inside me."

It is only recently that we have learned how creatively and constructively we may use dreams. The Senoi are a primitive tribe of about 12,000 people who live in the Malaysian jungle. Their life is relatively bountiful, easy, and peaceful, since other warlike tribes do not bother them because of their reputed magic. The Senoi are reported to have an almost complete absence of significant mental disturbance because of their highly developed self-awareness and self-control.

The entire fabric of the Senoi community, from intrapsychic matters to tribal government, is determined by the way they use their dreams. From earliest childhood, the Senoi are taught to use messages from their dreams to guide their interpersonal and intrapersonal lives. Moreover, they learn to use the messages to achieve more harmonious mental processes. For them, except during childhood, terrifying dreams and nightmares are non-existent.

The Senoi dreamer always confronts and conquers his or her dream enemy. Any figure, no matter how friendly in appearance, that attacks or simply does not help is an enemy. The Senoi never run from a threatening figure. They stand their ground, advance upon the enemy, and attack. If a Senoi dreams of being attacked by a friend, the next day he or she goes to the friend and tells the latter of the dream. Because of some unintentional act, the dreamer may have offended the friend. If the dreamer hurts someone in a dream, he or she goes to that person, apologizes, and gives him or her a gift. If a friend is exposed to some danger in a dream, the Senoi warns that friend and they try to diagnose the danger together. Every dream is made to have a positive outcome. The Senoi creatively learn to bring about a pleasurable or satisfying outcome to their dreams.

We have much to learn from the Senoi. Particularly, when we have disturbing, repetitive dreams, we can take control of them and finally give them a positive twist. People who do this report an end to such dreams.

We need to learn, therefore, not to fear our dreams, but to profit from them. We are trying to tell ourselves something. Whether we use a Freudian, Jungian, Reichian, Gestalt, or Senoi approach (or some amalgam of all of them), dreams can be instrumental in helping us to be more self-aware and self-controlled, as well as more sensitive to others and to our environment. It would be most valuable to try to remember dreams, write them down, keep a dream journal, and note the style and changes that take place. Discussion with intimates of our dreams not only provides different viewpoints, but also fosters sensitivity and communication, especially within families. When children have disturbing dreams, soothing them is necessary, but not sufficient. The children are trying to tell themselves and their parents something. Teaching them to appreciate, respect, and understand their dreams will help them to appreciate, respect, and understand themselves—and maybe, their parents, too.

Summary

Sleep, one of the oldest and most common activities of mankind, is only now beginning to be understood. Certainly, an activity that takes up fully one-third of our lives must serve important functions. The restorative powers of sleep, both physical and mental, are vital to our well-being, and we should ensure that nature's course runs as smoothly and efficiently as possible. Disturbances in sleep will affect our waking lives, and difficulties in our conscious life will show up in sleep.

Recent research on sleeping has found that every night's sleep follows the same pattern through four distinct phases and back again several times. In one stage, the phenomenon of rapid eye movements, which occur when we dream, has allowed us to learn about dreaming.

Patterns of sleep do, however, vary with individuals and change with age. Many of these patterns are learned and can consequently be relearned if they involve us in inconvenience or difficulty. Particularly in childhood, disturbances in sleep are often related to larger emotional difficulties. During this period, it is most important that such disturbances be dealt with when they occur, since problems in childhood strongly influence our later habits and behavior.

Many people are plagued with insomnia, which can be due to any number of physical and psychological factors. Learning to relax and to let sleep come naturally is the optimal way of overcoming this difficulty, since reliance on medication is ineffective over a long period and can result in serious adverse side effects.

Dreams, although seeming to be strange and illogical, follow a logic of their own, and we can discover much about the workings of our unconscious from learning to understand our dreams. Freud proposed certain ways of going about this, and others—Jung, Reich, and Fritz Perls—have elaborated their own methods. But such interest in the language of dreams is not confined to modern psychologists. We can learn a great deal about how to understand and use our dreams productively from other cultural groups like the Senoi.

We live much of our lives ignoring and repressing parts of our nature. If this ignorance goes too far, we become strangers to ourselves and victims of forces we do not understand. Dreams allow us to get back in touch with our whole selves. They are not foolish, irrational occurrences, but messages we send ourselves. Much of our growth, happiness and productivity depends on how carefully and seriously we read these messages. Nature, sly and subtle as always, has given us the opportunity to peer down into the darkness below our conscious personalities. Who would miss such a chance?

4
Playing

Freud thought that an adjusted person was identified by his or her ability to love and to work. Nowadays, with an increase in leisure, more money to spend, and a more fluid sense of sexual roles, the ability to play must also be added to our definition of a productive and adjusted individual. At first glance, playing seems to be the easiest and most natural of all activities: children take to it immediately, and animals— puppies and kittens—are masters at it. But as we get older, as responsibilities pile up, tensions increase, and we labor under a mounting awareness of our adult roles and positions in society, play is apt to become more and more a thing of the past—mere kid stuff. Or if we set about deliberately, with teeth clenched, to do our play and recreation, we are not playing at all. The cut-throat weekly tennis matches, the grim poker games, and other such joyless exercises are merely transpositions of the strains and competition of our work onto the field of recreation. Play is the most free and goalless of activities, and if it becomes contaminated by the mind-set of work, we have foregone one of the richest and most pleasurable activities available to us.

We play for many reasons—to prepare us for a later role, to gain recognition, to develop and sustain friendships, to promote health and relaxation—but all these are secondary purposes. The primary characteristic of play is simple volition: we arise before dawn, drive long distances, engage in the most strenuous of exertions, and abide by the most arbitrary and constricting rules simply because we want to.

Although play can serve many functions, and indeed, society uses it to teach children some of the lessons and skills they must have later in life, in its pure form it is one of the most human activities we know. Essentially, play is engaged in for its own sake, and although we may play to win, true play requires no goal outside the simple pleasure of its own performance.

Frequently play involves a set of arbitrary rules, often quite formidable in their complexity and subtlety—as anyone knows who has taken a European to a baseball game or who has watched a Rugby match in England. And the characteristic of "good" play is the interest it summons up and sustains in us. It often involves the cultivation of a high degree of skill and knowledge. Play may be as satisfying as anything we do.

Play, however, is not an entirely isolated activity, separated from other aspects of our lives. We may see this in the different ways play relates to our larger lives during various stages of our growth. Infants, for example, use play to discover the regularity and predictability of their physical and social world; adolescents, to integrate themselves into a society of peers and competitors; and adults, to compensate for the rigors of the working world and to fulfill fantasies and needs that are not satisfied elsewhere.

Play begins very shortly after birth. Actually, it would be proper to say that the first instance of play is observed when the infant becomes aware of his or her environment. The pleasurable attention to repeated stimuli, movement, and sound is the earliest form of play. The baby who toys with his or her fingers, hair, or clothes or who experiments with coos and gurgles is playing when he or she shows pleasure or repose in the act. In this earliest play, and for many months afterward, repetition is all-important. It is as if the baby is learning the predictable nature of his or her world, its physical laws and dimensions. Everything is new and needs to be poked, pushed, tasted, smelled, felt, viewed and—from the infant's perspective—swallowed. For all of these reasons, parents are very watchful people!

In early games, the child is delighted both by surprise and by discovering again and again that things turn out the same and will not disappear. It is as if the child wishes to prove that he or she will not be faced with the loss and separation first experienced during birth and thereafter when mother and her surrogates were not immediately present to minister to the child's needs. Possibly, that is why little children love to hear the same story told over and over again in exactly the same fashion.

Between the eighth and ninth month, play becomes more organized, especially in relation to other children. Between the fourteenth and eighteenth month, cooperation and the social use of play material usually develop. Play becomes more social and involves group games as the child grows older. The number of recreational activities actually declines with age. This is particularly evident with adolescents who engage in relatively few activities—one or two sports, tinkering with cars, dating, dancing, and watching TV.

Play is a positive good in itself, and it is all too often used negatively. Parents often use it to distract their kids, to get them out of the way, and to counteract boredom: "You're so listless. Go out and play!" Play cannot be forced, and if a parent conveys this negative attitude, the child may learn to associate play with coercion. The child will rightfully resent it, and the play itself will be half-hearted and bored. A child who is encouraged to play, helped with it, given the toys (which can be almost anything), or just left alone to play is far less likely to get bored. Boredom may also be a symptom of a lack of stimulation. Moderate stimulation is essential for mental equilibrium. When it is lacking, emotional difficulties follow.

This has been demonstrated many times in sensory deprivation studies.

By early adolescence, sports and games serve the function of teaching the growing person about his or her society and the ways he or she may fit into it. Play is, in a sense, training for life. Indeed, it has been said that the nineteenth century British Empire was made possible by the training English school boys received on the playing fields. In any case, adolescents' sense of who they are and how they relate to their social world is to some extent determined by their experience of games and sports. What follows has been more apparently true of boys than girls, but with the loosening of rigid sex roles and the growing freedom of girls to participate in these important socializing activities, our generalizations will hold for both sexes.

Although children must locate themselves in a family, which often includes competitive siblings, it is in adolescent games that they first learn to balance and correlate the dual functions of competition and cooperation in a larger social sense. Children play for pleasure and they play to win. The way they respond to winning and losing is a good indication of the way they will act under pressure, frustration, competition, and triumph in later life.

In addition, sports and games often provide adolescents with the first opportunities for sustained and intense effort at developing and perfecting skills. Nowadays, much is given to children, but young basketball or chess players are achieving—by their own efforts—something they can take pride in. The lessons learned here are extremely important, for the adolescents are measuring themselves, their skills, strength, speed, or cleverness against an external set of values which they have voluntarily undertaken to observe. They learn what they are and are not capable of, and must find a way of accepting the limitations of their ages and abilities.

Finally, adolescents come into contact with the realities of the social world, since success in group activities often determines the social hierarchies that prevail in the school years. Position in the hierarchy depends partly on skill and intelligence, partly on luck or plain unfairness. This is, perhaps, not as we would want it, but that's the way the world operates. Children's perceptions of groups, of who is in and who is out, the smooth operations of status and its unjust judgments, is an important part of adolescents' moral and psychological education. The way they respond—with outrage, resignation, or a realistic assessment—is integral to the conscious attitudes and actions that they will develop as they grow.

The child in us remains with us all our lives, as does the need for and pleasure from play. The transactional analyst says that we need to let our child out to play frequently and regularly. Often, we ignore this part of ourselves or let it atrophy to our detriment. The Protestant ethic, or its distorted interpretation, has suggested to many Americans and Western Europeans that play is to be eschewed in favor of work and purpose, despite the fact that play, balanced with work, can relax, recharge, stimulate, and enhance the capacity for work. If we ignore this need, we are less zestful, prematurely aged, and less interested and interesting. Sometimes, we have to learn to play all over again. More pointedly, we need to unlearn poor habits of play or of play contaminated by other purposes.

Play can become saturated with competitiveness and thus lose its playfulness. Frequently, it takes on compulsive qualities. The person who plays tennis or golf with a vengeance is really working at it, and brings to it much of the goal-oriented and driven qualities that characterize a work attitude. Its voluntary aspect becomes minimized, and relaxation and pleasure are lost. The "workaholic" and the driven competitor lose the sense of play and often suffer tension and coldness as a consequence. At first, it may be a contradiction in terms, but one would do well to deliberately set aside time for recreation and to assume an attitude of looseness and flexibility. The volitional quality will follow.

Recreation means what it says, to re-create, to reorganize our activities and attitudes in the service of ourselves. This implies eliminating all imperatives—shoulds, musts, have to's—and instead doing what we want to do. Similarly, the meaning of vacation essentially implies a vacating, an emptying of burdens and stresses. It is a period of respite, intermission, and rest—really, a time to play. When we return from a "vacation" exhausted or tense, when we have set ourselves all sorts of goals, such as having to see everything, do so much, be so many places, we really have displaced our work attitude onto another locale. Of course, there are people who seem to thrive on work (see discussion of cardiovascular conditions in chapter on Health), but play signifies less concern with why we are doing something than with how it makes us feel. It is good to let out our own personal child to play and frolic.

Age need not be a handicap. In fact, the contrary can be true. In later years, in retirement or after the children have left the house, more time becomes available, perhaps even more money, and, in general, one feels more entitled to one's own pleasures and satisfactions. Play now can keep us youthful. We have all seen young people who seem prematurely old because of an absence of playfulness, and old people who are young at heart and in attitude. Some people learn this ability with years. Hobbies and interests bring zest to old age and cause the years to drop away. A young person who has forgotten how to play has become a zestless young crab who can look forward only to becoming a cantankerous old crab in later years.

Games

A game is a special kind of play that is characterized by rules, no matter how arbitrary. It is played to win. There are many valuable by-products of games in addition to their fun, creativity, and fantasy. They promote the learning of rules and regulations, of reality or of replicas of reality. They teach cooperation, roles, and a wide variety of skills, including technical ones. Games played with others are one of the prototypes for forming and negotiating friendships. They are practice sessions for many of the activities of life that are to follow. Games provide a way of expressing tensions, anger, curiosity, and affection. At the very least, they allow us to add to our repertoire of recreation and to vary our means of communication and amusement. They also divert us from other more functional activities that are devoted to survival, production, or performance for ulterior ends.

An element of power can enter into and contaminate games when they become too competitive. When this happens, we have moved away from play into some other kind of activity. This is not to say that such a development is necessarily undesirable. It all depends on what value we place on competition, on defeating opponents, or on learning to perform well under stress. Still, we should consider whether or not games are the most appropriate means of expressing these values. More often than not, competition creeps insidiously into games because it is a habit or perhaps even a neurotic tendency.

The person who always plays competitively, who cannot end the poker session until he or she has won, who plays tennis so ferociously that it no longer is a friendly activity, who cannot wait to beat his or her spouse at scrabble, does so because he or she "can't" do it any other way. Underlying this rather annoying habit may be a deeper need for assertion and superiority, and games are hardly the most appropriate vehicle for understanding and satisfying such motivation. In these cases, the value of games, their freedom, fantasy, and fun, is lost. A similar contamination can be observed in some people's sexual activity, where the pleasure and satisfaction of this activity is corrupted by power.

Children learn the spirit in which they play largely from their families. If the need of a child to win is extremely strong, he or she may be looking for a kind of recognition and status which cannot be found in games. For both children and adults, signs of tension, frustration, and compulsiveness in games point to deeper life patterns. It is always wise to reflect on why we do something in a particular way and, more important, why we are unable to do it differently.

For many people, especially couples, games may be the easiest way of communicating and getting close. While this is certainly not the optimal vehicle for intimacy, it can be a constructive, warm, and meaningful form of communication. It is certainly preferable to people isolated in their own pursuits such as reading in separate corners or gluing themselves to the television set in insulated psychic compartments. In any case, the value of these games does not lie in winning or losing but in communication, playfulness, attention, and sharing.

Sports

Sports are games that emphasize physical skills, dexterity and coordination as well as mental and tactical cleverness. They may be solitary activities or involve groups. All that has been said about the psychological aspects of games applies to sports, except that here, certain characteristics like mastery, winning, coping with losing, and performance for other participants and spectators play a more prominent role.

The element of competition is emphasized, the purposefulness more keen, and conflict and work factors more liable to play a significant part in sports than in other games. This can be all to the good of the player, since the release of energy, constructive competitiveness, and even the resolution of conflict and frustration are sound activities when not taken too far. This can be true for the spectator as well. Everything, however, can be perverted. Throughout this book, readers are asked to observe the activity in question, to look at themselves and to observe how that activity makes them feel. When compulsiveness, rigidity, frustration, urgency, depression, or nagging feelings are associated with the activity, they have reason to suspect neurotic behavior, no matter what the supposed purpose of that activity.

Little League baseball is a case in point. Presumably, its purpose is to provide an activity where little boys, and now girls, first and foremost derive pleasure. Second, it is hoped by many parents and promoters of the League that cooperation, self-confidence, and physical well-being will be developed. But at a Little League game, what we may find is an adult manager snarling at a little tyke, parents venting their fury, frustration, and anguish at umpires, managers, players, and even their own children. Adults are obviously displaying their own vicarious insecurities. Whatever is learned by the youngsters besides baseball skills is of questionable value.

Adult sports can be no less reprehensible, and they too establish a miserable model for children. Legalized mayhem in professional hockey and assaultive behavior by soccer, baseball, and football spectators are not uncommon. The professionalization and commercialization of these sports is an example of what can happen to wholesome and pleasurable activities, but we don't need a television network to pervert and corrupt a sport. Nevertheless, engagement in a sport— especially on a regular basis—can have many of the advantages of play in its most constructive sense and promote psychological and physical well-being.

Hobbies

Hobbies are specialized games for older children and adults. They may involve collecting, making things, developing some kind of expertise or a store of information. As with all games, their primary motivation is the pleasure that comes from doing them, although with such hobbies as cabinet making or sewing, the secondary purposes can be considerable. The motivation to engage in them can range from a simple desire to fill up spare time, to an inescapable need to write poetry. They can be a harmless amusement or the most private and personalized activities in our lives.

Imbalances or disturbances in emotional life can manifest themselves in what we have called contaminations of these free, volitional activities. The antique collector who forgets about the beauty of the objects he or she owns in favor of a desire to make money, the stamp collector who uses his or her hobby to retreat from family life and to impose an order on the collection that he or she cannot achieve in other functions, or the person who reads history night after night or will not vary his or her schedule of watching sports on television is being driven by rather than choosing a hobby. More important, that person is ignoring the needs and pressures that are impoverishing his or her life. Hobbies used for this reason are only stop-gap measures and will never make up for a larger deprivation. If a person's life is getting narrower and narrower as it constricts around a hobby, he or she should take stock of life and perhaps seek the help of a therapist.

On the other hand, hobbies represent one of the most wholesome and pleasurable of activities. While many spend their leisure hours "killing time," napping, or sitting passively in front of the television, people who possess interesting hobbies have the opportunity to express themselves, perfect their knowledge, and, most important, to actively create their own pleasure and satisfaction. Because the choice of a hobby is a personal act, it allows people to engage in an activity for themselves alone, free of the constraints, responsibilities, and roles of the workaday world. It can be a free space in our lives, an uncontaminated area of self-cultivation and interest. Many people have lost the ability to be alone with themselves in a positive and active sense. We are in no better company than when we are enjoying ourselves, creating our own pleasure, observing ourselves grow in knowledge and skill. It is not all of life, but it is an important part.

Music

If we think about it, one of the remarkable things about the modern world is the extraordinary proliferation and ubiquity of music. The most dedicated music lover of the last century would have been lucky to have heard the nine Beethoven symphonies a few times. Now, for twenty-five or thirty dollars, he or she can have them on the phonograph constantly. Our world is surrounded—perhaps saturated—by music of all kinds. We go shopping: first we snap off the radio in our apartment, get on the elevator where Muzak has thoughtfully been provided, get into a cab where the driver's taste blares at us, and walk into the supermarket where we are lulled by homogenized music. Music can be a great joy and consolation, but it can also be padding to lull the mind and keep the world away.

A word needs to be said about "good" music. Any music that pleases, relaxes, or energizes is good. There is no bad music. Music, however, that focuses on false sentimentality, sensational sex, or mind-blasting vulgarity narrows and limits the listener, just as pap writing and comics do. "Good" music, like "good" art and "good" books, seems in general to be more permanent and mind-expanding and to provide a repertoire for fuller, diversified, and challenging experience. To the degree that we have a stock of interests, amusements, and inspiring or engrossing pursuits that we can dip in to, we will feel enriched, stimulated, and less likely to experience boredom, emptiness, and depression.

Sometimes, however, the eclectic or dilletante is really compulsive. That person masks the feeling that he or she is missing out, is fearful of involvement, and despairs of mastering anything because it has to be mastered and perfected. Perhaps he or she just has not learned how to focus attention. In such an event, pleasure is drained from music, and art becomes a chore.

There are critical periods during which the engendering of life-long appreciation of music can be encouraged. This is especially true of the first five years of life. Again, but not so optimal, are the prepubertal years, and then during the early teens. Thereafter, it is possible but more difficult to develop musical tastes, inasmuch as personality styles and modes of expression, perceiving, and processing the environment have largely been set. The most significant task is to provide children with diversified and enriching experience in music and art and to associate it with pleasant conditions. This ensures the child an excellent opportunity to appreciate beauty for his or her whole life and to avoid boredom and stultification.

A common cause of family tension and conflict is adolescent taste in music, in particular, the requirement that music be played at deafening volume. The nostalgic parent may well wonder why his or her offspring will not be satisfied with something like those nice Sinatra records which furnished his or her own adolescent aesthetic life. That parent would be well advised to remember a little more carefully: the frenzied and hysterical Sinatra fans swooning and shrieking at the sight of their idol were not so different from their modern counterparts, and they summoned up a similar dismay in their own parents. In fact, one of the functions of music for the adolescent is to set a distance from his or her parents' world.

In adolescence, young people begin to define themselves in terms of their peer groups, and often turn away from membership in the family. In flaunting their deviant and extreme musical tastes, they are partly asserting the fact of their difference from adults. This need of young people should be understood and respected.

Nonetheless, adolescents' need to demonstrate individuality must be balanced against their responsibility and courtesy toward the family. Some kind of understanding should be reached by mutual discussion and respect. Rock may not be played at highest volumes at all hours. It is a useful lesson for both young people and their parents to learn how to coordinate their own taste and needs with an appreciation for the feelings of others. If the playing of loud music has a hostile and defiant quality, the reasons for this should be explored. It may have a legitimate cause, or it may represent a more serious doubt about the young person's role and identity. Parents responding with anger and intolerance will only increase the teen-ager's defiance.

Conversely, sensitive and introspective young people often discover classical music during their teens. This involvement can be as subtly frightening as that of their noisier peers, since it can mean a similar withdrawal from the family into their own rarefied world. Again, this need for withdrawal and self-definition should be respected, and at the same time, parents should be aware of excessive solitude and self-involvement. Nevertheless, the young person who turns to Brahms to find an acknowledgment of his or her confusing world of ideals, sexuality, and identity is luckier than most.

Learning then that the most personal thoughts and fantasies have been experienced before, that there is an eloquent and powerful language for feelings, and that strength of emotion can mean depth as well as loudness, is an extraordinarily important and subtle lesson that will continue to help, console, and energize a person throughout his or her entire lifetime.

The discovery of a new form of expression and experience need not be confined to adolescence. Many adults, from young parents to the retired, have found their lives enriched and varied by learning to play an instrument or undertaking the study of a new musical mode. Like learning a foreign language, the time for mastery of a musical instrument seems optimal in childhood, so the adult student should not hope to become a Horowitz or a Stern. But the acquisition of a new skill, however imperfect, can be enormously satisfying. One's appreciation for music can be deepened and focused. A new world can open up. Finally, the opportunities for communication and sharing are immense when one includes another in his or her new discoveries and experiences.

Other Arts

What we have said about music holds true for the visual arts. The same values of relaxation, excitement, and self-expression hold here, and the person who finds the image for his or her own inner thoughts and emotions in a painting or sculpture has made a valuable discovery.

The taste for art, like that for music, is frequently begun in childhood, although this world is accessible to people of all ages. Children who are encouraged to express themselves with finger-paints and crayons and whose expression is understood and valued stand a good chance of deriving pleasure and meaning in later life from communicating with the great masters of the past. Artistic expression, however, is an intensely personal act, even for the youngest, and parents— especially well-meaning ones—should respect the integrity of their children's endeavors. Children may abandon their fledgling artistic efforts if their parents' reactions are excessive or fraudulent or if they insist that they see something in the work that the child had not intended. Let the child interpret and discuss his or her own work. This will allow an important and subtle form of communication to develop. The child's intention in a painting he or she has done in school can be surprisingly abstract. Cute or sentimental responses can stifle the child's first attempts at expression just as they would an adult's.

A love for art, visual or otherwise, can be instilled partly by the experience being a family affair, surrounded by enthusiasm, curiosity, and fun. Visits to museums, concerts, and theaters can provide some of the happiest and richest memories of childhood if they are not strained, phony, or pedagogical. Children are some of our best practical psychologists, and if parents undertake such outings in a spirit of pleasureless obligation, the child will respond accordingly to this glum, joyless exercise. For the child, art may well become an exercise in hypocrisy and false feeling. If the parents have no artistic tastes of their own, it is better to let the child make his or her own discoveries. Parents can, in any case, respond to their child's achievements with interest, excitement, and even admiration.

Adulthood and old age often provide the opportunity to develop skills and interests that previously lay dormant. A deprived childhood or busy adulthood often leave no time for cultivation of the aesthetic sense, but as one fulfills the requirements of adult life and grows more intimate with the self, a yearning for art may often arise. This is a good time to develop these interests.

A course, formal or informal, in art appreciation can dramatically expand our range of pleasure and enthusiasm, or a new hobby in painting or sculpture can provide much zest. Few of us are gifted enough to become a recognized artist; we should therefore try to cultivate the satisfaction of the activity itself at the personal level. The discipline and hard work of the serious artist are perhaps not for us and should not be a source of anxiety. Pleasure in color and form, the satisfaction of any completed work, the sense of discovery, and the intimacy that comes from self-expression are extremely important experiences. They are worth cultivating in themselves.

Dance

Dancing can be pleasurable and invigorating in its own right. It can also further relationships and intimacy as well. Some Fundamentalists condemn dancing because they recognize its sensual nature and see that erotic stimulation can be part of it. Yet these are good reasons for enjoying dancing.

Ballet and more formal kinds of dancing require great discipline, and their satisfactions are correspondingly great. Such forms can be subtle means of self-expression and ways of achieving intimacy with our bodies and feelings. Moreover, the achievement of the athletic skill necessary to execute the classical steps is a great accomplishment. On the other hand, the discipline required by this art form can become masochistic and tinged with anxiety. Dance is no way of defeating the aging process and can be no substitute for the usual forms of intimacy and communication. As with all the activities we are discussing in this section, our involvement should be judged by the pleasure, interest, and excitement we feel. If we find ourselves becoming anxious, compulsive, or unduly frustrated, it is a good idea to consider our motives and to inquire into what needs we are trying to fulfill—to ask if other activities provide more appropriate vehicles.

Reading

We have included reading under the topic of play, but we leave the discussion of certain of its aspects to the chapter on Coping. Reading to children by loving, interested adults is close to, if not another form of nourishment. Indeed, Freud postulated that visual and oral stimulation are linked and remain so in the primary process or unconscious. To help ensure a child's love of reading, its earliest, pre-school tendencies can be nurtured and encouraged, often as easily as by the availability of books in the home and their frequent use. A critical period is just past puberty—thirteen to fifteen years of age. Just as there is a spurt of growth and interest in the world around them, teen-agers may turn to books. If the experience is rewarded by interesting books and encouragement, the teen-ager will most likely love reading thereafter. What corrupts this gratification is the not infrequent association of reading with homework. Reading is then seen as a chore, a task to perform for others which has no personal value or interest in and of itself.

The goal is to cultivate the pleasure of reading in the child, to discover what pleases him or her, and to provide the opportunity and environment to develop this pursuit. Early exposure to classics appropriate to each age leaves its mark, and books presented as gifts, tokens of affection, or rewards will help the child associate reading with pleasure. A child who is rewarded with encouragement and conditioned by a family that enjoys reading and discussing will most likely continue to enjoy it for the rest of his or her life.

Reading, for both child and adult, can serve important functions in psychic life. It provides a welcome relief and withdrawal from the pressures of social and professional life and an opportunity to regain acquaintance with one's inner nature, particularly one's fantasy life. The identification with figures of fiction, the immersion in an exotic setting and life style, the vicarious participation in dangers and adventures, are needs that do not leave us with childhood. Adult, serious reading, however, does more than this. It works with these primal needs and relates them to moral and social values.

People who find themselves inordinately attached to

overly sentimentalized fiction might inquire about what facets of their lives are not being satisfied by their real life experiences. The place to correct such deficiencies is, of course, life itself. And if one finds that he or she judges real life by the fantasies summoned up by fiction, condemning the former as unexciting or pale by comparison, a serious imbalance in his or her sense of reality may be suggested.

Television

The arch competitor and possible inhibitor of reading and all other sports, games, and hobbies is television. Not only is it used as an alternative or supplement to custodial care in hospitals, asylums, prisons, and nursing homes, but it is the most permanent and widely used baby sitter in millions of homes. It has been called a wasteland—chewing gum for the mind.

There is something addictive (or at least habituating) as well as hypnotic about television. Unlike reading, which requires an active involvement by the readers, television encourages, even demands, passive surrender by the viewers to the tiny spectacle before them. Their perceptions are forced upon them, and television's explicitness leaves little room for individual fantasy. Television becomes fixated upon and stared at even when viewers feel boredom or distaste. They will stare at the screen during the most boring, irrelevant, and insulting commercials. Indeed, many are observed to continue to gaze at a blank screen with only a geometric signal flashing on it.

TV can be used as an avoidance of life, reality, and intimacy. Along with other popular soporifics, drugs, alcohol, and distractions, television allows the person to avoid a sense of depression, frustration, tension, and the need for human contact.

There is considerable controversy about whether the viewing of television encourages aggression and maladjustment in children. Defenders of television argue that children will watch only what they are interested in to begin with, and, in any case, what they watch only reflects the culture in which they are growing up. Critics answer that the viewing habits of adults and the young can be shaped and directed into constructive, creative channels while they are being entertained. Certainly, there is evidence that commercials geared toward children are often rank propaganda, often misleading them into feeling they are miserable unless they can persuade their parents to purchase an inferior or even unhealthy product. And persuade children they do! Recently, a defense offered by a teen-age murderer in California was that he was merely repeating an act he had viewed on television. His defense did not hold up, but the fact that it was offered seriously in a court suggests a body of opinion that supports this possibility.

None of the studies on the effects of television violence is absolutely conclusive, but certain things are clear. Children's behavior is extremely influenceable by what they see—particularly by the actions of role models. Attractive, successful, and admirable television figures who assert their masculinity with guns and fists are teaching a not too subtle lesson to their young viewers. A child who spends hours a day before the tube seeing that the solution to frustration is violence knows what to do the next time he or she is annoyed by a playmate. Children learn to respect violence and aggressive behavior and to ignore the more difficult, subtle, and less glamorous solutions to problems.

But most of all, the conception of civilized society and relations among people become warped. A child who regularly views bullet-ridden corpses and human beings beaten into unconsciousness forms ideas about what is permissible in human conduct. The dehumanization of life, the tendency to regard people as objects or numbers, the drying up of empathy and compassion are all encouraged by the indiscriminate viewing of violence meant to entertain.

Still, the defenders of television programming have a valid point. A healthy, feeling child will, most likely, not be unduly influenced by television violence. Children prone to violence will be more likely than others to take violent cues. The issue, however, may be more complicated and involve the operations of a child's fantasy life. Children who have a healthy ability to indulge in fantasy and to express it in appropriate ways are probably relatively immune from infection from TV. Those, however, who for one reason or another are afraid of their own fantasies and are unable to experience or express them fully are more likely to allow what they see to provide the contents of their inner lives. These children are most subject to influence from television, movies, comics, and their peers.

In any case, it is difficult to argue that violence of any kind can have a wholesome effect on young viewers. There are better ways of spending the years of childhood than by mindlessly watching inanity and brutality. Forbidding this activity will be only doubtfully effective—providing alternatives is the wisest course.

Lest the reader get the impression that television has a predominantly negative influence, we wish to stress its powerful positive features. First, it is a learning tool par excellence. When it is combined imaginatively with entertainment and education, its success can be outstanding. Public television in particular has been noteworthy in this respect. "Sesame Street," for example, has hooked millions of pre-schoolers and their parents. They watch it with pleasure and learn about numbers, economics, relationships, and so on. Studies have shown that faithful watching of this program alone significantly increases the information and scholastic aptitudes of children.

Good quality television, of which there is an appreciable amount, can and does provide artistic and educational programs and stimulates a creative involvement in the viewer. It can have the quality of play or recreation combined with education. If one were largely to restrict oneself to the National Educational Television Network for a year, we speculate that a viewer would attain the equivalent of a liberal arts education, for one is exposed to the best in the arts, music, dance, science, politics, philosophy, and considerably more.

So television, like most other things in life, can be used or abused. It behooves parents to structure the viewing of their children, determining with them what is interesting and entertaining and at the same time geared toward developing appreciation for what stimulates fantasy, thinking, aesthetics, and significant events and productions of other people.

Too often, while the parent complains of the TV addiction of the child, the adult is really at some level relieved that the child is off his or her hands and is distracted. The adult would be well advised to observe his or her own viewing habits. Does the Sunday football widow get some message about her relationship with her husband? Does compulsive watching of soaps tell the housewife that she is depressed or wishes to escape from a non-stimulating reality? And if sex cannot precede the eleven o'clock news, late talk shows, or the late, late show—provided one does not fall asleep—what does that say? Television is a tool, an instrument that we can use in any number of ways. We choose our books, our food, our friends. Why should we accept whatever television fare some group of executives and salespeople have determined will make them money? We have the choice.

Summary

Much of our lives is spent doing what we think we have to do. From our paid jobs to our roles as parents and spouses, from doing the laundry to performing in bed, we are only partly ourselves. It is in play, however, that we come closest to being ourselves and ourselves alone. Here we can choose what it is that gives us most pleasure and satisfaction.

The chief characteristic of play is its lack of ulterior motive—we do it for its own sake. In doing so, we enrich our mental lives, relax from tension, take satisfaction in real achievement, and emerge ready to confront the world. A healthy and well-balanced emotional life, it has become clear, depends partly on our ability to play.

It may seem strange, in view of this, to speak of the pathology of play, but this phrase merely means play that has become something else. If play is put to the service of other activities, if we do it to assert something about ourselves— our strength, superiority, youth, or cleverness—we have lost the benefits of this most useful and exhilarating activity. Similarly, if we become anxious, compulsive, or depressed while playing, we are no longer playing.

Play is not the withdrawal from life, and if we find that we are using hobbies and interests to kill time or to avoid tension, frustration, and boredom, we would do well to see what there is about our real lives that leaves us unsatisfied. In addition, there is also the danger that our free-time activities can impinge on our larger lives. A morbid involvement in sentimental novels or violent television can pervert our values and our ability to lead a full and free life.

We can help ensure that children develop an interest and enthusiasm for reading and art by providing appropriate cultural activities for them and by making such activities a source of pleasure and excitement. The optimal age for learning an artistic skill is commonly in childhood, but such activities are available to us throughout our lives.

The varieties of play are as broad as the human imagination, and the need to play is as enduring as the need to be ourselves. The healthy adult keeps the child in him or her alive throughout life, and just as all children need love, nourishment, and care, they need to play.

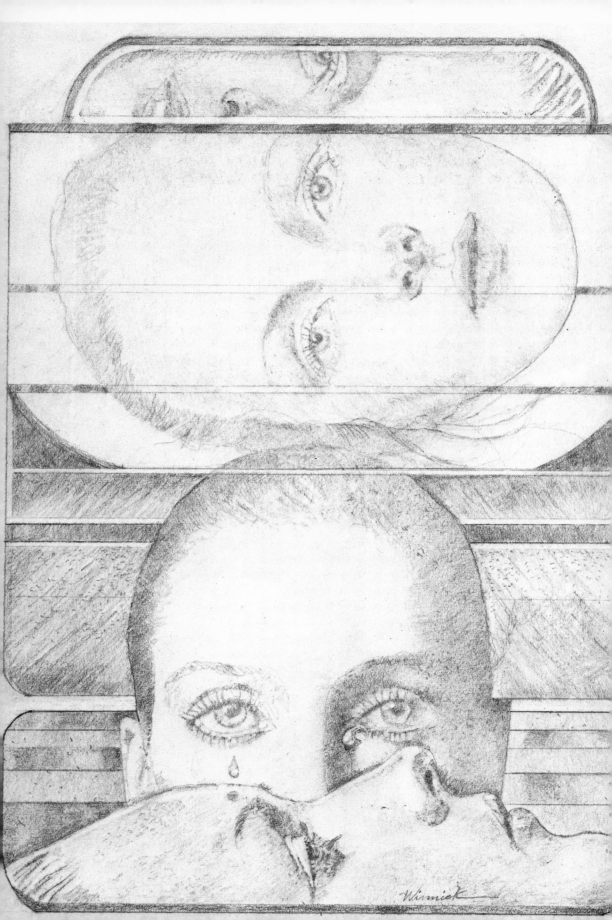

5
Thinking, Feelings, and Fantasy

There are two ways in which we process our experience of the world and of ourselves: thinking and feeling. Sometimes these are very separate processes, but more often they are mixed. We can be very emotional about what we think, or we can be very thoughtful about what we feel.

Thinking

To think, it is necessary first to distinguish between the outer world and ourselves. Until then we are merely perceiving, reacting, and emoting. We do not know what is real or unreal, we have no opinions, judgments, values, or beliefs, and we can make no decisions. The moment we differentiate ourselves from the world, we have a piece of information, knowledge—we are discriminating between figure and ground. The moment the infant voluntarily—not in a reflexive way—spits out something bitter or closes his or her eyes against a glaring light, he or she has learned something, has made a judgment, a decision. And in the infant, this is when rudimentary thinking begins.

Certain individuals never fully learn to tell the difference or to maintain the separation of the world of other individuals and themselves. They are said to have thought disorders. Paranoids, for example, ascribe influences, motives, and actions to others, vague "they's," the world, and even to inanimate objects. Such people have projected their thoughts onto someone or something else, because paranoids do not perceive the world as separate from themselves.

Thinking is the ability to reason; to tell the difference between what is real and what is unreal; to form judgments, opinions, beliefs, and values, and to operate on some logical system; to perceive and weigh options and to make decisions.

The Development of Thought

Although some of Swiss psychologist Jean Piaget's concepts are difficult and obscure, his main ideas are relatively straight-forward and interesting. Basically, he discovered that the thought processes of children are qualitatively different from their adult counterparts. It is not that children think less well than adults; they think differently. Piaget outlined the development of thought from its infant form to the threshhold of adult thinking in four stages. As far as we know, the order of these stages is constant across all cultures and styles of child rearing. The rate at which a child moves through these stages may vary, but the order of the stages is always the same. One stage cannot begin before the preceding one has developed. Parents should bear this in mind in their expectations of children, whether it involves toilet training or the child's taking on any number of responsibilities.

Piaget called the first stage the "sensory-motor" period, which occurs during the first two years of life. During this stage, infants learn to coordinate certain inborn reflexes into patterns of behavior called schemata, which are used to secure certain things from the environment. Infants learn that they do not have to wait passively for their parents to shake their rattles; they can grasp and shake the toys themselves. Generally speaking, children learn three profound lessons here: self-identification, efficacy, and causality. They learn that external reality consists of objects in space that are different from the self. They learn to separate figure from ground and to understand that objects endure when they cannot be seen. Infants' endlessly engrossing games of peek-a-boo help teach them this lesson. Moreover, the infants learn efficacy, the sense that they are competent to effect changes in their environment. Finally, they begin to assume causality, the belief that causes precede effects and that physical action, not wishing, is necessary to change objects.

The second stage, which occurs between the ages of two and seven years, is called "pre-operational thought." Here children learn to represent the external world internally by means of symbols and language. They begin to understand the concept of classes, that paper cut-outs can be arranged into circles, triangles, and so forth. This discovery of language and symbolic representation allows children to think about their experiences and to make plans for the future. The limitations to this kind of thought are the infants' tendency to reason by simile and their inability to transcend egocentric perceptions. That is, if I give a card with a dog on one side and a cat on the other to a child to inspect, and then hold it up with the dog-side facing the child, almost all three-year-olds can tell me what *I* see, but only one-half of all two-year-olds can perform the task.

The third stage, "concrete operations," occurs between the ages of seven and eleven. Here children learn to develop an organized system for dealing with events in the outside world. They understand arithmetic, the idea of classes, measurement, and the principle of conservation—that the amount of something remains the same although its shape may change. If you have a child from five to seven years old, you can perform a fascinating experiment. Take two glasses, one tall and narrow, the other short and wider. Have the child pour some liquid into the first glass and then pour from the first into the second. Most five-year-olds will insist that there is more liquid in the tall glass (because the height of the liquid is greater); a seven-year-old will probably understand that the glasses contain the same amount of liquid. A six-year-old might be quite confused. But a child who makes the right decision has mastered the idea of conservation.

The fourth and final stage, the gateway to adult and sophisticated thought, begins around the age of eleven and is called "formal operations." Here young people are finally able to think independently of visible and concrete experience by having recourse to purely mental and symbolic thought. Here the signs of abstract thought make their first appearance. Young people can now entertain hypothetical arguments, can distinguish examples from the substance of an argument, and can proceed entirely by verbal description and analysis.

These are not only extremely interesting things to know about the development of thinking, but they are useful as well. They teach us that a child's capacity for thought is strictly limited by what stage he or she has achieved. Unless a child is prodigiously gifted, it will do no good at all to explain a logical argument that he or she is incapable of understanding. The teaching of arithmetic, for example, must be geared to the mental capacities of the student, and more complicated moral judgments, like the ability to see things from someone else's point of view, also depend on the achieved stage of cognitive development. Significantly, it has been found that a child moves from one stage to the next only when his or her previous mental organization is inadequate to deal with his or her world. That is, mental growth depends on a degree of moderate frustration and surprise. The importance of providing a stimulating and moderately challenging environment for a growing child is apparent.

The Development of Moral Thinking

Lawrence Kohlberg, an American psychologist, has used Piaget's scheme to devise a similar developmental pattern for a child's capacity for making moral judgments. Again, the order of stages is unvarying, although the rate at which the child progresses depends on many factors. Significantly, some people never achieve the highest stage. Kohlberg divides this development into three levels, each of which is further subdivided into two stages.

On the first, the "preconventional" level, moral values are derived from external consequences, rather than from standards of authority. The earlier stage of this level is an orientation around results. Actions are judged wrong if they result in punishment or trouble. A later stage judges actions by their ability to satisfy needs. Here, the beginning of a perception of the needs of others first emerges.

On the second, or "conventional," level, value resides in conformity, conventions, and rules. Children adopt a "good boy" and "nice girl" posture aimed at pleasing others and winning their approval. The influence of stereotypes is very strong. At a slightly higher stage, children or even adults who have not gotten any farther, will judge actions by their correspondence to authority and law and order. Adherence to rules and a belief in social order are paramount.

On the highest, or "postconventional," level, morality resides in internal and socially shared standards of right and wrong. The first stage of this level is basically contractual and legalistic, qualified by a sense of the rights of others and of the relativity of moral judgment. The highest stage revolves around the idea of conscience and abstract values. Ethics are self-imposed, and the moral individual is concerned that his or her system of values be consistent and logical. He or she becomes interested in trust and respect for the individuality of others, rather than in some codified set of rules and laws.

An extremely interesting discussion can be had with a child by proposing some situation demanding a moral judgment and by discussing his or her evaluation. For example, there are two children, one of whom breaks a glass intentionally, while the other overturns a whole set of china accidentally. Who has committed the "worse" transgression? It is fascinating to see how different the perceptions of moral values can be. But most important, we can use Kohlberg's scheme to judge the adequacy of our own moral evaluation. Are we still at the stage of accepting the judgments of authority figures, or have we taken the responsibility of forming our own ethical system?

Thinking and Language

Thinking is linked to language. It is only when we acquire language that we can engage in secondary process thinking. It is necessary for us to put our thoughts into words for us to think clearly and consistently. Sometimes, this does not appear evident, and we use such terms as instinctive and intuitive. But this only means that the verbal process is subtle, subliminal, or that it controls a series of instinctive and automatic responses. We can't think without information, and the best, if not the only, way to store information and to retrieve it is to link it with words. The greater the vocabulary and the flexibility and control of words, the more effective and easy the thinking.

It is very likely that certain languages allow for different kinds of perceptions and thought more easily than others. The American linguist, Benjamin Lee Whorf, thought that the mental life of a culture, its perceptions, categories of thought, and thought processes themselves were shaped by its language. Eskimos have seven different words for various kinds of snow, while to New Yorkers, snow is snow. Ancient Greek has an intricate and highly developed system of tenses, while Estonian, with its complex system of noun declensions, encourages a great sensitivity to the spatial arrangement of reality. Languages that distinguish between polite and informal modes of address accommodate more elaborate and careful codes of manners than do languages that do not make this distinction.

It is a general rule that someone who uses language carefully and who has a wide range of linguistic expressions readily available will find it easier to perceive and think adequately than someone whose language is less precise. Linguistic richness can have many forms. It can be a precise and large vocabulary or a colorful and powerful slang. But in all cases, there is attention to expressing oneself with precision and nuance. Correct language can become stilted, and slang or dialect can be sloppy and lazy. The danger is greater with the latter. A shrug of the shoulders, a ready-made cliché, or lazy and imprecise habits of expression can reflect and lead to an impoverishment of perception and thought as well as inadequate powers of communication. Since language is not only determined by thought processes, but in turn influences the power and quality of thinking, it is important to stress from earliest childhood the development and enjoyment of fluent, rich, and expressive language. Because reading is very instrumental in promoting language skills, encouraging reading is most important. (See the discussions of reading in the chapters on Playing and Coping.)

Thinking tends to rigidify and narrow with age if stimulation and encouragement are not appropriate and sufficient. But barring brain damage or deterioration, there is no evidence to indicate that age in itself causes thinking to deteriorate. A gradual limitation of options, a decreased interest in life, or a despair about possibilities can lead to an unnecessary mental rigidity.

Feeling

We are all born with a capacity for emotion. The newborn infant manifests frustration, anxiety, rage, and pleasure. It then becomes the task of the child and the parents to channel and harness these emotions constructively. This is one of the most arduous and complicated tasks for human beings, although everyone tries to do it. If we are not tutored well in using rather than being ruled by our feelings, we and the people around us are subject to suffering, irrationality, and destructive behavior. If, on the other hand, we are taught to fear and to suppress our emotions, our feelings become relatively inaccessible to us. In such instances, we are prone to obsessiveness, guilt, and an inability to express anger or to experience pleasure. Emotions are our biological reactions to stimulation, both to what is gratifying and necessary for survival and to what is stressful and threatening.

Unfortunately, we often learn to ignore or stifle our emotions. First, we learn that we may not express or even feel such emotions as anger and pain, lest we court disapproval and punishment. So we learn not to be our real selves. Arthur Janov, the discoverer and practitioner of Primal Scream Therapy, bases his entire treatment and philosophy on this fact. All children, Janov says, learn that if they are literally to survive, they must be good little boys and girls and repudiate many of their needs and impulses. They become false people, incapable of real feeling or experience, storing up an ever-increasing reservoir of pain and unmet needs. The price they pay is emotional deadness, cruelty, and any number of psychosomatic diseases. Janov's therapy consists of liberating the initial experience of pain and repudiation in a violent and soul-shattering series of "primal screams."

Whether or not we want to follow Janov's analysis through all of its implications, we can agree that denying emotions results in the inability to feel fully or, in a certain sense, to be. We learn to perform rather than to respond or act spontaneously. Moreover, various emotions go underground and get expressed indirectly, often perniciously. They get dammed up only to pour out in an emotional torrent that can be very destructive. The retention of feelings such as anger and pain can also operate insidiously on our bodies, as we will see in the section on psychosomatic disorders in the chapter on Health.

Perhaps the severest penalty we pay for not feeling and not adequately expressing our emotions is the way this denial distorts us. When we learn to deny pain and anger, we learn at the same time to ignore or insufficiently draw upon our feelings of affection and pleasure. Excessive refusal to acknowledge our own anger and pain results in the inability to love or to feel. Once we begin to deny the feeling side of our personality, we begin to seriously distort and mutilate our personality, and it is an arduous task to set the proportions right again.

Much of the therapy of C. G. Jung, the great Swiss psychologist and psychiatrist, is an attempt to restore balance to a psyche that has denied part of its functioning. For him, although certain tendencies in the personality—the basic feeling or thinking type, or the introverted or extraverted orientation—are partly determined by inborn temperament, the course of most people's lives is to develop one aspect of the psyche—thinking, feeling, sensation, or intuition—at the expense of the others. A psychological crisis is often precipitated by the recognition that the personality has gotten seriously unbalanced. Frequently this happens at the mid-life crisis. (See the sections on the forties in the chapters on Change and Stages.) Jung's subtle and complex therapy is meant to recover and reactivate the possibilities that have been denied all one's life and to develop all the functions that make for a well-balanced individual. All of us need some correction, but those who have not been taught to deny their emotional natures are luckier than most.

As parents, it is extremely important for us to encourage the experience and expression of feelings in children, although appropriate channels for these expressions must be found. The contrary has too often been the case. Males have been instilled with the idea that to be masculine they must inhibit the expression and even the experience of pain and sentiment. If they do not, they feel and are seen as weak and feminine. Females, even as little girls, are taught to suppress any aggressive and ambitious tendencies lest they be viewed as unfeminine. These lessons are so emphatically learned and conditioned that, despite the judgments of these boys and girls in adult life to the contrary, their behavior is forever ruled by these stereotypes—to the distinct disadvantage of themselves and their intimates. Cultural and ethnic factors play a part as well. The Anglo-Saxon culture stereotypically puts a premium on stoicism and control of feelings, while such ethnic groups as Italians and Irish value toughness in the men and role conformity in women.

To reiterate, feelings are part of the human condition. They are to be respected, attended to, understood, and given appropriate channels for expression. To do so makes for a balanced individual. To do otherwise promotes an inhibited, rigid, or tense person.

All too often, one spouse complains that the other does not express feelings. Usually, but not necessarily, this is the complaint of the wife. Her husband, she laments, is always in his head and does not really communicate. The male spouse, on the other hand, does not know what the other is talking about. Here we have the classic instance of a feeling-type person married to a thinking-type. They chose each other for that reason, usually subliminally, and could not abide someone of their own orientation. This very choice, however, often makes for disparity in communication and in sensitivity to each other as time goes on. Of course, these apparent differences may be symptomatic of a power struggle between the two. More will be said on this in the chapter on Relating. At this point, however, we may note that for the relationship to continue, each partner must make an attempt both to communicate his or her own feelings and sense of values and to understand and respect the other's point of view. Marriage, in this sense, must at least partly be a process of mutual education and collaboration. Differences in thought and feeling between two partners in marriage can be a cause of conflict, but they can also be the source of growth and enrichment.

Anger

We see the expression of rage from birth on. Restricting a baby's movements causes rage, as can any frustration. Anger seems to be the power the body uses to overcome obstacles and to combat threat. Becoming aware of anger reveals to us what is frustrating, thwarting, or threatening to us. Awareness permits us not only to understand why we are angry, but to decide whether and how to express, suppress, or divert the feeling. In fact, we really do not have a choice: a pent-up anger will express itself indirectly as irritation or bitchiness, erupt in explosions or be turned back on ourselves, causing depression or psychosomatic illness. Expressed anger, on the other hand, permits us to learn more appropriate channels of expression and to deal with frustration in effective ways.

To deny rage or to believe we can avoid becoming angry is irrational. Anger is a natural reaction to an imperfect world. This is not to suggest that we cannot reduce substantially the triggers for rage, moderate our expression, or find more suitable modes of behavior. But the proscription, "Don't get angry," or worse, "You are bad if you get angry," is most harmful as well as unreasonable. Too often the child generalizes the prohibition against anger to one against any expression of aggression or even of assertion. Females particularly have been subject to this unreasonable demand, and many have grown up fearful of their own self-assertion and personal success. (See the sections on work and success and failure in the chapter on Coping.)

Moderate and appropriate aggression means merely moving an obstacle out of one's way or moving purposefully toward a goal. To repress or suppress aggressive tendencies is to become passive, wishy-washy, or indecisive. Assertion means determining a position, an opinion, or a conviction and taking a stand on it. To be non-assertive is to become martyred or to be set up for victimization. Many of us learn to be "nice guys," which means that we express our anger, aggressiveness, or assertion indirectly, usually by trying to make the other person feel guilty or mean in comparison to us. Surely, this is an inefficient and inappropriate way of relating to others. This problem is so prevalent, again especially for women, that assertiveness training has become quite common.

Anxiety

Anxiety is a diffuse feeling of apprehension or dread. It is different from fear, which is directed toward something specific. Harry Stack Sullivan thought that anxiety is a reaction to separation. The prototypical separation is birth—separation from the all-protective, all-nurturing womb. This is followed by the separations of weaning, the first day at school, graduation from high school, and at times, marriage, if this event is perceived as separation from the nuclear home. Sullivan believed that anxiety, as discriminated from fear, always was related to an interpersonal factor, specifically disapproval or the withholding of love.

What can be definitively said is that anxiety is a signal of psychological danger, which results from a conflict between competing motives or from a forbidden, dangerous impulse. Because of its diffuseness and lack of specificity, it is necessary to fathom its causes by identifying the trigger and by becoming aware of what reactions are thereby stimulated. It is only then that anxiety can be dealt with directly. On the other hand, Fritz Perls, the Gestalt psychologist, pointed out that some kinds of anxiety are healthy signals of change— really forms of excitement. It is always important to keep the distinction clear. Those who have been taught to be timid and self-effacing often confuse their experience of excitement with fear and anxiety.

All psychological disturbances involve anxiety, although the defenses against it may disguise that fact. The defenses themselves may be recognized as symptoms. (More will be said on that topic in the chapter on Behavior Disturbances.) With acute anxiety, especially when it is felt to be overwhelming, a variety of medications may be prescribed. (See the discussion of drug therapy in the chapter on Behavior Disturbances and in the Glossary.) Of course, this does not resolve the anxiety, but the precipitating disturbance may disappear or be minimized by the time the medication is suspended. It is much more effective and permanent to comprehend the anxiety-provoking situation and to confront the issues. There are various ways to do this, and these will be discussed in the chapter on Change, but counseling or psychotherapy is often the most reliable and effective course.

Guilt

Guilt is a secondary feeling. That is to say, we learn to say we feel guilty when we wish to avoid facing another feeling or action. Primary feelings are in reaction to the environment, interpersonal or otherwise. They have somatic correlates.

Guilt, on the other hand, is a cognitive, intellectual response. The guilty person believes that he or she has violated some value. To feel guilty, one has to have made a judgment that one has done or wished to do something one should not. Being ruled by moral imperatives has been described as the tyranny of the "shoulds," and Albert Ellis has called it "mustabation"—that is, "I must do this," "I must do that," and so on.

To avoid suffering the crushing weight of guilt, it may be helpful to eschew dictates that tell us we *have* to do something, that bespeak of obligations and responsibilities as "shoulds," or that are concerned only with the standards of others. Instead, it is more useful to determine what we want to do and to act accordingly. This means deciding for ourselves what option is best, what in the long run will be most appropriate for us and for those whom we care about, and then deciding in favor of that which weighs more positively than negatively. Almost always, this means settling for the least imperfect, rather than the perfect, solution.

For example, a friend is in the hospital, and I hate to go to hospitals. If I feel I should visit him, it is my obligation. If I don't go, I will feel guilty. On the other hand, I really hate going, and if I go, I will resent both my friend and myself. But if I really believe it more appropriate to visit the hospitalized friend—it will make him feel good and I will feel better about it in the long run—I go because I want to and have consciously decided to do so. The consequence is no guilt and usually less resentment. But the decision is by no means perfect.

Earlier, in the chapter on Eating, we noted that the need for contact is so strong that if babies are not held, cuddled, and fondled, they suffer severely, become apathetic, and can even develop marasmus, in which they literally sicken and die. This need for contact as well as for intimacy is experienced as feelings of love, affection, and tenderness. Both love and guilt, or the fear of the loss of love, essentially describe the human condition.

The satisfaction of these feelings of love, affection, and tenderness results in happiness and contentment. Their deprivation causes anxiety, depression, and frustration. There is no one who really does not want intimacy, although deprivation may have made him or her so guarded and cynical that he or she seems determined to deny and frustrate any attempts at closeness.

Without a close relationship, we are at least a little crazy. In fact, Sullivan defined sanity as a consensual validation—a sharing of perceived reality—with another. Yet the paradox

Love, Affection, and Tenderness

remains that so many fear intimacy and avoid close involvement. They opt for loneliness, isolation, and even alienation despite the attendant misery. This is because they have found rejection so painful that they will not risk it again. Or they may feel that involvement will bring demands they will not or cannot meet, or they fear at some level that their very identity will be swallowed up and destroyed in the process of involvement. Many may seem to be delaying commitment to relationships because of the press of work, economic duress, or a legion of other "reality" considerations. Actually, these people (even those who seem to be embedded in relationships) consciously or otherwise rationalize their fear of closeness. The gain—avoidance of pain and crushing rejection—is small because of the chronic ache. The penalty is high: loneliness, isolation, and alienation.

Such people are awkward or untutored in giving and receiving intimacy, even when they crave it. The seeds of this problem are sown in early childhood when demonstrative affection was scarce, unpredictable, or attached to demands for performance or submission. The parent who gave "love" to the child in such instances did so only on the condition that the child surrender his or her autonomy and not be a separate, distinct individual. The child carries this script into adulthood and still feels, if not believes, that intimacy will occasion the same threats.

Many people view love as an easy, natural process, but what they probably mean is the act of falling in love. Eric Fromm clearly elucidated the nature of what he called "productive love." Such love requires care, responsibility, respect, and knowledge. Without caring and responsibility, feelings consist essentially of passion or insurance against loneliness. What many people call love is merely a mutual comfort society. Some cynic described love for the young as passion, for the mature as mutual dependence, and for the old as concern for each other's survival. Productive love, according to Fromm, requires concern not only for the other person's physical welfare, but also for the growth and development of all his or her human powers. Care and responsibility alone deteriorate into possessiveness and domination. Respect and knowledge are also required. Thus it is not only necessary to see a person as he or she is but also to be aware of that individual's uniqueness.

We believe that love involves receiving from as much as giving to the other person. We put it this way because in our experience—contrary to usual perceptions—there is greater difficulty in taking from the other. By taking, we mean something active which includes a communicated recognition, comprehension, and appreciation of the act. All feelings, not the least of which is love, require a continuous effort at identifying its presence and vicissitudes, expressing feelings appropriately, and doing so with sensitivity to the other's as well as to one's own experience. This is a life-long task, the benefits of which are a passionate and compassionate life.

Fantasy

Fantasy is the interface between thinking and feeling. It is that activity of inner life that suspends some or most of reality considerations while expressing emotions, usually in subdued form. Like dreams, it is governed by the principle of wish fulfillment, but unlike dreams, it is primarily conscious, or at least preconscious (that is, available for our introspection if we study it). There are, however, unconscious elements to fantasy. As we shall see, fantasy, like other mental processes, may serve a productive function or become distorted and lead to aberrations.

Fantasy precedes thinking proper and probably exists very soon after birth. The infant cries, and a breast or bottle is placed in his or her mouth. The child wriggles, and his or her diaper is changed. So the baby feels at one with the world. He or she is omnipotent, and merely has to imagine or fantasize—and it happens. Some of this fantasy of omnipotence, this belief in magic, stays with most of us to a greater or lesser degree for the rest of our lives. Autistic children and psychotics (who will be discussed in the chapter on Behavior Disturbances) are preoccupied with, sometimes live almost exclusively in, their fantasies.

Young children use fantasy as a form of play. It not only provides pleasure but serves as a way of compensating for a sense of inadequacy and unfulfilled dreams. It also provides an outlet for frustrations and thwarted emotions. Fantasy can be a healthy outlet, especially for only and lonely children. Playing grown up, playing a favorite TV character with or without an imaginary companion is normal and useful. In fact, fantasy can serve as a rehearsal for future behavior and as an experiment in mastery. Again, if this behavior becomes exaggerated and significantly supercedes interactions with the real, outside world, mental disorders are suggested which may become exacerbated if not dealt with. On the other hand, fantasy may provide a rich source of creativity. It is essential in all of the arts and probably the sciences as well.

Daydreams are a more or less structured variation of fantasy. We are conscious of our daydreams and can vary them pretty much at will. Some daydreams are repetitive. When they are chronic, they indicate some of the problems of fantasy in general, but are more capable of being changed by an act of will.

The daydreams of children vary enormously, but generally are compensations for what is lacking or wished for. They are also role-defined and culturally determined. Little boys have different daydreams from little girls. And daydreams change with age. With the advent of puberty, sexuality occupies a considerable portion of fantasy life.

When adult fantasy or daydreaming runs into hours rather than minutes, there is a void in the person's life. Reverie replaces action, and this can become habitual. It may happen at work or shortly after rising. With a cup of coffee in one hand, a cigarette in the other, the individual stares off into space. Often this is a symptom of depression.

Fantasy can be structured for us. Absorption in television, movies, spectator sports, and pap reading may be little more than organized fantasy. Such absorption suggests a passive submission to repetitive and predictable content, rather than an active involvement or a stimulating interaction with challenging ideas and feelings. (See the discussion on television in the chapter on Playing.)

For older people, reverie and daydreams appear more common. There often is less opportunity for action, and the mind turns backwards to review pleasant and nostalgic experiences. But even here, stimulated minds engaged in active pursuits make for healthier and more adjusted lives.

Summary

From the moment of birth, we are more than passive responders to the external world. We react individually and originally in two major modes: thinking and feeling. Throughout our lives, our sense of who we are and how content we are with our condition will depend on the interaction of these two kinds of responses. The ability to think well, to make accurate valuations and effective decisions, is a developmental process, the foundations for which are established in the first dozen or so years, but which continues until we die.

We can help ensure a satisfactory and continuing development by taking pride in and exercising our mental powers, much as we care for our physical strength and vigor. With children it is especially important to encourage the pleasures and satisfactions of fluent and expressive language, as well as to provide the materials for its exercise in the form of a rich vocabulary and acquaintance with the expression of other people through reading and shared significant communication. Later in life it is important to keep up our mental muscle tone by engaging in novel and stimulating mental exercise.

Similarly, our emotional life requires appropriate respect, understanding and exercise. Emotions are a biological inheritance and provide a mode of contact with ourselves and the external world. Their free expression and experience are to be encouraged. As we do so, we learn to be responsible for actions that flow from such emotions. Suppression of emotions or guilt over them is neither a healthy nor effective way of dealing with them. Instead, we will profit by being comfortable with and realistic about emotions and by learning to assess the profits and costs involved in acting upon them. It is here that a healthy interaction of thinking and feeling proves most useful.

Genuine love for another person involves care, responsibility, respect, and knowledge. In contrast, fantasy is an intermediate kind of mental activity that serves healthy and productive functions when indulged in moderately. But fantasy can become pathological if it becomes excessive or replaces real emotional or cognitive interaction with the world and ourselves.

6
Coping

Coping is overcoming obstacles or contesting, as in combat. Only under such ideal conditions as in intrauterine life and during breast feeding do we have the experience of being one with the world. For the rest of life, we contend with a world of frustrations, threats, and obstacles. To survive and achieve a reasonably adjusted life, we must learn to cope. This means learning as much as possible about the world we live in and ourselves. We need to recognize the realities that face us, to appreciate rather than to deny or flee problems, to clarify the options and to exercise the most appropriate ones. This often involves effort, risk, and pain. But this is coping.

All of what we have said stresses the significance of learning, particularly in school. And it emphasizes the need to recognize and use our powers of work, negotiate, earn and use money, and to deal with success and failure.

Learning

Learning is the acquisition of information, skills, ideas, and responses that are translated into new behavior. It involves perception, memory, intelligence, motivation, response from the environment, and altered behavior. To learn something about the world it is first necessary to perceive the environment. The more senses we use, the more information we derive from the world, and the more intensively and extensively we learn. As the baby attends to sight and sound, for example, it learns to direct its attention to those visual and auditory stimuli which are associated with rewards such as feeding and being held and comforted. Its behavior is reinforced and becomes more specific and focused, rather than chaotic and aimless. In short, the baby is learning.

Perceptual disturbances, visual or auditory, can interfere with normal learning. They may be subtle, since the difficulty may not lie in the sense organ of the eye or ear itself, but in the brain, where the stimuli are processed. It is necessary, therefore, for the infant or child to be tested for perceptual disturbances. This becomes especially important if such signs as inattentiveness, mishearing, or a difficulty in completing tasks or following directions are noted. Often a perceptual disturbance is at the root of a learning problem.

It has become the vogue to label a huge variety of learning problems or suspected problems as learning disabilities. Indeed, there is a group who call themselves learning disability specialists. There does not seem to be a consensus, however, on what a learning disability is, although there is at least the implication that brain damage is involved, no matter how minimal. If there is a learning disability, and such factors as behavioral problems or poor motivation (and, yes, poor teaching) are not noted, then it is assumed that there is brain damage. Such assumptions are often baseless, merely presumptive, or, at best, untenable without any substantive evidence.

For many children, what may appear to be "minimal brain damage" may in fact be incomplete maturation. Their brains and perceptual apparatus have not fully developed yet. Hyperactive children, for example, may be part of this group. Certain motoric exercises, including dance and Tai Chi, may be very helpful in this respect and are offered in gym classes of sophisticated school systems. (See the discussion on hyperactivity in the chapter on Behavior Disturbances.) Moreover, a host of behavioral problems, including anxiety, phobias, and depression, may intervene in the learning process. So a label of brain damage or learning disability may prejudice the consideration of other more treatable factors.

There are considerable differences in individual powers of memory, both in terms of how much and how fast information can be processed and retrieved at will. These powers are not correlated directly with intelligence. Of course, for a superior intelligence, one needs an excellent memory, but remarkable or even prodigious memories can be possessed by people of sub-normal intelligence. An interesting case is the idiot savant. Such individuals function at a very low, even moronic, level (that is, severe mental retardation), but demonstrate phenomenal rote memory.

Memory

Memory, like physical strength and dexterity, can be developed to an extraordinary degree, depending on the value the individual and his or her culture place on it. In fact, when writing was first introduced into Western culture, some people objected that it would make people rely less on their memories, and that they would become lazy. We know this, of course, because someone thought to write his objections down. But in England in the seventeenth century, it was not uncommon to find quite ordinary people who had memorized the entire Bible. And today in small Arab villages, there are usually numbers of adolescent boys who know the entire Koran by heart. Both the *Iliad* and *Odyssey* were recited from memory, and many African villages have historians who can recite genealogies for the past few hundred years.

The simplest memory process is for absent objects and situations. Memory of this type may be measured in terms of delayed reactions, the ability to retain the image of something that is absent. Delayed reactions are observed as early as three months of age, and gradually increase with age. By the end of the second year, the interval of delayed reaction is fifteen minutes or more. In some pre-school children it is as long as thirty-four days. The upper limit of memory span is not reached until the teens. Ability to recall narratives and to report past events also increases gradually with age. All tests of memory except delayed reaction require the use of linguistic responses. Therefore, improvement in memory performance as an individual becomes older may be attributed in part to the acquisition of language.

The ability to recall past events holds up well with age but begins noticeably to decline in the fifties and precipitously after the sixties. Even the ability to define words, which holds up through most of the age range, shows a precipitous decline around seventy years of age. The ability to recall new material, including learning new ideas, sharply and steadily decreases from the age of twenty. On the average, older people show relatively little decline in the ability to receive new impressions, but suffer greatly in their ability to form new associations necessary for learning new material. Their learning process seems to suffer from their decreased flexibility and adaptability. The brighter older people are to begin with, the better they are able to retain the efficiency of their learning ability; a good deal of this seems to be due to their greater flexibility and continued activity in the intellectual field.

Many factors contribute to memory impairment. One, of course, may be some form of cerebral pathology—brain damage. A fairly rare form is the relatively early manifestation in the fifties or sixties of Alzheimer's Disease. Its symptoms are some confusion about time, space, and person and a loss of memory for recent but not distant events. This disease is associated with the active degeneration of nerve cells in the cortex—the surface of the brain. The symptoms of Alzheimer's Disease are rare, although they correspond generally to senility in more elderly people. It is now believed, however, that malnutrition and lack of intellectual stimulation exacerbate, if not cause, a good deal of senility. (See the discussion of organic brain syndromes in the chapter on Behavior Disturbances.)

Cloudy or faulty memory may be a sign of somatic or central nervous system disorders. It may be a consequence of a trauma or injury to the head. The use of alcohol may also be responsible. Or it may merely be a consequence of fatigue. Generally, however, memory disturbances are a function of anxiety and depression. Lapses of memory and the inability to recall pertinent and important facts are excellent cues that we may be suffering from psychological problems.

It has been convincingly demonstrated that memory does not spontaneously decay by itself. Forgetting is an active process. It may be due simply to interference from surrounding stimuli or to a more psychologically motivated need to forget things that cause anxiety. If you notice a pattern in your memory lapses, or if your forgetfulness is associated with a particular event or person, it is a good idea to inquire into the possible causes of anxiety.

Memory is like a muscle. We may be born with small muscles, but we can exercise and develop them. There are various techniques and tricks to improve our memories which we shall discuss later in the section on study. An enriching environment where the acquisition of information, experiences and ideas—no matter how esoteric—is valued, promotes the enjoyment and development of memory. Although there is a myth that the collection of too much extraneous and trivial information will crowd out our memories, the contrary is true. The capacity of a normal human memory is virtually inexhaustible. Most informed people, those who demonstrate remarkable memories, are broadly ranging rather than narrow in focus. Of course, they may have gifted memories to begin with, but they know how to use them. Using our memory muscle clearly develops its power.

Intelligence

The controversy about what intelligence is has raged for decades. One theorist, in irony or frustration, concluded that intelligence is what intelligence tests measure. Although a tautology, such circular thinking has informed much testing and labeling as well as academic and vocational decisions. We may consider intelligence as the ability to perceive and to organize our percepts into ideas, attitudes, opinions, and values that permit us to understand what is going on around and within us. Intelligence is the ability to comprehend, to process the input of experience.

Intelligence, however, should not be confused with learning. Learning involves a change in behavior; intelligence is the ability to learn. We can be intelligent and learn very little. Sometimes we say that a person is intellectual but unintelligent. By that, we mean that the individual appears to have intelligence but shows little of it in his or her behavior. He or she does not learn. On the other hand, we must possess some basic intelligence if we are to learn.

It is easily observable that at birth there are wide differences in intelligence. Some babies respond alertly to their environment, take their world in, seem to process the stimulation and are able to learn rapidly. Here it is not the learning itself but the ability to learn that we are calling intelligence. Thus, high scores on achievement tests tell us only that the individual has learned more than his or her peers. This is a most important fact, of course, but it does not tell us that low scorers will not be able to achieve or learn more given certain pertinent factors.

That genetic factors play a significant part in the possession of intelligence is borne out in the correlation of intelligence test scores of parents and children, siblings, fraternal twins, and identical twins, in ascending order of correlation. These studies are extremely difficult to perform correctly, primarily because it is almost impossible to separate genetic from environmental factors. If a set of twins shows similar IQs, is it because of their genetic endowment or because of a shared upbringing? To solve this question, researchers have studied sets of identical twins (i.e., those with the same genetic endowment) who were separated after birth, and found a very high correlation in test scores. From this, some have concluded that genetic factors account for about 80% of varibility in intelligence and the environment for about 20%.

Still, the question is more complex than that. So-called "normal" IQ scores (i.e., between 85 and 115) account for 68% of the population, and this range is adequate for dealing with most of the situations we are likely to confront. Indeed, the average IQ for eminent nuclear physicists was found to be in the 130s, far below a level approaching that of genius. So it all depends on what one does with one's intelligence, how actively one uses it, and to what uses one puts it.

No one knows what intelligence is, and a most basic question about intelligence still has to be answered: is intelligence a single trait applicable to any number of tasks or is it a combination of separate traits that are not transferable from one task to another? IQ tests try to measure a general trait and may overlook or underestimate a particular specialized talent. Is a person with a moderately high over-all intelligence more gifted than someone with a specialized talent? It all depends on the way we interpret IQ scores and on the uses to which we put such information. In any case, it has not been established that there is any correlation between IQ and creativity.

Intelligence is enormously malleable, and certain socioeconomic environments emphasize the development of talents that other environments do not. It is quite clear that IQ tests are very selective about which talents they will measure. An uneducated rural person may be extremely gifted, but the way he or she has developed his or her intelligence may not register on a test designed for educated, urban people.

We have said that intelligence is the ability to comprehend one's world. It is not to be confused with learning or the motivation to apply learning. Certainly, the comprehension of one's world and the application of this comprehension differs dramatically in a village in the Brazilian jungle and a cooperative apartment in Manhattan.

What is true in this technical world is that verbal and abstract skills grow increasingly important. The crucial issue is not to assess intellectual function, but to tap, develop, and motivate its expression. This is the responsibility of society and particularly of parents, schools, and the media.

For practical purposes, it is not very useful to distinguish among basic intelligence, perceptual and memory ability, environmental factors, and motivation—except for people of exceptionally high and low intelligence. It may not even be possible to make these distinctions theoretically. In practice, there is an interaction of these variables. The drive to apply one's abilities, the encouragement to do so, and the rewards that may follow all result in intelligent behavior, including learning and achievement. Put another way, non-intellective, personality factors such as motivation, anxiety, and the experience of failure or reward greatly influence the quality of performance.

Mental Retardation

By conservative estimate, 3% of the American population, or more than six million children and adults, are mentally retarded. According to this estimate, mental retardation is twice as prevalent as blindness, polio, cerebral palsy, and rheumatic heart conditions combined.

In the past, people referred to disorders of intelligence as mental deficiency and classified the mentally handicapped as morons, imbeciles, and idiots. The implication was that such conditions were discrete and separate from the rest of mankind. But too often this was an unworkable approach for several reasons, and we now use the terms mild, moderate, and severe retardation. This newer classification suggests a more complicated concept that includes social and cultural functioning.

Approximately one-quarter of all retarded people suffer from the effects of some physical defect. It may be genetic, as in the case of some dominant gene, Down's Syndrome (mongolism), or Rh incompatability. It may be due to such infections during the mother's pregnancy as syphilis, encephalitis, or rubella. Or it may be due to trauma during pregnancy or at birth caused by radiation, toxic agents, lead poisoning, or cerebral injury. Improper instrument delivery has also been responsible in the past for much damage to intellectual functioning.

Seventy-five percent of retarded people, however, fail to reveal any physiological disorder. They are labeled "familial retardates." Because they perform more poorly than normals on a variety of experimental tasks, they are considered by many theoreticians to suffer from some unobservable defect.

This is arguable. In any event, for those adults who have a mental age of nine, or an IQ of 50, there has been considerable evidence to suggest that they merely fall statistically in the lower 3% of the population. That is, they occupy a certain range in the natural distribution of intelligence.

Let us turn our attention for the moment to the severely retarded, the physiologically or exogenously defective. They are a relatively rare group. Idiots are technically people whose IQs are below 25. They cannot be taught connected speech or to defend themselves from danger. Imbeciles are people whose IQs are between 25 and 49; they are usually unable to defend themselves and cannot earn a living. At one time, it was believed that instrument delivery accounted for a considerable number of the severely retarded. Remarkable strides in chromosomal and endocrine research, knowledge of nutrition and the effects of oxygen deprivation during birth, and information about drugs, alcohol, smoking, and in-adequate nutrition have given us ways of minimizing the tragedy of severe retardation.

The predominant number of retarded people—those with mental ages of nine to twelve—have the intellectual ability and resources to meet the minimal demands of society. They can dress, prepare meals, travel, hold down a job, and pay rent and other bills. In the 1930s, there were more than 118 jobs suitable for individuals with a mental age of five to twelve. In 1956, it was observed that 54% of jobs required no schooling beyond the elementary level.

A test group of children with IQs of between 50 and 70 were followed up into their fifties. By their mid-thirties and forties, over 15% had died—twice the national average. Of the dead—mostly males—one-third had died violently. However, more than one-third were economically self-supporting. Fewer than half received welfare support. About 18% were institutionalized for mental retardation or psychosis. Less than the average number were married. These had an average of 2.03 children, slightly below the average rate. Of great significance, the children tested between 50 and 138, with an average IQ of 95! This, despite considerable social, cultural, and economic disadvantages in the homes the children grew up in. Only two of these children were institutionalized for mental retardation. The original group had an average divorce rate, more than the average incidence of living in single family homes, and more than half of them owned their own homes. The men were mostly laborers, the women house-keepers. Forty percent had some involvement with the law. A significant number retested in the 80s—or dull normal functioning. Therefore, this group who had tested as mentally retarded as children functioned in their fifties intellectually, physically, and socially far above expectation.

Studies of simple or mild mental deficiency have demonstrated that the longer these retarded people remained in their original homes, the lower their IQs were likely to be. Upon transfer to privileged institutions where there was a ratio of two employees to each seven children, the pattern of IQ reversed itself. For those between eighteen and fifty years of age, however, community living was found to enhance the IQ score. Put another way, the longer children live in very depressed environments (including those where the mother is mentally defective), the lower those children's average IQs are likely to be.

The parents of a mentally defective child must consider a variety of factors: their emotional, physical, and economic resources, the impact on other children, and the implications for the deficient child. The more severe the handicap, the greater the tax on psychological and other resources, and the more limited the advantages. Guilt can be a poor rationale, especially when it becomes confused with responsibility. A severely retarded child who is kept at home for misguided reasons, only to be institutionalized later, can occasion tragic and heart-rending results for all involved. On the other hand, a mildly and even moderately retarded child can be a source and recipient of extraordinary pleasure and satisfaction, provided deliberate planning and professional guidance are utilized. It is extraordinary what results can be obtained with love, understanding, respect, effort, and, most of all, realistic expectations.

Tests such as the Vineland Maturity Scale and the Worcester Scale of Social Attainment gauge social competency rather than pure mental ability. While these techniques make use of observation, the study of the person in his or her actual environment provides a more useful and accurate diagnosis. Factors that are relatively independent of intelligence test scores, such as social competency and general personality characteristics, are most relevant in the diagnosis, labeling, and placement of retarded people. These non-intellective factors can largely be learned.

Schools, government, and private agencies have effective programs to help retarded people. These programs can be greatly augmented by the concerned and informed participation of parents; the great enemies of such programs are ignorance, prejudice, and unimaginative bureaucrats. Whatever the limitations of tests, they are invaluable when supplemented by alert observation in the early years of life when potential retardation can be identified and most effectively compensated for and ameliorated. Signals are poor attention, spotty memory, speech and motor difficulty, poor learning of dress and toilet skills, and diffuse anxiety. These clues may also signal a host of other difficulties, including sensory disorders. But these conditions, especially anxiety and continued failure, can be mitigated by special, sensitive consideration and creative planning.

School

Our first experience of having to cope in a comprehensive way with a strange environment is often at school. It is here that we are called upon, with greater or lesser urgency, to use our intelligence, learning ability, and social skills. It is in this organized, usually less emotionally protective, setting that we taste success and failure in large doses. Here we first find out that we are not so special. We are more on our own.

The first day of school is a big event in our lives. Almost all of us remember it, and if we don't, that may tell us something important. Did mommy have to take us by the hand—and daddy, too, for good measure? Or did they accompany us out of their own need? Was it a day of dread and silence, punctuated by crying, nausea, or stiff resistance? Or were we chafing at the bit, eager to get started in this new adventure? And when we got to school, how did we behave? Did we start by making friends, trying to please others, performing for the teacher, or getting into trouble? In short, the ability to cope and the techniques of coping we had already learned were brought into play.

The same event is repeated for every later, important, novel situation: the first group of friends, the club, the first date, the new school, the interview, the new job, meeting our date's parents, marriage, hospitalization—all the way through life. The desire to conform and please versus the fear of performing and the need to rebel, the attempt to get along with others versus the tendency to withdraw, the movement toward or away from peers and adults have already been learned in the home. And so has the experience of learning, succeeding, and failing.

It is the responsibility of the school to reinforce and broaden positive coping skills and to reshape negative ones. Unfortunately, this responsibility is not always understood, considered, or implemented. Picking a good school, if you have the choice, ranks with the most important decisions. We may not have such options, but monitoring and influencing the educational process is always possible.

A fairly common phenomenon is school phobia. This occurs in children who are deathly afraid of attending school. Their fears may be expressed as sheer anxiety, rage, rebellion, or psychosomatic illness. If children in such a state were to be coerced into attending school, the likelihood of their learning anything is minimal, and the negative consequences are serious. These children may have learned to fear performing or competing for attention with their peers, who may represent symbolic siblings. The children may dread separation and abandonment by their parents. Or their fear may represent their parents' own unconscious separation and abandonment dread. As so often happens throughout childhood and adolescence, the children may be acting out the parents' secret fears, needs, and desires.

Working with phobic children almost always requires working with the parents. Ignoring or only partially resolving the phobias fairly ensures future emotional scars and neurotic learning problems. Quick and effective attention generally results in success, but children with school phobias do require professional attention, at the very least, consultation with school psychologists. Parents would be well advised not to challenge, shame, or coerce their children, but rather to understand with them what they are afraid of. This can best be done with support and honest and sympathetic talk. Undoubtedly, the parents of school phobics, if honest and courageous, can empathize with their children's fears and share similar experiences of their own with them.

It is in school that we encounter expectancy head on. We expect things of ourselves, as do our parents and society in the guise of classmates and teachers. Expectancy is a spectre that will ride herd on us for the rest of our lives. It will haunt us, prod us, taunt us, and challenge us. Without such a ghost, we would be far more tranquil, but also more apathetic and dull. This spectre is not such a bad spirit. It is only when parents, society, and then our own incorporating selves turn it (with the best of intentions) into a demanding demon that we become its slaves.

The Rosenthal studies in California demonstrate that expectancies of the teacher tangibly influence school achievement and even intellectual performance. Children were arbitrarily designated as bright, normal, and dull, and the teachers so advised. The "bright" children, even if dull, improved significantly on scholastic tasks and even on IQ tests. The "dull" children, even if superior, performed dismally, even on IQ tests. The same results were obtained when the study was repeated in Chicago. The implications for the self-fulfilling prophecies of the teacher are evident. That is why attractive, charming, and verbal children (and adults) often fare so well. The pernicious possibilities for the minority child—black, Hispanic, and Indian, for example—are frightening.

Often, failure in school is a sign of more general problems that go unrecognized and untreated. Most children with reading problems also have other serious problems with mental health. In addition, a first grade child with reading problems may simply be less physically mature than the rest of his or her age group, and may have difficulty learning to read because of a difficulty with coordinated eye movement.

More than 60% of black and Hispanic students in the New York City school system drop out of high school, and many of those who graduate do poorly on the Scholastic Aptitude Test, which is used as an admissions criterion by many colleges. Mastery learning, a system developed by Professor Benjamin Bloom, is being used with some of these students. This technique is a form of programmed instruction in which a student who answers incorrectly must review the basic question before going on to the next step. The system is based on the supposition that every child except those who are physiologically disabled can learn. Given sufficient amounts of time for tasks in the classroom and a structured curriculum, Dr. Bloom maintains that every student can achieve academic success. Indeed, convincing New York students that they can learn seems to have had marked success in terms of their achievement.

Nationally, there are 700,000 drop-outs each year, most of them at the secondary level. The primary factor seems to be inadequate language development and a consequent inability to read and write. The preponderant number are in the 75 to 90 IQ range and come from poor and culturally deprived homes. Often there is no father, a disorganized home life, and poor family interactions. Language skills are not practical, school material is irrelevant to their lives, and there are low expectations from teachers. The biggest problem of drop-outs is their inability, after school years, to read, write, and calculate effectively.

There are other reasons for dropping out of school, especially among middle class children. Quite often it is a sign of discontent and rebellion felt toward the family but expressed against society and its most tangible symbol—the school. Dropping out of school is almost always an unhappy occurrence, but it is a symptom far more benign than the inner emotional distress that occasions it. It is far more important to address the causes than the symptoms. A school drop-out can, and often does, succeed in life, but almost always at great emotional price. Rather than heaping greater pressure on the drop-out or pushing him or her to get fixed up, family therapy is indicated, since there is a good probability that the family system is disturbed.

The problem of the drop-out, however, may be only the most blatant failure of the educational system. Although most Americans do learn to read, their competence may be so minimal or their associations with reading or with any kind of intellectual activity so noxious that they remain at the level of the functional illiterate. Nearly half of all Americans never read a book of any kind. Thirty-nine percent read only newspapers and magazines. And fully six percent never read anything at all.

Children's first experiences of success or failure in school can leave a mark on them which, if not indelible, is difficult to erase. It may well determine their attitude and performance not only throughout the rest of their school careers, but later in life as they confront other tasks and expectations. The only thing they may have learned in school is that they are failures. Parents are advised, therefore, to be particularly sensitive to timing their expectations and to tailoring them to individual rates of learning and maturation in their children.

Late bloomers, especially, can have a hard time of it if premature or otherwise unreasonable demands are placed on them. This is especially true of mathematical and abstract reasoning abilities, which show a large variation in rate of maturation. By the time the skills ripen, the habit of expecting to fail may be well established. It is no wonder that many of us are phobic of mathematics. Readiness to understand and perform is an individual difference and needs to be recognized and appreciated by parents and educators alike. Although genuine learning problems need to be recognized and treated, many late bloomers, if they have sufficient drive, desire, and if they haven't been harmed while they waited to mature, have come to flourish when they were ready and the circumstances favorable.

There is an art to study. For some it can be a science. But for too many it is a haphazard, sink-or-swim procedure. Yet learning the techniques and skills of studying is the prerequisite coping tool for school. Effective studying gives a sense of success to the student, whereas inefficient study conditions a sense of failure, anxiety, and even phobic avoidance of things academic or pedagogic.

Study

Taking notes can be extremely useful. The first order of note taking is to devise a system of short sentences, phrases, and abbreviations that are meaningful and readable to the note taker. The second order is to gauge what the lecturer is trying to say. More helpful than notes taken during the lecture might be a summary based on the major points the teacher was making, but this decision depends to a large extent on the nature of the material and the relative importance of details.

In reading assignments, it is helpful sometimes first to read the summary of each section, and then to skim through the section, paying particular attention to topical and concluding sentences. On the second reading, it may be reinforcing to read aloud, even if you are basically a visual person. Underlining and checking sections can be as much a hindrance to many as overwhelming notes. Summarizing the writer's major points in writing and finally reading the summary again are good techniques.

It is not a good idea to read alone. Good company is the companionship of a dictionary, glossary, and encyclopedia, provided these are sensibly rather than compulsively used. In the chapter on Thinking, we discussed how words influence thinking. They also aid learning, as do technical and informational terms and concepts.

The use of all resources possible, including family, friends and libraries, is extremely helpful. Too many students, however, only know how to employ the Dewey Decimal System and the index catalogue, if that. Learning how to use a library is a most useful skill for those who are concerned with learning and the acquisition of information.

Studying for an exam can be done efficiently or it can be a waste of time. Understanding generally how memory works can help make studying more productive. There are basically three processes involved: registration, consolidation, and retrieval. These processes are connected, and the efficiency and sureness of retrieval depends to a great extent on the thoroughness of the previous two processes.

We can retain and store memory best if the information we wish to memorize is processed in a structured manner. Psychologists call this "depth of processing." The more we previously know about what we are memorizing and the more we can connect it with previous knowledge, the better chance we have of retaining it and summoning it up at will. Cramming is one of the least efficient means of learning, and learning while asleep with tape recorders is almost entirely useless. It is usually best to space study sessions, allowing an interval between each.

Earlier, we compared memory to a muscle that can be strengthened through exercise. We may also say that memory is like a library. The more we cross-file and duplicate information, the better able we are to locate and use the desired bit of information. In other words, it is important to take in the information in an active way, understanding it and relating it to what we already know.

For memorizing lists, using rhythms and rhymes can be helpful ("Thirty days has September . . ."). So can subdividing lists into component parts. Instead of memorizing the fifteen causes of World War I, it is more efficient to break the causes down into categories: six economic, three diplomatic, etc. But generally, studying is most efficient if it is preceded by a rather deep and structured understanding of the material in the first place. This means not putting off studying until the final exam. It begins when we first encounter information, in reading or in class.

Social Skills

Most social skills are not so much taught as learned by modeling on family figures. What is learned in the family for approval, however, may be well nigh disastrous in the world at large. All schools, of course, should prepare their students for life, but they are often far from adequate, especially when it comes to manners and techniques of relating. Too often, the shy, withdrawn, and even schizoid child is rewarded for passive behavior because he or she does not make waves. A style that leads to loneliness and isolation is thereby reinforced.

Social skills are inextricably bound up with our personality development. A happy, adjusted child has an easier time acquiring social skills, and, conversely, good skills make for greater happiness and adjustment. It is easier to teach these skills in the first place than to later reshape more basic and complicated personality strata. At a very early age, however, it is essential to learn how to speak, dress, smile, frown, laugh, and so on, not so much to fit in as to learn to communicate and relate easily. Later on, especially if we have learned these amenities poorly, we may use them either to conform or to rebel, to please or to distance others. But for little children, these are the tools for relating, for coping with the world interpersonally.

Throughout life we learn to capitalize on our assets. If sweetness is our suit, we play sweetness cards so regularly that it becomes our style. So may fluency, vivacity, brightness, radiant smiles, charm, and so on. There is a danger here. Someone with good looks learns early on that his or her appearance beguiles others, gets a favorable response, better grades, and even wins trust. The dependence on this or any one trait generates a sense of shallowness and conveys it to others. Such unidimensionality, no matter how popular or successful the person becomes, is almost always accompanied by insecurity.

An unusually large number of people suffer from shyness. In many adults, this may be masked from others and even from the self by charm, verbal facility, aggressiveness, wit, and cheerfulness. The cues to shyness are the compulsivity of these compensations and the associated tension when relating to others. In smaller children, shyness is obvious in excessive timidity, seclusiveness, and passivity. Xenophobia, the fear of strangers, is particularly obvious. The factors that produce shyness seem to be shy or over-protective parents. The only child, or the youngest one, is the most likely candidate for this condition. He or she has learned to feel that he or she cannot trust people outside of the family or that people will detect the child's worthlessness. Often, family techniques for discipline have been the subtle or gross use of humiliation, guilt, or shame.

While shyness disappears or is largely mitigated for most children with the advent of school and other experiences of socialization, for others it remains a painful inhibitor to experiencing satisfaction with other people. With pre-school children, it is helpful to promote play with other babies and to ensure pleasantness and encouragement when fear is evinced. Nursery school is recommended, and later, camp. There, as well as in school, assignment of tasks, offices, and positions that interest the child and win recognition and approval are recommended. Sometimes it is useful to compromise with the child's need to "no see me!" by encouraging anonymity with costume, an assumed role, or play-acting. A peer group is most important, although for very shy children, younger, less threatening children are often the best type of companions.

For older children and adults, specialized interpersonal situations prove helpful, such as speech and drama classes, clubs, and groups where a particular interest or skill wins acceptance and approval. Group therapy is a most valuable experience for those shy and uncertain in interpersonal skills. Assertiveness training groups have become very popular and are easily available.

Work

Work is the expenditure of effort and energy to produce something or to move around an obstacle in order to attain a goal. Work is goal-oriented, although the process of work can secondarily be as pleasurable as play, where gratification is the primary characteristic.

For children, study, household chores, baby sitting, clean-up squads in school, and so on are work activities defined by specific goals, rewards, and approval. For about the first ten years of life, work is externalized—it is the demand or pressure of the outside world that motivates us to work. It is notable that children in their teens will ordinarily work with greater alacrity for those outside the family, even if the task is more onerous and less generously remunerated. Here, the social approval of the "stranger" or outside society is a more potent reinforcer than the rewards to be expected within the family.

Some people never internalize the desirability of work because of cultural and personality factors, and will work only when coerced into reluctant and sporadic effort. Such a person has learned to labor only for immediate gratification. Long-term goals are fuzzy or distrusted. In poor families or ones in which personality difficulties are rife, the unpredictability of rewards and the bleak opportunities for advancement promote the association of work with the idea of a necessary and unnecessary evil.

A basic fact of life is that a job occupies by far the greatest portion of our waking lives. If it is tedious and non-rewarding, it would appear that priorities are mixed up, although the necessity to eat or the imperfect planning of our society frequently imposes that situation on us. Calling our work our "job" often implies a resignation to a slot we're stuck in, whereas the term "career" and "profession" suggest pride and choice. We have the option to plan and prepare ourselves as well as we can for the work we will feel most suited for, but family, school, and society have the obligation to enable us to attain that position and at least provide us with choices suited to our skills and talents.

We have just said that work predominates our active adult life. If it doesn't, we are categorized as bums, hedonists, or parasites, depending on our assets and social class. But for most of us, work is an integral part of our identities. We think of ourselves—and others do too—largely on the basis of what our jobs are. One of the first questions we ask on meeting someone new is what he or she works at, and we relate to him or her accordingly. This is so true that we may be more responsive to or intimidated by a bore in a prestigious job than an interesting, alert person who does mundane work. To identify so exclusively with our work tends to narrow and stultify us. This is another reason to balance work with gratifying avocation, stimulating pursuits, and meaningful recreation. (See the chapter on Playing.)

Most people choose and stay at a job because of real or imagined job security. This sometimes is a reality consideration, but does generate a TGIF (Thank Goodness It's Friday) mentality. Often, however, this is not a reality consideration, but an expression of a more generalized personality insecurity. During the Depression, many college graduates sought the only job security they could find in federal employment, such as with the Post Office. In better times, numerous lawyers, accountants, and teachers remained in jobs that they were overqualified for, bored with, and paid less for, because of "security."

The task for every worker is to weigh security against job satisfaction. The lower down the job scale and the more menial the skills required, the more security is defined in terms of keeping a job, receiving the best possible paycheck, and winning fringe benefits such as pensions. Blue collar workers (and increasingly, white collar workers) have unions and governmental legislation to assist them. Unions also provide a sense of identity, potency, and pride. But workers often remain on or leave a job because of personality conflicts, despite other rationales that are offered.

To see and appreciate the finished product and to have an ownership in the production may be more of a choice than is realized, and this is certainly within the capability of management. It has been known for a long time that salutary and pleasant work conditions, as well as real interest in production, make for greater productivity, stability, and decreased absenteeism.

The most common reason for abrupt or unhappy job termination is interpersonal difficulty rather than intolerable conditions. It is far easier to externalize the difficulty than to face the problem within ourselves. Acting out—doing something impulsive rather than facing our feelings and attitudes—very frequently is manifested by quitting or getting fired. Conversely, losing a job can be a crushing blow to our pride and sense of identity and often is accompanied by emotional or psychosomatic disturbances. When problems arise on the job, vocational counseling or psychotherapy is well advised.

There are particular factors that are important for people in the work they do. For some, the relationship to authority as well as the need for their own autonomy is an issue. They are happier being their own bosses, even if this means greater stress, more insecurity, and even less emolument. Or they may have the drive to make it on their own, to get a bigger slice. What is important here is to recognize the needs, the risks, the assets, and the limitations and to be willing to take a risk.

When feasible, the selection of a second career may be a vital decision. For those women who have chosen or found themselves in the role of mother or housewife, this is especially true. As the children grow up, the role of these women changes dramatically, and their satisfactions and very identity are at stake.

Working in itself presents a role conflict for most women, although this prejudice is slowly abating. (We will discuss this in the section on success and failure.) There is a disturbing paradox, however. In the United States, more than 50% of the work force is female. In the lower socio-economic classes, women may have to work to survive economically. The almost universal aspiration to own one's own home increasingly demands a second income even for middle-class families.

But the working mother is criticized and criticizes herself for neglecting her family. Mamma is supposed to take care of the family, provide hot meals, clean house, and to avoid "ring around the collar." But many women not only through necessity but through choice would rather devote a significant portion of their time to their outside work. If a woman has clarified her goals and has decided that she is job oriented, then the entire family needs to evaluate their roles within the home. Role flexibility and interchangeability seem to be the answer. Perhaps an Emancipation Proclamation such as that for slavery is required. The Equal Rights Amendment for women would be far too modest, since it does not speak for the equality of roles. Be that as it may, support groups for all concerned are recommended.

For many in mid-life, the challenge, the stimulation, and new options available in a second career are promising, although they may also be frightening and threatening to security. Counseling or psychotherapy may well be indicated at this juncture in life. This is especially true when the issue of retirement arises for the individual. (This is discussed in the chapter on Stages.)

A word on the workaholic. Like any addict, a workaholic cannot do without a continuous supply of a drug—in this case, work. He or she consequently avoids recreation, relaxation, and intimate relating. Throughout this book, we stress the fact that compulsivity is a neurotic symptom. Where urgency, imperatives, and exaggeration characterize behavior, there is maladjustment. The person married to his or her work cannot be married to anyone else, and is probably limited in his or her ability to experience intimacy. This work compulsion, no matter how rationalized, is a compensation for a fear of relating or of seeking more balanced gratifications. The rewards, of course, can be great in terms of money and success, but the price of alienation and tension are often greater. (See the discussion of stress in the chapter on Health.) Workaholics can be a great boon to everybody except their intimates (if any) and themselves.

Money

Money is the medium we use to purchase another's labor or the product of that labor. This simple fact becomes obscured by the most complicated and profound personal factors. How we come by money, the opportunities to do so, and the options for its expenditure color our reactions to its real or imagined significance to the extent that our mental health depends on it. We will fight and die for it.

Almost more than any other object, money takes on a symbolic value. We say that if only we were rich, our problems would go away. At some level, we are referring not to the realities of its purchase power so much as to its symbolic value to us of love, power, and strength. It becomes an extension of our selves. Of course, money can buy a cosmetic rehabilitation of a person. Even when we strip away badges of office and expensive clothes, the naked individual may have purchased contact lenses, a toupee, capped teeth, face lifts, plastic breasts, or revitalization at a health spa. He or she may have also bought an excellent education, culture, and the approval of others.

The very way we think of ourselves and others reinforces the contamination of self-image with money. To be known as one of the lower, middle, or upper class connotes considerable emotional and perceptual differences. These differences percolate up into spiritual considerations, so that the rich are sometimes thought of—and not only by themselves—as superior in ways other than monetary, and the poor seem somehow—and not only to others—undeserving and worthless.

Freud believed that money has a strong association with anality. The very first possession we have the choice of letting go (spending) or retaining (hoarding) is our feces. It is the part of us that we treasure and want to keep as long as we can. If we do associate money with anality, then conflicts about it may mean that we think of money as a precious part of ourselves or as "filthy lucre" to be treated with disdain.

It is as security, however, that money takes on such a great significance. Because security, though important for all of us, is tenuous for many, a concrete representation of it is desperately desired. This can be served by possessions, sometimes of the most esoteric nature, such as collections of bottle caps or pebbles, or sometimes in the form of chattel, which used to include numerous wives and still is symbolized by having many children. But it is money and its possession which signifies to most people a sense of security. Many a man or woman will claim to be able to die happily if only there is a fat bankbook or large insurance policy close at hand.

Money can come to represent a substitute for power, potency, love, and human value whether for the self or for another. If the parent rewards "good performance" tangibly or bestows affection essentially in monetary terms, then this substitution is understandable. If the child learns that he or she must virtually buy love in the family, he or she will believe that it is literally necessary to do so as an adult. This is why economic net worth becomes equated with personal worth for so many adults. The more money a person has, the more valued he or she will feel. Irrational use of money—miserliness, squandering, or impulsive buying—often represents a conflicted and compulsive drive to be loved.

With respect to marital difficulties, differences over money surpass any other issue—including sex, child rearing, and family loyalties. The disparity in the meaning of money for spouses and their lack of frank discussion about this cause enormous bitterness and misunderstanding. Money, as well as sex, becomes the vehicle for power struggles. Conventionally (but not necessarily), the male uses money in this struggle and the female uses sex. Yet they both want security, love, and gratification. This displacement is one of the greatest travesties of relationships.

Some of this difficulty may be precluded by the early teaching—through precept and example—of the value of money and of its difference from other values. Demonstrative parental and familial affection is much more important than gifts. Children's worth needs to be based on their humanness and relatedness, not on their purchasing power or physical or social skills. Learning the significance of money, how it may be earned and how it may be exchanged for meaningful value, is learning how to cope with the adult world.

Learning about budgeting, banking, credit, and debt financing—as unpalatable as this may seem to some—is necessary. Couples ignorant or confused about these issues have a much higher risk of foundering. Many a male suffers a sense of inadequacy for lack of this knowledge. Many more females and young people are held in de facto subjugation for the same reason. Whether or not money is a necessary evil, its acquisition and management are significant in maintaining a sense of self-respect and adequacy.

Power is the mental or physical capacity to act. It is the energy we have available to work or to influence others. It is the capacity for recognizing and then exercising various options. The

Power

expression of our individuality in its variety is the power we all have. Therefore, the possibility of choice and of effecting change is a power almost always available to us from early childhood, and certainly in adulthood. Yet so often we feel powerless. This is almost always because we believe we cannot make the perfect choice, especially since we don't even know what that choice might be. To make the least imperfect decision is within our power, but we often do not recognize the option.

Another reason for a sense of powerlessness is our clinging to a belief in our omnipotence. As infants we all felt an absolute sense of power; we only had to cry, squirm, or even fantasize to have our every wish promptly attended to. The illusion that we are still omnipotent or can become so stays with us to a greater or lesser degree, and we believe in magic or bestow this power on real or imagined others. When the discrepancy between this fantasy and reality becomes apparent, we feel powerless.

The power we yearn for is to have our every whim satisfied—again. If we are very good or very beautiful or very strong or very rich, we believe we can have this power. Often our belief is reinforced to some degree, and so our illusion is maintained. When it is not reinforced, we seek power indirectly by getting our way in a devious manner. These strategies do not have to be, and usually are not, conscious. Psychological symptoms frequently serve the purpose of expressing our power over others, despite the meager results and stiff penalty.

The positive use of power is flexible coping—using our various skills and techniques to secure gratification and remove obstacles. Assertiveness is a meaningful expression of power and enhances our self-respect and confidence. Because so many of us are insecure in our power, we engage in constant power struggles to prove some point, primarily to ourselves. The strong seek to disenfranchise the weak—often the child and the female. The weak then retaliate because they have considerable instruments of power, such as withholding love, sex, or approval. But real power is the attainment of these very things as well as recognition and understanding.

Whenever there is a break in communication, there is a power struggle going on. It may begin with ignorance or faulty information, but the consequent frustration, resentment, and anger tell the person that he or she is not having his or her needs met. This is another way of saying he or she feels powerless. So that person will struggle to regain this power in whatever way he or she can. A considerable amount of parent—child, child—child, and marital strife is an expression of this struggle.

A remarkable occurrence is that in the quest for power, we often invest the other person with so much of it. We may say, "If only he would . . ." or "She makes me feel so helpless and frustrated." Of course, this is nonsense. We appear to give away our power of choice and action, but we hold on to it and manifest it instead in martyred and neurotic behavior. That is, we seek to gain what we want—intimacy, recognition, and understanding—indirectly, and we lose most of it in the process. We confuse power with money or exterior symbols of achievement or performance, and obsessively, even frantically, drive ourselves to have more and more of the wrong thing. We tell ourselves that with power we will have success. Although this is possible if we sacrifice the original psychological needs for the secondary ones of status, this is hardly a meaningful success.

All reinforcements of behavior are administered from a basis of power. There are four sources. The first, clearly perceived by the infant and child, is physical. Both parents exercise it, but the father is soon perceived as possessing more of it. This is particularly true in lower-class families. If the child learns that this power is not esteemed by society, disillusionment and damaged identification with the father may follow. The second source is sexual. What the parents actually or apparently achieve with this potency serves as a model throughout life and may saturate sexual roles with power struggles. In a single parent home or one where a single parent dominates, considerable distortion of sex as power may be learned. The third source of power is wisdom and logic. This is the most subtle form of power and also the most profound. It is usually only when a child is much older that he or she can truly perceive this power. Different socio-economic classes and cultural groups place different premiums on it, and society varies its evaluation of it at different times. The fourth source is social and economic influence: who the parents know, where they can go, and what they can buy and possess impress most children. If the parents use this source as behavior reinforcers, the child may well learn to inhibit physical power but also to devalue wisdom and logic. It has been said before: the power of love may become corrupted into the love of power.

The basic issue of personal power is recognizing our strengths, assets, and what our choices are, and finding the best way of exploiting them. The identification and use of power is generally a mystery for individuals, organizations, and nations. For individuals, the meaning of power changes as they grow older. At all ages it is the expression of the self. With smaller children, however, it is overlaid with the ability to win

approval of others. Many people operate on that basis thereafter. Older people, who lose physical strength, youthful looks,
and vocational opportunities, often believe they are losing
their power and therefore substitute indirect expressions of it,
such as familial or political potency. Since males often equate
sexual vigor with power, when they lose their potency (usually
with age), they compensate with ambition.

The power residing in creativity, aesthetics, and benign
influence on others and the environment, however, may be
nurtured and grow throughout life. Our spiritual side, perhaps
our greatest power, increases with age. This is what we must
learn and teach our children.

Success and Failure

Webster defines success as the attainment of wealth, favor,
and eminence. These are external criteria. Elsewhere we have
seen that adherence to the standards of others rather than to
our own internal value system breeds insecurity and discontent. What to others seems our success may not mean that to
us at all. Success, as we define it, is attaining what you really
desire. In general, however, our society correlates success
with excelling in the socio-economic, vocational expectations
of society or that part of society important to us. More precisely, it is the recognition of that attainment that connotes
success.

Many do not know that they are compelled to strive to
meet the expectations of others, such as parents. This generates conflict and often sabotage, consciously or otherwise. We
are conditioned very early to cherish our own standards or to
conform to parental or societal standards. From an early agen
we learn to see ourselves as winners or losers, and from this
perception we may derive a life style. We may also learn that
an essential ingredient of success is competition: for us to
succeed, others must fail, or vice versa.

The issue of competition has been instilled in a very
peculiar way in the minds of most women. They are not supposed to be better than males except in those pursuits designated as feminine (which do not really meet cultural criteria
of success). Certainly, women are not supposed to be more
successful than their dates or spouses. Those women who
nevertheless do become successful are disparaged as masculine, maladjusted, or paradoxically, not really successful as
people (it is not unusual for us to change criteria when it suits
our psychological purposes). Many women, therefore, seem to
fear success. Actually, they fear failure to get the approval of
others.

Apart from real differences in opportunities, lowered expectations and lack of resilience in response to failure help

explain underachievement in women. It has been found that women typically have lower expectations for success, are more likely to assume personal responsibility for failure, and are more likely than men to evidence what has been called the low expectancy pattern for their successes and failures.

In a study, highly successful women expressed discomfort about pressure and intense competition as well as the lack of social support for their contributions. They questioned whether they had adopted their culture's, parents', or husbands' definitions of success rather than their own. They wondered whether they had swallowed whole the prevailing notion of success in order to please others. Yet most of these successful women had *not* adopted the dominant culture's view of success.

There have been various theories about why people fear success. Freud believed that the attainment of success is identified for some with an unconscious forbidden wish—namely the winning of the parent of the opposite sex, sexually or otherwise, and hostility towards the same sexed parent or siblings. Since the wish is taboo, external frustration is far more tolerable than the anxiety at having fulfilled the wish. That is, instead of the original parent being punitive, our own conscience is the tyrant. As long as success is within reach, the conflict is bearable, but if it is at hand, the conflict is too painful. Since success may be equated with aggression or exhibitionism, it must be inhibited.

Karen Horney postulated that we learn two lessons in our society: to be successful and competitive, and to be modest and unselfish. If the first lesson is over-stressed, we develop an inordinate fear of failure. If the second is overemphasized (as is true with many women), we develop an inordinate fear of success, or at least the inability to enjoy it. It is as if we must say, "It's not my fault."

The common denominator in all of these theories is the idea that success, by whatever definition, means competition and therefore courts envy, hostility, and retaliation from others. This seems to occur when parents acted as if parent—child conflicts were win-or-lose struggles, when parents made invidious comparisons between the child's skills and the parents abilities, when parents took over or excessively interfered with their child's activities, and when parents did not encourage the individuation or separation of the child.

Recent studies have discovered certain traits in those who fear success. These traits are a low self-esteem, a preoccupation with being evaluated and with the competitive implications of performing, a tendency to repudiate competence and to act as if luck or the help of others was responsible for success, and a tendency to become anxious in the face of imminent success and to sabotage or not enjoy it.

Therapy or counseling geared towards reconditioning these attitudes is often successful in disabusing people of these irrational notions. The thrust of such approaches is to eliminate or minimize the tyranny of imperatives like "shoulds," "musts" and "have to's" and to assist people in crystallizing their own standards, so that they feel more comfortable in choosing what they want to do.

Most of us have not learned how to cope with either success or failure. When success brings sudden and unusual recognition and affluence, many grow confused with increased options and changes in life style. Although they may have dreamt of this success as an index of security, they grow insecure because success requires change, and change is frightening. (See the chapter on Change.) Often they grow grandiose. It is as if success overwhelms and frustrates in the same way that deprivation does. The consequent irrational and omnipotent behavior is not so different from the tantrum behavior of infants.

All this is even truer of failure, which is even more frightening because it implies that we are inadequate, incompetent, and worthless. Of course, this is irrational. Not getting what we wanted signified failure to us when we were very young, and does so to many even when we are older. Either we get it all or we fail—we have not learned to distinguish disappointment from catastrophe. Actually, there are very few catastrophes, and they are almost exclusively restricted to loss of life or debilitating illness. Most often we experience disappointments, no matter how severe, not catastrophes.

Failure is part of the fabric of our lives. We fail in countless ways, every day. But too often, we are taught that we are not supposed to fail. Learning how to fail and to cope with failure is an essential lesson. Almost anyone can, at least at first, manage success. To manage failure, however, is to profit from experience. Without failure—in manageable doses—we cannot grow and develop. Therefore, it behooves parents to teach and encourage the management of success and failure to their children and to themselves as well.

The point of all this is that coping is pointed toward managing our lives so that we can obtain a maximum degree of gratification, including achievement and intimacy. Confused notions about what constitutes success; contamination of compulsive drives for working, money, and power; confusion of desire; and obligation to succeed all plague and defeat us in the search for success. It is critical, therefore, to teach and demonstrate to our children the individual nature of success. That is to say, parents, schools, and society have a responsibility to recognize and develop individual attributes and to express them in the service of individual as well as group goals. This is extraordinarily difficult, since it is so easy for us to project our own values, standards, and aspirations onto those for whom we have a position of authority and power. If we feel that success— whatever we mean by that—is eluding us, or that we are botching it up, then counseling or psychotherapy is indicated. Finally, success is relative and boils down to doing the best we can. We ourselves are the only obstacles to that goal.

Summary

If life were one unchanging series of predictable situations, we could find the one best way of dealing with life's problems and stay with that until we died. Such, of course, is not the case. As we grow out of infancy, life keeps changing: responsibilities change, rules shift, possibilities evaporate and materialize. Whether we like it or not, a new stage begins even before we have mastered the previous one. Most important, we ourselves change. What was once satisfying, challenging, and interesting for us can become stale and meaningless. Our powers as well as our interest and needs keep developing. Coping is the ability to recognize these changes and to adopt our expectations and strategies to obtain satisfaction and meaning in life.

Any situation in life represents the interaction of two enormously complex factors: the world and ourselves. Our ability to cope adequately depends to a large extent on our accurate assessment of these two mysteries. When we find we are frustrated, deprived, or that we are mishandling our affairs, we have frequently misjudged the true state of affairs in the world or have misunderstood our present needs and desires. Often this happens because we are at some level living or thinking as if we were back in a stage we long ago outgrew. The best strategy is always an honest and realistic appraisal of our present condition and a readiness to discard old ways of doing things.

Not everyone has the same abilities, and what abilities we do have change. There are realistic things we can do to develop whatever endowments we possess. Intelligence, alertness, and ability in general can be fostered by exercise and stimulation, whether we are talking about learning, work, or social skills. Difficulties in learning, memory, and intelligence may be due to some organic defect, but more commonly are the result of some early conflict or association between achievement and losing affection or approval.

Intelligence is a complex and malleable native capacity. It involves the ability to learn rather than how much has been learned or accomplished. Achievement, on the other hand, depends on intelligence, motivation, and other personality factors. Although there are differences in intelligence, the real task for parents and society in general is to develop the capacities people do possess. Even people who are mentally retarded can, if provided with suitable opportunities, function in adequate and productive ways.

Intimacy is difficult for people for whom love in childhood was contingent on performance or on surrendering their integrity or identity. They consequently learn to relinquish the possibility of intimacy. Frequently, we try to compensate for deep doubts we have about our worth by investing people, money, or status with values they do not really embody. These are almost always unsuccessful strategies, and lead to frustration and deprivation, which in turn lead to power struggles. In a similar way, we may fear success because of a learned association with forbidden competition. Finally, few of us have learned the appropriate management of failure, which we often confuse with catastrophe. But failure is a necessary part of our lives and enables us to learn and grow.

We can help ensure a more successful and gratifying life if we are attentive to what our real present needs are and if we make the attempt to free ourselves from many of the fears and conditions we accepted long before we could know any better. The range of possibilities open to us can be expanded immensely if we are willing to be realistic and to take risks.

It is not very useful to complain about how difficult life is or how everything changes. Our experience can be enriched and deepened if we look forward to these changes with a sense of adventure and a hopeful, realistic sense of our capacities. We all possess the power to take control over our lives and to actively will change. The effort, risk, and pain are not really the price we pay for change, but parts of the real satisfactions and pleasures that life in its variety can offer.

7
Identity and Roles

Our very first and our very last dilemma is "Who am I?" The Jewish sage Hillel asked: "If I am not for myself, who am I? If I am only for myself, what am I? If not now, when?" Almost all of us develop a sense of ourselves at the very beginning of our lives, which, no matter how refined or buffeted, persists with us to the very end. There may be novel or traumatic situations where we feel strange and unreal. Under extraordinary circumstances, such as during crises or while we are under the influence of drugs or alcohol, we may feel uncertain of ourselves and even wonder who we are. But there is a uniqueness, a "me-ness," that we almost always retain. Yet we continue to struggle to define this me-ness as separate from others and the rest of the world.

As we gain a more complex and truer sense of the self, we establish an identity that includes our current and past experiences, our physical and psychological image of ourselves, the roles and functions that we carry out or are expected to carry out, our character style, our affiliations, and our spirituality.

This sense of identity, however, develops and is not ready-made at birth. In the first weeks of life, the infant has a number of patterns or sensory-motor activities which Piaget calls schemata. Designed to maintain homeostasis, or internal organic balance, they include sucking, looking, listening, vocalizing, grasping, and diffuse motor behavior. Toward the end of the first month, the baby will gaze at objects. During the second month, the child will search with his or her eyes for the source of a sound. Already, the me is being differentiated from everything else. From the third month on, there is coordination between sight and hearing, and the child recognizes sound coming from a particular object with a particular appearance, or "not-me." During this period, he or she begins to coordinate hand movements with sucking.

Physically, the first "foreign" object we recognize as our own is our hands. We learn between the third and fourth month that hands are part of us and will always be with us. It takes most of the first year to form a general image of the body. We shall see in our discussion of body image that the completeness of this image varies for adults as well as for children. Strong, muscular elementary school-aged children are less anxious than fat or very thin children. They are also at least as well adjusted and are able to admit more to negative characteristics about themselves.

During this early period, we are sharpening our picture of what is "me" and what is "it." "Me" is what I know and can control. "It" is more alien and less controllable. For the infant, impulses, drives, and emotions are not perceived as "me" but as "it." Even mature people perceive what they fear or believe they cannot control in themselves as alien to their egos. We dissociate these perceptions, sensations, and even ideas, externalize them or project them onto others or onto inanimate objects. The phenomenon of animism, ascribing our feelings and traits to inanimate objects and to animals, is observable in small children and primitive people as well as superstitious modern people. It exists in our myths, folklore and art and literature as well as in our routine lives. We kick that "damn" post we stubbed our toe on or curse a car that won't start. Under stress we regress to this primitive, unde-fined sense of self when we complain that "it" is impossible to do when we do not wish to acknowledge that "I cannot or will not do something." We say "it" makes me anxious rather than "I am confused about that."

What we have been calling the self Freudians designate as the ego. The "it" is called by its Latin name, id. Freud theorized that the ego emerged from the basic matrix of drives and impulses we are born with, which is closely related to the "it" above. The ego results from a conflict between the id and the frustrations of reality which require that gratifica-tion be delayed. Rather than merely wishing, we must now think or say, "I want, I can, I can't, I need" and so on. Our ego becomes crystallized during the period of active socialization—the Oedipal stage—roughly between two and a half and five and a half years, when we learn to accept who we are and our limitations in the family. If we do not resolve this adequately here, we remain confused about ourselves.

Ego psychologists present a different view of the ego and id, postulating that we are born with a conflict-free ego. Both ego and id emerge from the same undifferentiated mass of thought processes and sensations. At birth, we are curious and search for stimulation and mastery. In the first three or four months, we begin testing reality—we distinguish be-tween what we will or will not put into our mouths.

From a very early age, autistic children seem to be preoc-cupied with themselves to the virtual exclusion of everyone else. Closer observation will reveal, however, that they do not truly know who or even what they are. They do not have the clear self-image of even a five-year-old. (See the discussions of autism and childhood schizophrenia in the chapter on Be-havior Disturbances.)

Another deviant, but less rare, behavior pattern is narcis-sism. This is a fixation on an infantile wish to remain omnipotent—a grandiose desire to receive constant and in-tense attention. In mythology, Narcissus gazed into a pool and fell in love with his own reflection. A little bit of narcis-sism is healthy—it makes for optimism and self-caring—but when our most primitive yearnings to control and to be the center of our universe are fixated upon, we are prevented from having any real human contact. Narcissistic personalities constantly aggrandize themselves. They can only be in love with themselves. When there is not a constant stream of attention and adulation, the brittle sense of self may shatter with consequent depression, psychosis, or suicide. Narcissistic personalities may also idealize and adulate another. In that way, the other person expresses their basic and extreme wishes for themselves.

The schizophrenic, who is fixated on infantile yearnings and an unformed self-concept, may split up the personality into selves that are not fused into one entity. The paranoid, on the other hand, projects onto others those traits and wishes that he or she cannot accept into his or her own self. (See the discussions in the chapter on Behavior Disturbances.)

In a symbiotic relationship—the prototype of which is a gratified baby nursing from a contented mother—two (or more) people absolutely rely on each other to provide a sense of self. Take one away and the other collapses. We have all seen parent–child, teen-age, and couple relationships of this sort. But an entire group or culture can base its identity on a dependence on a group self. They establish a we–they relationship with the outside world. Outsiders are alien, menacing, and even non-human. While outsiders solidify the group's cohesion and identity, they are so different that they pose a threat of destruction and may therefore have to be destroyed. This is xenophobia. It provides the rationale for war, exploitation, prejudice, and even genocide. Its most dramatic form is cults in which the group-supported sense of self is so extreme and yet so fragile that mass suicide may follow a perceived threat from outsiders.

Most of us develop a flexible self-concept that allows us to perceive a benign outside world. This is predicated on a family having validated and rewarded who we are, and then having experienced similar validation and rewards with each larger circle of environment or milieu that we are exposed to. Finally, it is our society which shapes our self-concept. If it is open and supportive, then we will be open and supportive to others. It has been found that those who report self-acceptance tend to accept others—they view the world as friendly. Those, however, who are shaped by a society that is closed and repressive will keep to tight, closed circles and be hostile to strangers. If we like ourselves, then significant others—most probably our parents—convinced us that they liked us. If we respect ourselves, then significant others conveyed to us that they truly valued our expression and growth. This communication transcends words and may even contradict surface appearances. It has more to do with what the significant others demonstrated than with what they said.

College students whose traits and behavior were rewarded and valued when they were children reported a higher self-esteem. Studies of those with a high self-esteem found that they shared certain characteristics. As children they experienced acceptance, interest, affection, and warmth. Interestingly, this high esteem was associated with demands made upon them with firmness and care. Punishment was used for managing undesirable responses and did not involve undue harshness or the withdrawal of love. Those with low esteem experienced harshness, disrespect, and little guidance. There was an emphasis on punishment rather than reward. Force and the withdrawal of love were stressed. Finally, those with high esteem perceived the family as operating according to democratic processes with mutually agreed upon goals, rules, and limits.

The Self

The modeling behavior of our parents is extremely important in the formation of our identities. Freud believed that during the normal resolution of the Oedipal phase, the child identifies with the parent of the same sex. He or she literally incorporates the traits and characteristics of the same-sexed parent. We have all seen little boys of this age shaving like daddy and little girls playing house like mommy. Almost all theorists, no matter what their persuasion, agree that the identity formed during the first five years or so of life, whether it is weak or strong, is basically the one that persists throughout life. Harry Stack Sullivan described this acquisition as a self system, whereby this early identity is perpetuated and solidified by accepting only what is compatible with the perceived personality. We literally ignore, deny, or distort what conflicts with our previous sense of ourselves.

There are, however, influences that continue to shape our identities. Siblings, caretakers, teachers, relatives, and peer groups exert a strong influence. Sullivan believed that just prior to puberty, the relationship with a chum opens us up to both verification and modification of our self-percept. Peer group influence during adolescence is very prominent. For the first time, the significance of both sexes, how we see them and how they see us, becomes salient. The affiliation with a group or gang is enormously reassuring to the sense of self at this period. Those who have only two or three pals feel that they are outsiders, that they do not fit in. Such relationships become merely mutual comfort arrangements. The lack of any stable, relatively intimate relationships in adolescence results in a sense of being an oddball or misfit.

The search for identity, as Erikson described, reaches its acme during adolescence. Adolescents are neither children nor adults; they are unsure of sexual, vocational, and societal roles; they can dream of the future or fall back on the past. Or they can experiment. Since solitary experimentation is dangerous, once again the support of a peer group, a cause, or an ideal is vital. In young adulthood, the sense of identity relates to vocational, familial, and societal values. During the middle and later years, a successful resolution of identification depends on separating the sense of self from external values.

Body Image	There are sex differences in body concept. Traditionally, women have been assumed to be more narcissistic about their bodies than men. In the past, anxiety was reported to have been converted more often by women into somatic symptoms. Such a syndrome is diagnosed as hysteria—the very word now connoting a female difficulty. In recent decades, the hysterical syndrome has been less clear and has been compounded with a variety of other symptoms. Increasingly, men manifest hysteroid and narcissistic symptoms. (Narcissus, after all, was a man.)

Sexual differentiation, the accuracy and sureness with which we make sexual distinctions, apparently has a profound influence on a sense of body integrity or body distortion. Several studies suggest that the clarity of sexual differentiation can serve to predict sexual adjustment and general personality integration. Confused and overcompensated sexual identity seems related to a weak body image and results in, among other things, maladjusted sexual behavior. The degree of confusion or ignorance about the sexual features of our anatomy seems to be considerable. Many men not only labor under serious misapprehensions about the appearance and function of the female genitalia, even fusing them in their minds with the excretory system, but also suffer similar ignorance about their own anatomy. They are anxious about the "normal" size of a penis and irrationally overemphasize that dimension with a consequent feeling of impaired self-esteem. Even college educated women may be ignorant of their own anatomy and not know what the clitoris is. This information may have been selectively unattended to, as Sullivan would say, or inhibited because of its learned association with badness and dirtiness. To redress this distortion, consciousness raising workshops, particularly for women, are now stressing viewing and open discussion of the body.

The more definite and clear an individual's body images are, the greater his or her capacity to enter into intimate relationships. Persons with definite body boundaries show evidence of greater sexual interest and expressiveness than do those with vague or shifting boundaries. It seems that only those who are sure of the boundaries of their selves can merge them with others with pleasure and confidence. Women with a low level of anxiety about their bodies seem better able to obtain sexual enjoyment.

A variety of drugs result in a sense of body distortion ranging from subtle to gross experience. A normal person in unusual circumstances can experience patterns of body image similar to those which develop when individuals become schizophrenic or suffer certain types of brain pathology. It is a common phenomenon to feel that our hands are swollen when we have a headache or a hangover. When intoxicated or hyperventilating, we are prone to feel our heads as larger and hollow. Substances in our body quite readily affect our body images, even when these substances are not strong drugs and we are not schizophrenic.

Distorted body image is not an uncommon experience. We have seen in the chapter on Eating that obese and anorexic people suffer a distorted concept of their bodies. Some people who wear glasses, despite the huge number who do, feel a stigma, as do people who have lost their hair. Any exaggerated feature, such as a large or a small nose, big ears, small or buxom breasts, maloccluded teeth, shortness or tallness of stature, may be accompanied by a sense of differentness or inferiority. The same is true for handicaps, scars, and surgery. When the surgery is related to the sexual organs—and mastectomies and hysterectomies have become only too common—these feelings become compounded.

An interesting phenomenon is that attractive people seem to take the most pains with their grooming in order to look even more attractive. What seems to operate here is Sullivan's self system. A picture of the self is established, reinforced, and perpetuated. Conversely, if the self-image that is established is negative, the person despairs of receiving rewards and instead derives some grim satisfaction and security in maintaining the script, "Well, that's the way I look. Won't you love me anyhow?" We call this the Frog Syndrome—the fantasy that someday a prince or princess will kiss us into beauty. What happens instead is that meanwhile, we croak rather unappealingly and give people the message that if they come near us they will grow warts. On the other hand, there are people who are not especially endowed with attractive features (according to social norms) who, because they received considerable esteem from their parents, esteem themselves. They comport and groom themselves to emphasize their esteem and attractiveness—and they convey that message to others more successfully than low esteem "beautiful people."

The point of all this is for us to appreciate how intimately involved our sense of self is with our body image. The self is greater than our skills, our smarts, our charms, and our bodily appearance. But these components of the self—especially physical appearance—are projected onto the world and occasion either positive or negative reinforcement. Therefore, it is necessary to receive and give to our children both esteem and a sense of integrity for who we and they are as people, and to learn and teach an appreciation for the most enhanced (not necessarily ideal) image. This means early knowledge of the body and of methods to enhance its presentation by grooming and posture.

Somatotypes	Just as no two personalities are alike, no two bodies are identical. The influence of one upon the other is profound, based not only upon subtle biochemical but gross constitutional factors as well. The most thorough study of these interactions was conducted by W. H. Sheldon. He found three basic body types, which he designated as somatotypes. The bodies of endomorphs are soft and rounded, and their digestive viscera are massive. Another somatotypologist, Kretschmer, called such people pyknics, and they usually, but not necessarily, are those people we see as fat. Mesomorphy, the second type, is characterized by the relative predominance of muscle, bone, and connective tissue. The mesomorphic physique is normally heavy, hard, and rectangular in outline. Kretschmer called it the athletic type. Ectomorphy, the third type, is a relative predominance of linearity and fragility. In proportion to mass, ectomorphs have the greatest surface area and, thus, the greatest exposure to the outside world. Relative to their mass, they also have the largest brains and central nervous systems. Kretschmer called such people aesthenics. They are usually those we see as skinny. There is another large category called dysplasia, which is a disharmony between different regions of the same physique. For example, a body may be one somatotype in the region of the head and neck and another in the legs and trunk.

Kretschmer found correlations between body types and psychiatric syndromes. Manic depression was associated with pyknics (endomorphs) and schizophrenia with aesthenics (ectomorphs), athletics (mesomorphs), and dysplastics. Sheldon found a much more subtle interaction between somatotypes and temperament, although he did see tendencies in these types to the relative incidence of psychosomatic and somatic disorders. As examples, mesomorphs are relatively insensitive to pain and probably therefore are more aggressively disposed to the world. Ectomorphs are relatively more sensitive to both physical and psychological pain and tend to be more cautious, withdrawn, and cerebral.

We can affect the shape of our bodies, although Sheldon's precise measurements of indices such as bone ratios suggest relative life-long stability. But our bodies also mold our personality and our perception and expression of ourselves.

Jung described four types of temperament: thinking, sensation, intuition, and feeling. He theorized that we inherit, or at least very early on develop, these orientations. He stressed how important it is to recognize and not struggle against our basic orientation as well as to develop as much as possible our other temperamental facets. The same emphasis would seem to hold for body types.

Typologies are not entirely accurate. They are largely descriptive rather than explanatory and are based on statistical norms. Nevertheless, modes or clusters can be very revealing. The interaction of body and mind is profound. Indeed, the distinction between the two is only theoretical. Moreover, the multifarious reactions and reinforcements to our appearance solidify our self-concept, often at the expense of a free choice of options. The ectomorph can certainly participate in various athletics successfully, and the mesomorph need not be an insensitive clod.

Roles

Perhaps nothing else defines our self-concept so much as the roles we assume or have assigned to us. Roles are determined by any number of factors, such as gender, age, physical characteristics, mental traits, ethnic affiliations, education, job, locale, parents, siblings, friends, and even the car we drive. The list is inexhaustible. These factors may or may not be based on reality considerations, but they become our reality, for we are largely what our roles tell us to be.

Our gender immediately casts us into a life-long role. The moment some happy pediatrics nurse exclaims, "It's a boy!" or "It's a girl!" the die is cast. The expectations that our family and society have for our particular gender become imprinted—literally shape our behavior—and are, to a significant degree, unalterable. How we eat, walk, talk coordinate, perform in a variety of areas, experience pain or pleasure or beauty, feel, express our feelings, grow ill or stay healthy, fornicate, relate, and succeed or fail is pre-set to a considerable degree by the gender role we assume.

Actually, there can be enormous flexibility—even inter-changeability of tasks and vocational achievements—possible between the sexes. Only the most gross distinctions, such as bone structure, musculature, and body mass limit this achievement. And the limits seem less obvious all the time. This is particularly true with the advent of sophisticated technology, which has jarred the fixity of old roles. Neverthe-less, cultural traditions typically lag behind, especially when the entrenched power purveyors (in this case, male) seem-ingly benefit. Of course, they don't, since role rigidity and limitations of choice narrow self-expression for all concerned. (See the chapter on Sexuality.)

At mid-life, women frequently feel bereft of any meaning-ful role and men grow similarly apprehensive about theirs. Older women only too often are expected to play the role of little old ladies, and older men are relegated to the role of spectators of life. If they are still interested in sex, they are seen as dirty old men. Nothing so limits and warps self-concept and self-esteem as gender-bound, age-delimited roles.

The strongest determinant of our roles is gender, but this relatively clumsy two-fold distinction can do violence to the complexity and subtlety of our real natures—our needs, de-sires, talents, preferences. To think of oneself as only a man or woman and to limit one's behavior accordingly is to limit one's options and possibilities.

Traditionally, men are supposed to be "masculine" and women "feminine," and these categories are seen as polar op-posites. On standard tests of masculinity and femininity, you can score as one or the other, but not as both. Recent studies, however—particularly those of Sandra Bem of Stanford University—have tried to break out of these limiting assump-tions. Bem has found that men who rate themselves as highly masculine are relatively unable to perform certain human tasks which they see as feminine, such as playing with a kit-ten or consoling an unhappy fellow student. Highly feminine women were often found to be unable to engage in activities that they perceived as masculine. The limitations of this are that people who unthinkingly accept cultural sexual stereotypes deny part of their natures in doing so. Such men find it difficult to be nurturing and emotional while these women are ill-disposed to be independent and original.

Implicit in Bem's research is the possibility that fuller lives can be lived by people who are *both* highly masculine and feminine—who are, in Bem's terms, psychologically an-drogynous. This is not to advocate an abolition of sexual dif-ferences, a suggestion that is both silly and impossible. Rather, it is to suggest that our sense of self and the range of

activities we allow ourselves should not spring from a culturally imposed stereotype, but from a realistic knowledge of our
own nature.

Beyond gender, there is a nucleus of roles that define the
preponderance of our behavior, style, and attitudes. To know
that someone is a Northeastern urban American Irish
Catholic blue collar high school graduate or a Midwestern
suburban Scottish Presbyterian white collar college graduate
is to be able to predict, with some confidence, politics, dress,
speech, recreation, reading habits, and so on. Second only to
gender, our vocations impose the strongest identifications
and sense of self, often transcending religious, ethnic affiliations. It is not the person who assumes the roles, but the roles
that define the person.

The issue here is not that roles ought to be avoided. That
is impossible and even undesirable. Rather, rigid role definition narrows expression and limits choice. It is stultifying and
results in a brittle sense of self. Maslow described a hierarchy
of values that evolve during our lifetime. The first level is associated with our basic needs to survive. These involve the
physical needs of nurturance and shelter. Erikson, too, described an ontogenic, developmental series of stages that
characterize the evolution of the self. We have discussed
elsewhere these stages that move from basic trust to integrity.
(See the chapter on Stages.) We believe that integrity can
begin early in life. The different conditions that we face at
varying ages must be integrated into our self-concept, our
identity. To accomplish this at any age means we have
learned to respect ourselves and others because we have ourselves received respect. Respect means the appreciation and
development of each individual's uniqueness—including and
especially our own. It implies the granting of the full range of
choice and expression to all, irrespective of roles. This mutuality of respect involves the recognition of freedom of choice
for all.

Life Style

In this chapter, we have essentially been describing character
style—the expression of the self as circumscribed by a sense of
identity, individual characteristics, and an assumption of
roles. Life style includes patterns of behavior, modes of relating to the world and to others, and the vehicles for such expression. It is our general orientation to the world. When
people say to us that we have a traditional or a free life style,
they mean that we relate to the world in a fixed, predictable
manner or that we have an open, dynamic orientation. In the
same way that roles may rule us, our life style may encase the
way we live rather than be chosen for gratifying and produc-

tive living. Erich Fromm has written that the need for security becomes so important that we are willing to surrender our personal and collective autonomy for rigid structure and even tyrants. He calls this the escape from freedom.

It is a most difficult thing to let go of the patterns to which we have grown accustomed. And yet not to let go restricts either our own freedom or that of those around us. The fear of letting go is the fear of going out of control. That is why a rigid life style may be chosen and autonomy surrendered to a partner, a group, a society, or a religion. Security is the payoff, but at the expense of productivity, growth, and personal gratification. The latter, however, need not be sacrificed when the basic tenet of the affiliation stresses respect for the individual. Whenever people surrender power over their lives to another, they pay by feeling powerless.

The most definitive sense of self—a stable and productive identity—requires the recognition and development of spiritual powers. This is perhaps our greatest strength. For many, spirituality means religious belief and participation in an organized religion, but it need not be limited to such an alternative. Most basically, the development of our spirituality implies our sense of relationship to something larger than ourselves. At its simplest level, it can mean an involvement in the family, society, or some group, but at its highest level, a willingness to know and participate in the common experience of mankind or to leave ourselves open to the sense of belonging to nature, the human spirit, or the universe as a whole. The word religion, after all, simply means a bond between people and something higher.

Thus a deeply religious person may not practice a formal religion. His or her spiritual needs can be satisfied by the communal experience represented by art, by the deep appreciation of nature or by the self-imposed responsibility for humanity. In this view, the philosopher Bertrand Russell, who, although an atheist, spent the last decades of his life working actively for nuclear disarmament, was more genuinely religious than the average church-goer. We finally cannot be responsible for humanity, but a deep involvement in its welfare leads to a deeper sense of our own humanity.

To be fully human, we need to develop an individual system of values and a philosophy of life. People who know, as best they can, who they are or what they can be, must face both life and death. This requires a degree of selflessness, an ability to give ourselves up, with all our needs and ideas, to the world and to let go. In such a state, we truly possess nothing but the experience of being part of, perhaps at one with, the world.

At the same time, we need to be selfish. This is not pejorative. Selfishness means identifying our uniqueness and wants and striving for their fulfillment while being sensitive to the uniqueness and needs of others. Self-centeredness, on the other hand, implies preoccupation with me, me, me and an insensitivity to others. Such a narcissistic orientation precludes both validation and gratification from others. Think of sexuality—without mutual gratification, there is a hollowness, a lack of involvement, and an auto-erotic quality. There is little or no opportunity to receive the nurturance and contact so necessary for self-esteem and self-respect. Selfishness in a positive sense means self-actualization, the fulfillment of our potential for ourselves and for those about whom we care.

Summary

All but the most impaired possess a sense of self, a conviction of uniqueness that endures through all the changes that life brings. The stability and depth of this sense allows us to approach the world with confidence and openness. The basis for such a conviction is established early in childhood, probably in the first six years. We can help ensure in our children a clear and stable sense of identity by validating and rewarding them for who they are as people, by giving them guidance and affection, and by encouraging the experience and expression of their individuality. If these influences are absent or inappropriate, behavior disturbances such as paranoia, schizophrenia, and narcissism may be partly caused and are exacerbated. Just as our sense of ourselves is developed in childhood, so is our level of self-esteem. Those who have a high sense of self-esteem experienced warmth, acceptance and affection as children; guidance was given with care and sensitivity and did not involve a withdrawal of love.

Part of our sense of self comes from the sense we have of our own bodies. Although body image is largely determined by what our body is really like, there are important differences between the two. What is important for us psychologically is not so much what our bodies are as what effect they have on important others, particularly our parents. Body image, therefore, is largely an interpersonal affair. Our bodies may also change, while our body images remain the same. Fat people who have lost weight often require a long period of time before they truly stop thinking of themselves as fat.

In general, we are prone to attend only to those responses from the outside world which confirm our previous sense of ourselves. This can lead to a serious discrepancy between who we really are and how we think of ourselves. Still, the surer we are of ourselves, the more deeply we are convinced about who and what we are, the more open we are to experience and the greater are the possibilities of gratifying interactions with the world and with others. People who are accepting of themselves tend more easily to accept others.

Of course, we do not have an absolute choice about who we will be. Our gender, our basic body type, and our temperament are given to us at birth. In addition, society tends to impose roles on us which may or may not match our individual needs and talents. We do, however, have the power to choose what we will do with our endowment and what roles we will accept for ourselves. Our lives will be happier, fuller and more productive if we base our roles and life style on internal, individual needs and talents rather than accept impersonal stereotypes.

Our greatest strength is our spiritual side, which may or may not involve participation in an organized religion. Instead, it involves a sense of belonging to something larger than ourselves, whether it be nature, society, or the universe as a whole. The dilemma to be resolved is how to surrender our individual selves to a larger whole while at the same time maintaining a sense of uniqueness.

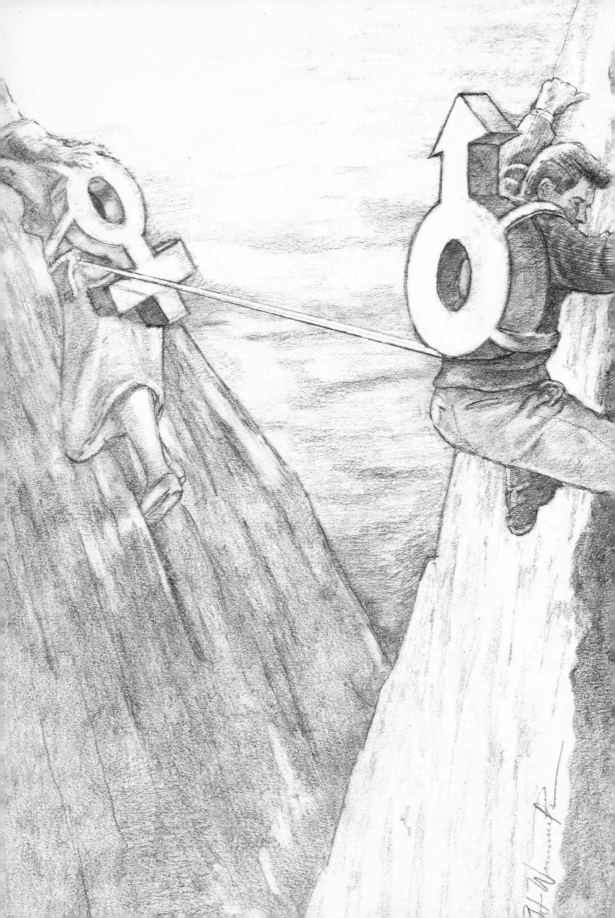

8
Sexuality

The most pervasive of the basic drives is sexuality. It influences every facet of our lives and colors our relationships, loves, dreams, fantasies, desires—our total identity. The arts, fashion, the media, mores, value systems, laws, education, and religion are significantly concerned with sex. When sexual drives are gratified meaningfully, we feel contented, adjusted, and whole. When they are frustrated, we feel confused and enraged.

The force of sexuality and its expression involve the most personal contact with another human being, with consequences of either intimacy or exploitation, comfort or threat. It is the most misunderstood, guarded, and distorted drive. Confused identification, warped communication, and emotional and physical disturbances are often the products of sexual disorder.

Freud understood this more than anyone else. It was he who systematically explored the significance of sexuality and largely based his theory of neuroses and psychoses on it. He believed that libido, or psychic energy, was essentially sexual in nature. When bottled up or perverted from its "true" object, it could cause emotional disturbances. Furthermore, Freud believed that the development of the personality depended on the expression of sexual energy at different periods—what he called the psychosexual stages.

The first, or oral, stage focuses on the erogenous zone involved in nourishment: the mouth, lips, and tongue. Fixation at this stage because of early trauma, deprivation, excessive stimulation, or regression to it due to severe stress is manifested by childish, dependent behavior characterized by a chronic need to be fed, literally or figuratively. This corresponds to a sucking phase, whereas the biting phase is characterized by cutting, rejecting behavior. These behaviors are most often symbolic or figurative in nature. Rather than wanting to be literally fed, an oral person may instead seek out people who will take care of him or her, may express unusual anxiety at, say, a Chinese restaurant, lest he or she not get a fair share of spare ribs. Similarly, someone fixated at the biting stage may employ excessive verbal energy and a "biting wit" as a means of expression.

The second, or anal, stage focuses on the erogenous zone involved in elimination, specifically the anus. Fixation or regression to this stage is manifested by withholding behavior, stubbornness, punctuality, excessive neatness, and miserliness. That is the anal retentive phase. The anal expulsive phase is characterized by explosive behavior, sadism, impulsivity, sloppiness, and procrastination.

Freud, a product of his male-oriented society, also posited a phallic phase, by which he meant a focus on the erogenous zone which includes the phallus and the large muscles associated with it. Fixation on or regression to this phase is manifested by aggressiveness, striving, and competition. The implications for females were ambiguous, however. If females demonstrated this behavior, then Freud explained it as penis envy, a theory that is currently being re-evaluated by clinicians as well as by feminists.

The final phase for Freud was the genital phase, which focuses on the genitals and is manifested by the ability to love, be intimate, and in general, by psychological adjustment. Theoretically, this is attained at the onset of puberty.

Freud, of course, built a more sophisticated and complicated psychosexual theory around these stages than is described here. Nevertheless, the rather literal stress on anatomy, male orientation, and the extolling of the genital phase have resulted in a simplistic conceptualization on one hand, and a difficulty of comprehension for many on the other. It does not require voluminous research to conclude that genitality is not sufficient for love, intimacy, or adjustment. For most people, such behavior is not attained until well into their third or fourth decade of life, if then, despite their "genital achievement." (See the chapter on Stages.)

What Freud most dramatically accomplished was to explain the significance of sexuality, especially infantile sexuality, in our lives and to inculcate an open-mindedness toward this extremely important human behavior. Concurrently, from the latter part of the nineteenth to the first third of the twentieth century, Havelock Ellis was doing the same in his psychosocial writings, research, and case material. In the 1930s, Kinsey began his research, which resulted in his enormously influential books, *Sexual Behavior in the Human Male* and *Sexual Behavior in the Human Female*. These works revolutionized modern attitudes toward sexuality.

Identity, Gender, and Typing

The most recent scientific evidence suggests that while heredity contributes to physical, mental, and behavioral sexual differences, these differences are largely shaped by culture. Apparently, there is no such thing as a simple male hormone or a female hormone. The female produces the same three hormones as the male, but in different proportions—far more estrogen and progesterone than testosterone. In both men and women, it seems that testosterone is the hormone that stimulates sexual desire. All people would have a female anatomy if it were not for a precise mixture of hormones at a critical time in prenatal development that triggers off a series of developments which ultimately make some fetuses male.

The sex ascribed to a baby is a social decision as well as a biological fact. Both biological endowment and cultural reinforcement determine the child's gender identity. Sometimes, when the two conflict, the important determinant for behavior is the biological one. Sex typing appears at about eighteen months and is firmly established before school starts. Such typing seems to be universal and is probably based on rewards and imitative behavior, but this is sex role rather than sex preference. Boys with older brothers and girls with older sisters form their sex type earlier than only children. Boys who identify with their fathers appear better adjusted, but the same is not true for girls who identify with their mothers. Cross identification—that is, partial identification with both parents—appears to be beneficial for both boys and girls.

There are boys who prefer to dress in girls' clothes, dislike playing with boys or their toys, and like dresses, wigs, and cosmetics. Such boys display feminine mannerisms, say they feel like women, and want to bear babies. They may have felt this way since they were two or three years old. Boys who manifest such cross-gender identity outnumber corresponding girls fifteen to one. A true, comprehensive cross-gender identity occurs in one person out of 100,000. Gender disturbance is usually noticed when a child enters school. The child usually suffers severe secondary psychological problems. There is evidence that gender disturbed children will not outgrow such behavior without intervention or favorable life circumstances or psychotherapy. The greatest promise for help appears to be social learning approaches, although many of these people are not changed by such therapy.

Gender disturbance seems to be caused, or at least encouraged, by being rewarded consciously or unconsciously by the parent of the opposite sex. A mother frustrated, enraged, or disillusioned by the physical or psychological absence of her husband (or her father in the first instance) may act out her needs on her little boy. She treats him the way she would like to have been treated as the little girl lavished with attention. Moreover, by keeping him as a little girl, she forestalls the inevitable rejection and desertion she expects from males. A cold, withdrawn, or punitive father also precludes successful identification by his son. Conversely, a father who wants a son in his own image, who wishes to act out vicariously his own needs, will reward boyish behavior in his daughter. A cold, withdrawn, punitive mother will reinforce this identification with the father, as will the collusion of a mother who also vicariously wishes her daughter were a son. Gender disturbance calls for early intervention with the parents as well as the child. Family therapy would be optimal, but counseling of both or at least one motivated parent is indicated.

Infantile Sexuality

Perhaps Freud's most controversial contribution was his delineation of the universality and significance of infantile sexuality. The resistence to this fact was all the more bitter, since the phenomenon had been observable for thousands of years. To all those who have been parents, the observation of infantile sexuality has been inescapable. All of us have been children, but many of us have repressed sexual memories from that period. In the past, and possibly still today, upset infants were soothed by caressing their genitals. The need for modern society to deny sexuality, especially in children, however, has been strong. Kinsey verified that arousal and sex play in children is extensive. Most of this pre-adolescent sex play occurs between the ages of eight and thirteen, although some of it occurs at every age from earliest childhood to adolescence. An excessive preoccupation by the child with sexual matters may signify an anxiety over sexuality or over self-identity. So too may a markedly indifferent attitude.

The sexual drive is at first not focussed on any particular person. Only as the child develops does he or she learn to direct sexual drive toward partners, under certain conditions and locations.

A study of sex education in the United States in 1957 established four goals of such training: to inculcate the taboo against incest, to discourage masturbation, to guard against sex play with other children, and to control information in order to limit and postpone sexual gratification. There were, significantly, no rewards, only inhibitions.

Although these conclusions were drawn in 1957, and despite the avowed greater permissiveness and encouragement of sex education in the 1960s and '70s, a 1978 survey revealed that even though the vast majority of parents agreed that pre-adolescent children should know about the pleasurable aspects of sex, fewer than 15% of mothers and 8% of fathers said they ever talked to their children about sexual intercourse. Even fewer had told their children about contraception or venereal disease.

Knowledge of the body and of the sexual process is both necessary and desirable for adjusted and contented living. Limits imposed on this information because of fear or misguided reasoning limit self-expression, intimacy, and relatedness. From the very earliest age, therefore, an open and intelligent attitude toward sex is valuable. Parents are not always the best informed nor free of their own conflicts and distortions. Fortunately, there are appropriate materials available for all ages.

Freud wrote of a latency period, roughly between five years and the onset of puberty, during which sexual activity is largely repressed. This has not been completely confirmed by such research as that of Kinsey. True, sexuality for the older child is less sanctioned by society and the outlets are fewer than for the adolescent and the adult, but studies show that experimentation and masturbatory behavior are active during this period.

Puberty

The onset of puberty occurs at an average age of thirteen years for females, in association with the menarche, the first menstrual flow, and is preceded by the appearance of secondary hair and the development of breasts. For males, the average age is fourteen and is associated with the ejaculatory response. It is preceded by the development of secondary hair and the lowering of the voice. The average age varies considerably and is influenced by cultural, ethnic, climatic, and dietary considerations. At this time, there is a revival of the early sexual drive in full force. The incomplete resolution of sexual relatedness to the parent of the opposite sex is reencountered now, but with the added physical and psychological factor of genital competency. The transition from childhood to adulthood is accentuated by hormonal changes and intensified sexual appetite.

Menstruation

It is surprising how often the young female is not prepared for her menarche. For many, it is a frightening time, for others disconcerting, and for almost all, exciting. The mother's attitude toward this event, expressed or implicit, is particularly crucial. The experience of peers also has a significant impact. The menarche is an occasion to celebrate the fruition of the healthy development of the body and the entrance into adulthood for the young female.

Menopause

Approximately in the forties, perhaps, in the fifties, menstruation becomes irregular and gradually ceases. This is called the menopause. There are hormonal changes attendant to the process, and it is important to become educated about them, but, other than certain mineral and vitamin (in rarer instances, endocrinal) deficiencies, menopause is another natural status. Certainly, there is not necessarily any associated change of sex drive. (Indeed, this may increase, probably because of a diminished concern about pregnancy as a possible consequence of the sex act, and a late acceptance of one's sexuality.) For those women who have been conflicted about their sexuality, who have been compulsively engaged with the role of Mother, or who fear growing older, the cessation of their menses may be depressing—sometimes, seriously so. Support groups, books, and treatment from a well-informed, compassionate physician can each contribute positively to one's experience of menopause.

The male, too, at this age, is wrestling with his change of role and acceptance of physical as well as chronological aging. In acute cases, psychotherapy may be indicated. Conversation with other men or support groups may be useful at this stage of life just as a general forum for exchange of the experience of this aging process.

Pregnancy

Pregnancy is a condition to which every female devotes enormous consideration. It may reflect her yearnings or apprehensions, her sense of fulfillment or aversion. It is a natural state, and yet carries with it extraordinary significance and change of status. Pregnancy is involved with identity and coping, of course, but it is particularly relevant to a woman's sexuality.

As such, the attitudes toward pregnancy in particular may be as conflicted as they are toward sex in general. Unfortunately, many people, both women and men, experience feelings of shame about what used to be called "that delicate condition." The fashion industry has counted on such prejudice, and produces lines of clothes that include bathing suits and nightgowns. There is no reason (other than financial) why any woman cannot be stylishly dressed well into the ninth month.

Women, into very late pregnancy, typically are not "delicate," and can do most everything they choose—including having enjoyable sex. When a woman (and, secondarily, her husband and family) can accept her sexuality, she can also accept her body image—whatever its form. For some, particularly for very young women, pregnant women's groups offer support and validation.

The positive resolution of sexuality and identity for some women is achieved with pregnancy. It results in a feeling of fulfillment—of being a woman who is becoming a mother. There is no other experience that equals that of sustaining, nurturing, and producing another human being within the boundaries of one's very own, familiar body. All those who have not been pregnant—no matter how imaginative, creative, and productive—can only guess, but not experience this miracle. The more fully the pregnancy is consciously experienced, as in natural childbirth, and with an active participation by the father in labor and delivery, the more both parents can come to share and understand this collaborative productivity.

Yet, despite its touted glories, the female, understandably may harbor various fears regarding pregnancy. She may fear the discomforts of pregnancy: that she may suffer morning sickness, and/or frequent nausea and back pains. She may fear post-partum disfigurement, discolorations, or stretch marks, the pain of an episiotomy, the scar of a Caesarean-section, varicose veins, and so on. She may be very apprehensive about the actual pain of labor and delivery. She may even fear dying herself. To belay the irrationality of these fears, and to minimize such possibilities, education in child bearing is vitally important. The choice of a competent obstetrician is all-important—one who will take the time to discuss these concerns. Again, a pregnant women's group can be helpful. Information on diet, medication, smoking, drinking, avoidance of pollution, radiation, and contact with such diseases as German Measles, exercise, methods of delivery (such as LaMaze) and involvement of the father are extremely important. The fear of a stillborn or "damaged" child is relevant as well. For the mother who will be having her first child when she is in her mid-thirties, discussion is indicated—with her obstetrician—as to the consideration of having amniocyntesis. This procedure is relatively mild and efficient, and can detect such problems in the unborn child as Down's Syndrome (Mongolism).

The fear of dying often represents the fear of the death of one's own personal child. That is to say, the advent of motherhood, concretely and profoundly destroys the illusion that one (the mother or father) can still remain a child and continue to be mothered. Putting it another way, there is fear of the attendant responsibilities of parenthood. That is why so many are fearful, or elect not, to become a parent. When this fear is intense, psychological counseling is suggested.

Conversely, many potential parents fear infertility. Much of the same psychology as above pertains. The fear of sterility is also the fear that one cannot or should not be adult. Often, with the adoption of a child, the otherwise "sterile" person becomes fertile. Consultation with obstreticians, urologists, and fertility clinics are valuable.

Relevant to pregnancy, we recognize, are the attitudes and knowledge one has about birth control. Among other issues, technological advances in contraception have given women much more choice about sexual experience. Religious and other personal considerations aside, the female has independence now from either avoiding sex or assuming a chronic breeding role. Such independence has always involved conflict, if not guilt, about sexuality and role. (The development of oral contraception for males, just as vasectomy, will place greater responsibility on men.)

To complicate matters, the birth control procedures have varying degrees of efficiency and, as with oral contraception, may occasion health concerns. Choice of birth control calls for responsibility and education. Consultation with physicians and planned parenthood associations are suggested.

Birth Control

Both sexes have similar phases during the sexual act: an excitement phase, a plateau phase, an orgasmic phase, and a resolution phase. Both sexes demonstrate an increase in blood pressure, breathing, heart beat, and muscular tension. The variation of sexual response for individuals, however, is very great. Surveys reveal that males report having an average of between two and three orgasms per week, but some report as many as twenty or more. While some females report fewer than one orgasm per week, others report multiple climaxes each time they engage in sex. Many females report a low interest in sex, but there are also males who go for years without experiencing an ejaculation. Physiological factors play a part, of course, but it has been said with a great deal of truth that the brain is the most important sex organ.

A significant discrepancy between male and female sexual responsiveness is their disparate phases of development in adulthood. Males report a steadily declining activity from their teens (about four and a half orgasms per week) through their sixties (one per week). Thirty percent of men report sexual inactivity in their seventies. Females, on the other hand, report an increasing sexual intensity that builds gradually but maximizes in their fifties. Gail Sheehy, in her book, *Passages*, describes this phenomenon as "The Diamond." That is, males and females are closest in sexual responsiveness until their mid-teens, diverge widely, and then approach each other again in their late fifties. Again, while hormonal differences may account for some of this divergence, it is cultural factors such as expected roles and societal prohibitions that undoubtedly play a prominent part.

Sexual Responsiveness

Masturbation

Masturbation has been so controversial that even its definition has not been agreed upon. There are some who would say it need not even be conscious. The broadest interpretation would include any intended stimulation of the genital area, whether by touching, rubbing, fondling, or even tensing the muscles. By this definition, few if any of us would be excluded from masturbatory behavior at some time in our lives. In 1948, Kinsey found that 96% of American men and 66% of women admitted to having engaged in the practice.

Yet the proscriptions against this behavior have approached the proportions of an eleventh commandment. Indeed, religious interdictions against masturbation are most specific. The conflict between intensity of drive and prohibition has resulted in one of the major wellsprings of guilt. And guilt always inspires irrationality. Consequently, such myths as masturbation resulting in blindness, insanity, and moral enfeeblement abound. Fear, rather than counteracting guilt, intensifies it.

As a sign of the times, there is hardly a sex manual that does not contain specific discussions of, and instructions for, masturbation. Indeed, many recommend that women engage in this practice as a way of dissolving inhibitions and of understanding and appreciating their orgasmic response.

What of the child who engages in frequent and conspicuous masturbatory behavior? Permissiveness does not mean abdication from the necessity of socialization and the establishment of boundaries. The issue here is the appropriateness of this behavior in public, rather than its intrinsic wrongfulness or dirtiness. Such behavior, however, may signify a need for sexual information, a deprivation of contact and affection, or some interpersonal difficulty. When such is not the case, excessive, conspicuous masturbatory behavior generally subsides because a stimulating environment for a child competes successfully for his or her attention. If the behavior does not subside, the familial and personal environment of the child needs to be explored and adjusted.

Fantasy

The predominant theme of our daytime fantasy and of our dreams, in either subtle or gross form, is sexuality. This is not so difficult to understand, since it is the most monitored and inhibited of the basic drives. Because of similar although less precise prohibitions, aggressive fantasies probably take second place. It is the rare person who reports no sexual fantasy. In all probability, that individual is extremely repressed in most of his or her behavior and emotions.

In a study, 65% of married women reported fantasizing during sex with their husbands. Another 28% had fleeting thoughts of someone else. The two most popular themes were being with another man, such as a former lover, familiar actor, or casual friend, and of being forced into sex by an ardent, faceless male. Only 7% reported no fantasy. Sixty percent reported that they sometimes fantasized an imaginary lover during intercourse, and 18% reported having this fantasy very frequently. There seemed to be no relationship between these fantasies and marital adjustment, except those who had positive, pleasant thoughts (20%) reached orgasm all the time, and those who had negative thoughts (16%) never experienced orgasm, or they experienced it as unpleasant.

There are fewer reports on male sexual fantasy, perhaps because it seems to be more likely to be acted out in the media, film, novels, and advertising. What reports there are seem to coincide largely with those of females, except that the males are doing the forcing or they are delighting several females at once. In the 1950s, *Playboy* magazine contributed to the start of an era of voyeurism and sexual freedom. Many bolder magazines, such as *Penthouse*, followed, along with nudity and explicit sex in the theater and in films. These sources provide many people — particularly males — with instant, prepackaged sex fantasy.

Heterosexuality

In the next chapter, we shall discuss one of the most difficult human behaviors—a meaningful, stable relationship based on mutual respect. When the relationship is a sexual one between two people, it involves all that is personal and interpersonal: a sense of identity, of sexual role, an ability to give and receive pleasure, a capacity to cope with power and competition, an ability to communicate and trust. This trust includes sharing the most intensely private parts of the self, including the surrender of the usual body boundaries. It means the conscious exposure of vulnerability which can result in the most painful rejection or intimate acceptance. In the face of lifelong training to describe sex and even the body as forbidden, it is no wonder that difficulties in this area are both common and myriad. For many, a satisfactory resolution is not achieved until past the third decade of life.

A gratifying sexual relationship presumes a merging of lust and tenderness. One without the other results in a distorted union. Lust alone implies exploitation, self-centeredness, and diminished regard for the other. Sexual pleasure may be a consequence, but it is not a loving act. Tenderness alone implies a cool relationship that may be compassionate, but without passion it also is not a loving act. It often flows more out of obligation and the need to please the other rather than the self. Certain moral and religious

teachings promote this attitude. If sex is allowed only to pro-
create children or to serve a mate, it is not conducive to the
mingling of lust and tenderness. When sexual performance,
the need to prove oneself as a man or woman sexually, is perceived as integral to the sexual act, mutuality, respect, and
trust—not to mention pleasure—are hardly possible.

What needs to be understood, and is so frequently not
appreciated, is that the objective of sex is gratification, both
physical and mental, for *both* partners. Nothing more,
nothing less. When that objective is understood and practiced,
both pleasure and intimacy result. How sex takes place and
the manner of its performance are relatively less important.
Sex without love is limiting and often stultifying. Love without sex often occasions the same consequence.

After having stressed the importance of attitude in sexuality, we by no means wish to minimize the importance of
timing and technique. It is certainly no less important than
in any other human endeavor. The petting and necking that
take place so passionately in the teens and often long after are
important, if not necessary, as training in attitude, timing,
and technique for the lovemaking that is to follow. This is
true both for foreplay, which is almost always necessary for
satisfactory coitus, and actual intercourse.

Incidentally, if gratification and intimacy are the goals,
why have coitus at all? The answer is that coitus is not necessary. Even cuddling and just holding each other can be emi-
nently satisfactory. There is, however, ample reason to believe, despite little scientific evidence, that coitus is the acme
of sexual gratification when there is a union of body and
mind, a maximum of contact, and a cooperation of passion
and tenderness before, during, and after orgasm that pro-
motes the keenest pleasure, closeness, and afterglow. The jux-
taposition and fit of genitals, the warmth and moisture, and
the optimal friction during intercourse, while bodies and
emotions are intertwined, combine to produce the highest
sense of closeness.

As for timing, there is usually a difference in arousal time
for males and females, due to both physiological and
psychological factors. Many males, at least when they are
younger, are, as they say, "hot to trot." The mere suggestion
of sex or a visual stimulus may occasion an erection. Since the
females may be much slower in arousal, the lubrication of
their genitals and their distension require more time. A
woman may first be arriving at a highly erotic pitch just
when the man has climaxed and would like to go to sleep.
This set of circumstances generates frustration and is an exceedingly common source of contention for couples if they are
uneasy about discussing their sexual experiences.

So, a protracted and imaginative foreplay is desirable. This includes verbal and non-verbal communication. The male who observes this principle will not only have a more intimate partner but will probably also experience a more satisfactory orgasm himself. Not infrequently, one or both partners are anxious about the act itself. Sometimes, time and experience resolve the problem, but this is chancy and too costly in frustration and bitterness. Psychological counseling in this event would be useful.

As for intercourse, frank communication and variation are as desirable here as in any act between two people. Because sex is so veiled in taboos and inhibitions, many people who love and otherwise trust each other are not frank in their communications about sex or are ignorant of its possibilities. Fortunately, there are excellent books on this subject. Creativity in foreplay, experimentation in intercourse, including a variety of positions, and communion in afterplay will enhance lovemaking for most people. Many university psychological centers and medical schools offer sexual enrichment programs and counseling.

Masters and Johnson, following on the heels of Kinsey's surveys, studied sexual behavior and introduced the specialization of sexual counseling and therapy. Among other things, they deal specifically with such difficulties as premature ejaculation, impotence, frigidity and sexual dysfunction in its many forms.

Premature ejaculation is a very common affliction among males. Premature may be a relative consideration based on subjective criteria. It may be defined, however, as including ejaculation prior to, during, or seconds after penetration, or after less than half a dozen thrusts. Almost always this condition is due to anxiety over performance or over the nature of the sex act. A significant component of this anxiety may be hostility toward the female in question and females in general. Freudians believe that castration fear underlies this symptom. At some level, the male fears that his penis will be damaged or hurt because he has learned that his sexual behavior is taboo. Unusually delayed ejaculation may be the opposite, with similar psychological dynamics.

Masters and Johnson report a 95% success rate using a rapid, efficient technique. They employ what they call the Squeeze, or a version of Seamans', Technique. What is involved is a desensitization procedure wherein the partner applies pressure to the glans penis as soon as the ejaculatory response is signaled—there is approximately a thirty second warning period—until flaccidity results. This is done repeatedly until penile sensitivity is diminished and the ejaculatory response delayed.

Although the Squeeze Technique has considerable and efficient success, it has been our experience that many males discontinue treatment before they achieve success. It is as if there were a wish to avoid success in sex or they derive some gain from their symptoms. Others regress to their original behavior seemingly for spontaneous reasons. Therefore, what appears to be called for in many cases is both behavior modification such as the Squeeze Technique and counseling or psychotherapy.

Another common sexual difficulty suffered by males is secondary impotence. It is called secondary because it is not the result of a primary physical disability, but secondary to some psychological disorder. The difficulty is the inability to gain or sustain an erection. The performance factor seems to be the most common cause of anxiety. As males get older, there is a decreasing ability to initiate and maintain an erection, but not an absence of this function. If, in addition, there is tension, some crisis, or intensified "demands" by his partner, the added pressure on the male may result in impotence. Typically, the male makes the condition worse by worrying, and the fear escalates. The behavioral technique utilized includes the establishment of relaxed conditions with minimal requirements for performance. Emphasis is placed on pleasure, touch, and fondling. Essentially, support is provided and, again, psychological clarification and support are essential. Also essential is knowledge by both partners that the female can be well satisfied even in the absence of an erection.

What has been called frigidity in females, but which is an umbrella term for lack of responsiveness, indifference, or aversion to the sexual act, is quite common. Sometimes, the inability to achieve, or more precisely the omission of, orgasm is included in the label. It has been variously reported that one-third to one-half of females experience this condition, at least during intercourse. Perhaps two-thirds frequently do not reach climax during intercourse. With such numbers, we can hardly speak of pathology. Rather, clitoral stimulation as a source of orgasm is to be recognized as an accepted factor in sexual behavior. Masters and Johnson recommend that females familiarize themselves with their bodies and that they masturbate in order to lower inhibitions and to demonstrate as well as reinforce the experience of orgasm.

With respect to the generalized sexual dysfunction of couples, a combined procedure of relaxation, an emphasis on giving and receiving pleasure, desensitizing, and stimulating by reading and films are recommended by Masters and Johnson and others. Doubtless, these procedures are valuable in furthering personal and mutual confidence as well as interpersonal and sensual communication. It is essential to reiterate that mechanics and technique are useful but do not obviate understanding one's own and another's motives, apprehensions, and desires. And this requires understanding and respect, which often means individual, couple, or group counseling.

A homosexual person is one who prefers to develop erotic relations with someone of the same sex. In other words, the label refers to the choice of sexual partners and in itself says nothing about the person who is homosexual. The varieties of homosexuality are complex, ranging from those who have had only one homosexual experience in their lives, or who have refrained from such an experience but know that they are sexually responsive to members of their own sex, to those whose sexual experience has been without exception homosexual. In 1948, Kinsey found that 37% of all American males reported a homosexual experience to the point of orgasm between adolescence and old age. Later, he reported the corresponding statistic for women to be 20%. Thirteen percent of the male population, he found, were predominantly or exclusively homosexual. If anything, these figures represent an underestimate. In 1948 fewer people than now would admit to such practices, and the recent movement toward sexual liberation has allowed many more this alternative. These figures were fairly consistent across all socio-economic classes, educational levels, religious groups, and geographical areas. In summary, more than one in three males has had a homosexual experience to the point of orgasm, and about one in seven is more homosexual than heterosexual.

In the past, descriptions of the "typical" homosexual or theories about how people got to be that way were based on very unrepresentative samples—those who had been imprisoned or those who sought therapy to "cure" them of their orientation. Recently, however, researchers have been trying to find out what this population is really like, and as a result, many of these generalizations have been proven false. In reality, homosexuals are represented in all professions—doctors, politicians, clergy, police, and psychologists. Although some are easily identifiable by their mannerisms or modes of dress, by far the greatest number are indistinguishable from the population as a whole.

Several studies have been unable to find any higher incidence of psychological disorders or personal unhappiness among homosexuals. This is remarkable, considering the social, familial, and professional pressure that these people experience. The only commonality that has been determined is that they prefer to have sex with members of their own sex. In 1973, the Board of Trustees of the American Psychiatric As-

Homosexuality

sociation voted unanimously to remove homosexuality from their list of psychological disorders, and in 1974 the membership of that organization voted overwhelmingly to approve this decision. In 1975, the American Psychological Association did the same.

Few people are bothered by how someone becomes heterosexual, but this does seem to be an issue when it comes to homosexuality. Freud's notion, supported by a mass of evidence, was that all people are originally polymorphous and bisexual in nature. If this is so, then the choice of sexual partner is determined largely by environmental factors, particularly within the family. A distant or punitive father and a dominant but affectionate mother have been posited as a factor favoring male homosexuality. Complementarily, a cold, dominant mother and a warm, charismatic, or passive father have been thought to favor female homosexuality. The evidence for this view is inconclusive, and in any case, such a theory does not explain why many children from such families turn out to be heterosexual. Similarly, an initial sexual experience that is very rewarding or calamitous may influence sexual choice, although evidence here too is lacking. The most likely explanation, although it explains very little, is an initial predisposition which can be encouraged by environmental events.

People do not become homosexual or heterosexual through choice. Indeed, sexual orientation has developed before we are capable of a real decision. Still, there are choices to be made and aspects of sexuality to be understood that are available to homosexuals and heterosexuals alike. One sexual orientation is neither right nor wrong, but can be judged by the degree of freedom and satisfaction it offers. It is important for people not to use their condition as an excuse for lack of growth, productivity, intimacy, or happiness. No genuine life style can be built on rebellion or avoidance, and truly liberated homosexuals will not use their sexual orientation as a weapon against their families or as a way of refusing to confront anxiety—if it is present—over the opposite sex. Realistically, they must also be aware of the social animosity and limitations they will face at the hands of an ignorant and prejudiced society. The rewards and satisfactions offered by such a life style are correspondingly great, and people come to a realistic assessment of their lives by understanding the limitations and opportunities that any decision necessarily involves.

Much unnecessary unhappiness results when homosexuals decide to inform their families about their lives. Many people mistakenly believe homogenization is superior to diversity and label any deviation from norms as perversity.

Still, even the most loving and well-meaning of parents are subject to misinformation and cultural stereotypes. For the parents of a homosexual only child there is also a sense of genuine disappointment at knowing they probably will not be grandparents.

Coming to understand and respect a family member who is homosexual is a gradual process, and both parties must try to separate their real feelings from stereotypical attitudes. Mutual respect and honesty will allow the possibility of a deeper understanding and love within a family. The project for a family is not really to accept a homosexual child, but to continue to love and understand—as much as they have done before—a child who happens to be homosexual. Dr. Charles Silverstein has written an excellent book, *A Family Matter*, which is a guide to families who are struggling to come to terms with this issue.

A homosexual who is willing to examine his or her motives will have a firmer sense of identity and a more productive life if the choice of sexual style is volitional and informed. The same is true for the heterosexual, who does not, however, face so hostile a society. The heterosexual may also rebel sexually with promiscuous behavior. Both ways, rebellion or conformity, are compulsive and deprive the person of free expression. It is possible that the very oppositional tendencies noted in the sexual behavior of many homosexuals are expressed creatively in artistic and aesthetic contributions. Society generally benefits from diversity.

An interesting circumstance prevails nowadays. Since the life expectancy of females is longer, there is a larger number of living females than males. There are also more females in the first instance. Refusing to conform to an institution that they believe exploits and limits, many feminists do not marry or refuse to remarry. So there is a large pool of single, separated, divorced, or widowed females. By choice or by default, it appears that ever-increasing numbers seek the companionship, including sexual companionship, of their gender. This phenomenon has not yet been studied to any degree, but empirically the consequences appear more felicitous than not.

The sexual drive is experienced early in childhood. It may, and often does, last into old age. Prejudice and erroneous information have denied sexuality to our seniors. Children are dismayed to learn that their parents engage in sex into their late thirties or even forties. Parents are shocked to learn that grandpa and grandma are still sexually active. Only recently have we learned that people who have been sexually active all

Sex and the Adjusted Person

their lives and who, most importantly, have an open and be-nign attitude toward their sexuality can enjoy sex no matter how old they are chronologically. We saw in the chapter on Stages that chronology is only one—and often not the most important—determinant of aging.

Regular and normal sexual response occurs each night during sleep. Between four and seven times a night, both men and women will exhibit physical signs of sexual arousal dur-ing rapid eye movement sleep. This cycle has been found in studies with ninety year old subjects. Physical aging affects sexuality beginning around fifty, but sexual dysfunction is caused mostly by misunderstanding the changes. For men, delayed and partial erections, accompanied by slower and less intense reactions, are to be expected. For women, lubrica-tion and elasticity may be affected by age, but medicinal lu-bricants are helpful. The appropriate attitude and a prolonged and uninhibited foreplay can result in gratifying sexuality into the nineties.

A person capable of experiencing sex who also can cope with the responsibilities, implications, and conditions neces-sary for this behavior is able to enjoy it no matter what his or her age. Sex is a basic drive, the fulfillment of which pro-motes adjustment as well as gratification. Presumably there can be too much or too little sex, as in overeating and under-eating or oversleeping and undersleeping, but here the issue is usually attitudinal. When related to interpersonal issues of love and relationships as well as to self-expression, sexuality can be the cement that glues together the sense of self and the interrelationship with another. We agree with Freud in be-lieving that a whole and integrated person joyfully celebrates his or her own sexuality.

Summary

Sexuality is one of the strongest drives in human beings. It is also the drive most subject to prohibitions and taboos. Almost because of this it becomes the most pervasive, influencing almost all our activities and occupying an enormous portion of our fantasy life. It also offers the greatest possibilities of satisfaction, pleasure, intimacy, and a sense of relatedness to others. Any adequate definition of psychological adjustment would almost necessarily include the ability to express sexuality freely and to experience and give pleasure in the sexual act.

Sexuality does not begin with puberty, but manifests itself in the youngest of infants. It is only through the gradual process of socialization and the formation of an identity that this drive crystallizes into a specific orientation. It is essential that a growing child not learn to associate his or her developing sexuality with badness or dirtiness. All the evidence indicates that masturbation, if not excessive, is natural. Similarly, the onset of menstruation in girls is a time for the celebration of a developing body, not an occasion for dread and shamefulness. A child has a good chance of developing a positive sexual adjustment if sexual matters are discussed in the family with frankness and ease.

The greatest enemy of healthy sexuality is ignorance. Many people are ignorant of their own physiology and even less informed about the real differences between men and women. Rates of arousal are different for the two sexes, as are changes in excitability and interest as people get older. A frank understanding of our partner's needs and interests does much to avoid resentment and a sense of deprivation. A satisfactory sexual relationship depends on a balance of lust and tenderness and on mutual consideration of each other's needs.

Many kinds of sexual dysfunctions, premature ejaculation, secondary impotence, and frigidity, are quite common and may be experienced by most people during various times of their lives. Luckily, recent therapies and sexual counseling have been very effective in treating these problems.

Homosexuality, which was once thought of as a disability affecting a small number of perverts, is now recognized as a common sexual variation with no necessary connection to psychological disorder. No important differences have been found between homosexuals and heterosexuals except in the choice of sexual partners. One of the effects of gay liberation, however, is that many families are having to recognize and understand the homosexuality of one of their members. Honesty, understanding, and love, as usual, are the best ways for families to emerge from this crisis stronger and more loving than before.

9
Relating

Relating to another person is the most human of all behavior. It is also the most complicated and difficult. To know ourselves—our needs and fears, desires and conflicts, dreams and confusion, strengths and sensitivities—takes a lifetime of conscious effort to succeed even in part. Many give up almost before they begin. But difficult as this task of self-knowledge is, to enter the heart and mind of another is not only even more formidable, it is almost impossible. To begin to achieve this, we must allow the other person into our own private being, a delicate and frightening prospect. Yet all of us who are sane, and most who are not, crave this completion. So we struggle for the warmth, sustenance, and validation we get from another, or we despair of the alienation and coldness that result from a weak relationship or the lack of one.

Every relationship, from the most superficial to the most intimate, whether it be with a child, parent, friend, lover, or boss, is based on the mutuality of giving and getting. That is the contract, explicit or implicit. Interactions are satisfying, meaningful, and relatively free of frustration to the degree that the contract is understood by both parties and is open to definition and redefinition. More often than not, however, relationships are characterized by one-sided contracts in which we get less than we expect or give more than is welcome. All too often, these contracts are based on roles—The Child, The Mother, The Father, The Wife, The Husband, The Boss, The Worker—to which we attach our own private expectations. Never bothering to explain what we really understand and expect from such relationships, we assume that the other will come to share our view in time and that his or her own needs and desires will not change. We can and must use our sensitivity and intuition—what is the other feeling, thinking, and expecting, and does he or she know what I am feeling, thinking, and expecting? This is necessary but not sufficient. It suffices only to explicate, again and again and again, the nature of the relationship. Roles change, expectations change, we change. We too often are misunderstood because we don't understand ourselves and are therefore precluded from expressing our needs adequately or accurately. The essential ingredient of a rational relationship is a continuous process of open communication and redefinition.

The stumbling block to this full communication, however, is our vulnerability. If we open up to another, display our feelings, expose our sensitive spots to scrutiny, we can be scorned, derided, rejected, manipulated, destroyed. Note how this sense of vulnerability escalates. But this unwanted manipulation and annihilation only occur when we irrationally give such power to the other. That irrationality is a residue from our infantile past. We may even know this consciously, but we nevertheless erect barriers and facades between ourselves and everybody else. Jung called these masks personae. A great deal of our relating takes place behind these personae—we relate, make love, play, and work through psychological tissue paper.

We have been discussing the issue of making contact. At the opposite extreme is the problem of maintaining separation. The early severing of the umbilical cord may be successful physically but frequently not so psychically. We merely re-attach to an intimate other. The conflict between remaining merged, protected, and safe and becoming an individual, feeling free, autonomous, and vulnerable begins in the second year of life. The conflict reaches its peak in adolescence and the early twenties. It is never resolved for immature people. (See the discussions of adolescence and the twenties in the chapter on Stages.) Indeed, maturity can be thought of as an individuated identity that still remains desirous and capable of mutually interdependent relationships. This theme will be discussed throughout this chapter.

Our experience of being children is the prototype for all relationships. We learn here how to relate: we generate trust or mistrust, the ability to take and to give, to be esteemed and to esteem, and to be respected and to respect. The consummate relationship, for most of us, is to be parents ourselves, although this role may be manifested as teacher, philosopher, or artist.

Parenting

The major principles of being parents, as we see them, are guiding, but not dominating; teaching, but not proselytizing; encouraging, but also structuring; and giving as well as taking. Because being a parent is so difficult and because it is not entirely instinctive as it is for animals, we search, sometimes desperately, for answers. As a consequence, styles or fads of parenting come and go.

In the 1920s, the style was strict habit training. There were rigid schedules for feeding, sleeping, and toileting. There were formulas for everything. The forties ushered in an era of permissiveness. Now schedules were self-regulating, based solely on the demands of the child. Parents were told only what not to do. The works of Gesell and Ilg were largely instrumental in furthering this attitude. These books and articles included behavior profiles of children for different ages. They were largely descriptive, suggesting a laissez-faire attitude toward normative patterns that would develop in an inexorable fashion. These guidelines were perhaps too normative and did not pay sufficient attention to individual differences in child and parent.

The forties also ushered in the era of Spock, an era of permissiveness that confused respect and tolerance with lack of structure. Many believe that its consequences were blurred boundaries and diffused identities, rebellious attitudes, and the search for concrete truths that characterized children who attained their majority in the 1960s. Spock himself had a change of mind and revised his principles of permissiveness to one of "gentle structuring." He stressed the importance for parents to be comfortable, less guilty, and reasonably informed in their parenthood.

Research has shown that child care practices are less important than the spirit in which they are carried out. Unfortunately, it is more difficult to change attitudes than specific acts. There are, however, some general rules that all parents might observe. It is generally unwise for children older than four or five years to sleep or bathe with their parents. Unnecessarily hostile behavior should not be reinforced explicitly or covertly, although a child has a right to express appropriate anger and frustration. And, in general, using punishment more than reward can have consequences opposite to those intended. Other such rules are readily available in books and articles on child rearing, and parents do well to avail themselves of these resources. Similarly, sharing experiences and difficulties with other parents in study groups can be most profitable. Most important, however, is for parents to be aware of what motives inform their overt behavior. Ambivalent behavior—saying one thing and meaning another—can have disastrous results. So it is crucial that parents take upon themselves the responsibility of understanding what they really mean and of communicating it clearly. Finally, taking the advice of experts can be a good idea, but such hints should be tempered by a sense of individual differences in both child and parent.

Studies have demonstrated that children from warm and democratic homes are more socially outgoing, more active in school functions, and generally more assertive. The children from indulgent homes tended to be inactive, unaggressive, and socially unsuccessful. The children from restrictive homes, in which punishment was severe and the control autocratic, were more unpopular, quarrelsome, insensitive, and emotionally less stable. Maternal coldness, manifested either by punishment or uncaring permissiveness, was found to be associated with feeding problems, bed-wetting, aggressiveness, toilet training problems, and slow development of conscience.

Many studies have shown the dire consequences of maternal deprivation. "Hospitalism," the term for the effects of prolonged institutionalization, is a vitiated condition of body and mind. Separation from mothers, even those with whom

the child had a good relationship, for three or four months results in "anaclitic depression," a life-long sense of loss and
depressiveness. The critical period for separation trauma is
between six and eighteen months of age.

In routine, everyday events, the degree of distress a child
feels when his or her mother leaves can be diminished by the
mother giving the child information about her departure, including reassuring plans for future return and what the child
should do in her absence. Children whose mothers slip out
without saying anything about their departure show the most
separation distress; children whose mothers explain that they
are leaving and will return show less distress; and children
whose mothers not only explain that they are leaving but
suggest an activity the child can do in her absence show least
distress.

High quality non-maternal care does not appear to have
harmful effects on the pre-school child's maternal attachment,
intellectual development, or social-emotional behavior. Children experiencing substitute care and those reared exclusively at home show similar patterns of attachment to their
mothers. The intellectual development of middle-class children is shown to be little effected (diminished) when such
children are not reared exclusively by their parents. Educa-
tionally oriented day-care programs often have been found to
prevent the decline in intellectual developmental performance
frequently found in lower class home-reared children.

The loss of a parent has been found to be associated with
a large proportion of delinquent children and with depressed
and suicidal patients as well. The very same statistic is also
associated with people who have attained eminence. For both
groups, the death of the father rather than the mother seemed
to be more significant. Bereavement reaction has two possible paths. It can be an impetus for creative effort, a force for
good. It can have the opposite effect and stunt personality
growth, producing concomitant anti-social acts, destruction
of social relationships, and even the taking of one's own life.
At times, the child may become his or her own parent surrogate. In other words, parental loss can result in a sense of
severe insecurity or it can be compensated, even overcompensated, for in a keen need to master the environment. Probably,
the relationships to the dead and surviving parent, as well as
opportunities provided for the child, are all important.

There is definitive, growing evidence that fathers contribute
significantly to the development of sex roles, cognitive
abilities, and achievement motivation. The most desirable
characteristics of a father are warmth, acceptance, and involvement. The specific activities and behavior the father en-

Fathering

gages in with the child, as well as the father's relationships with other members of the family, appear most significant as does the quality rather than the amount of time he spends with his child. Among child psychologists, the tendency nowadays is to consider the importance of the father not solely as the masculine parent, radically different from the mother, but as an equally affectionate and involved parent. Being a parent is a difficult, complex and demanding role, and two more nearly equal parents are better able to fulfill the needs of their child than two figures who assume different functions and roles.

Not only do children identify with their parents, but the converse is true. We see in our children facets of ourselves, realistically or otherwise. This may generate pride, but the pride can become overweening, involving inexorable and unreasonable demands. We want the child to be what we dreamed of for ourselves and could not or would not achieve. The child is used as a link in our chain of immortality, just as our parents link us to the past. And so we may live vicariously through our children, denying them their right to separation and individuation.

Parents can subtly encourage their children to act out their own needs. For example, an enraged father, indignant with a son who has fathered a child out of wedlock, might suddenly wink and exclaim, "A chip off the old block, eh!" The long-suffering, martyred mother may encourage her daughter to withhold sex from her son-in-law to keep him in line—something she never dared to do with her own husband. Parents' irritation and fury with teen-agers is often a reaction to those negative qualities they feel in themselves. Vicarious motives and unconscious conflicts underly the often inconsistent behavior of parents. The child may seem to rebel against the obvious parental message, but unconsciously is responding to the concealed one, incurring wrath and disappointment for the sake of unspoken approval.

These double messages or double binds instigate considerable grief. In the extreme they even contribute to psychotic behavior. A parent can literally drive a child crazy with totally inconsistent messages: "I love you even though you cause me so much pain—I am giving up my life to raise you," or "You are the most important one in the world to me even though I almost died in childbirth." Often the double bind is a conflict of messages from both parents, as when the mother discourages any fighting as bad and the father decries nonaggression as weak.

A very frequent double message is often expressed through qualified affection. Certain cultural groups have particular difficulty here. Conflicted about being openly demonstrative, parents may display affection only with food or material gifts. Another very common expression of affection is teasing, which is affection larded with hostility or at least disparagement.

A curious but all too prevalent phenomenon is that behavior when the feelings and acts which we were discouraged from or fearful of expressing toward our own parents are manifested toward our children. This can happen with love as well as hate. Too often, we inflict upon our children not only what our parents inflicted upon us, but what we wish we could have answered them with. This is almost always unconscious.

It is extremely important to identify what our real motives toward our children are, to determine whether they are ambivalent or are rationally related to the present. To do this, it is necessary to ask ourselves why we are reacting in a certain way—especially if our behavior is intense, urgent, and imperative. We need to question what this behavior has to do with how we see or do not want to see ourselves, and how it may be related to our experience with our own parents.

The Family

Just as being a child is the prototype for relating, it is the family that provides the strongest influence on the child's learning. A successful family supplies a support system and a source of security. When this system is closely knit, familial, social, moral, interpersonal, and even educational development of the child is furthered more significantly by far than by any other social institution.

It can hardly be said that the family unit as we have known it traditionally is the definitive norm today. Separation and divorce are common, sometimes exceeding one out of four marriages. In New Jersey in 1977, there were 57,000 more applications for divorce than for marriage. In 1975, there were over one million divorces in the United States, twice as many as in 1966 and almost three times as many as in 1950. It is our guess, based on observation and clinical experience, that a significant number of "intact" families are intact in name only, held together by "propriety" or just plain inertia.

The Adopted Child

While a large number of young people claim they do not want children, an increasing number of people also wish to adopt them. Interestingly, non-fertile parents who adopt children then frequently have natural children. A factor would seem to be the psychological relaxation of anxiety about fertility and virility. Whereas the predominant motive in adoption seems to be parental love, as in child bearing itself, it may also be motivated by social expectations or the desire to cement a faltering marriage. This last is usually not a successful action. On the other hand, the deliberate choice to adopt a child very often results in rational, loving behavior.

If parents are clear about their own motives, they will have little difficulty in sharing the nature of their parent relationship with the adopted child. When such sharing is done early, frankly, and lovingly, the adopted child will almost always respond positively and warmly and develop a strong identification with his or her adopted parents, just as natural children do with theirs. It is the parents rather than the child who usually have a problem. Overcompensation and bending over backwards may generate uncertainty in the child. This is exacerbated when there are natural children in the family and when the adopted child is from a minority or foreign background. A very helpful measure in such instances is participation in groups of adoptive parents.

Domestic Violence

Families may be the wellspring of love and security, but there is evidence to suggest that they are also the setting and source for all kinds of aggression and violence, from simple verbal hostility through physical punishment and beatings to torture, maiming, and murder. Physical violence is ubiquitous not only in the United States and Britain, but in many other societies as well. Sixty to seventy percent of all couples have used physical violence at least once in their marriage, and about one out of four couples has experienced recurrent patterns of physical violence. (By violence, we mean any act intended to cause physical pain or injury.) In the United States, that is about 13 million couples.

About one out of every hundred husbands and wives has gone beyond kicking, slapping, or throwing things at a spouse to beating up a spouse in the year the survey was taken. About 5% had been involved in at least one beating during their marriage. Almost 4% reported the use of a knife or gun in the attack. In the United States alone, out of 47 million couples, almost 2 million witnessed a husband or wife wielding a knife or gun, and well over 2 million spouses had been beaten by their partner. If anything, these are underestimates, depending only on reported acts of violence. It is anyone's guess how many incidents go unreported.

In a study of 1,244 families with children from three to seventeen years old living at home, three out of four children had engaged in an act of violence against a brother or sister. Eight-tenths of a percent threatened to use a knife or a gun, and three-tenths actually did in the survey year. Projected to the United States population, that would be 138,000 children. Eighteen percent had at some time beaten up a brother or sister, and 5% had used a knife or gun at some time on a brother or sister.

Men who assault adult family members come from all races, socio-economic classes, and occupations, although there are higher percentages in certain sub-cultures. Sixty-three percent of men who batter were battered as children or have witnessed physical abuse in their families. Many of these men seem to have intense dependent relationships with their victims. They appear to fear losing their relationships and take extreme measures to control them. The men also have difficulty in identifying any of their emotions except anger, lumping together fear, anxiety, frustration, hurt, irritation, guilt, and disappointment as anger. Often they do not have the verbal skills to express their personal needs. While alcohol may be involved, it does not necessarily cause the violence. Stopping the drinking does not necessarily stop the battering.

Studies within and across societies suggest that the psychologically absent father leads to a "protest of masculinity," or a machismo pattern wherein sexual aggression is glorified. This is only one way in which cultural influences relate to domestic violence. If violence is approved of in society at large, then it will be expressed in the family.

Child Abuse

Over 80% of parents of children three to nine years old use physical punishment; when this goes beyond ordinary physical punishment, it is known as child abuse. Over one-third of fifteen- to seventeen-year-olds reported having been hit by their parents in the survey year. Twenty percent of parents had hit their child with some object, and more than 4% reported they had beaten the child up. Amazingly, almost 3% reported threatening the child with a knife or gun. For the population of children aged three to seventeen, about 1,200,000 had at some time in their lives been attacked by a parent with a lethal weapon.

Some have argued that the incidence of child abuse in the United States is related to the cultural sanctioning of violence. For example, in 1972, the incidence of homicide in the United States was 8.9 per 100,000, but only 0.9 in Great Britain. The assault and battery rate in Canada in 1968 was 28.6 per 100,000, while in the United States it was 141.0. The level of TV violence in the United States is higher than in Sweden, Britain, or Israel. A report from Los Angeles finds that one-quarter of all mothers spanked their infant children in the first six months of life, and nearly half spanked babies by the end of the first year.

The family unit, therefore, rather than instilling an example of intimacy and love, may too frequently serve as a breeding ground for alienation, cruelty, and violence. It is in the attitude and example of the parents, in their compatability in every sense, that a meaningful model for relations is established.

The Extended Family

A family consisting of grandparents as well as parents and children, either in the home or in close proximity, provides advantages as well as disadvantages. The advantages are an extended source of parenting and a sense of community heritage. The grandparents, shorn of their day–to–day responsibilities, can provide—even lavish—unadulterated non-conflicted affection, attention, and modeling. They receive love and contact in return. The parents are freed to live their lives more flexibly. Grandparents often compensate for parental deficiencies and provide surrogate parenting.

The disadvantages are the almost inevitable generational conflict over every issue from life style to child rearing. Parents whose own childhood was beset with conflict and tension may repeat this behavior with the grandparents, perhaps with a vengeance. The need for individuation and space may get stifled in an extended family. In such situations, separate domiciles and clear contracts—perhaps enunciated for the first time—are all-important. The rights and privileges of visitation are as essential and delicate as in a disrupted marriage.

The kibbutzim in Israel have experimented with raising children by a community, but with parental influence still prevailing. They resemble more the extended family, as do the communes in Western countries, although research in the latter is rather sparse. Nevertheless, the more traditional extended family of grandparents and the close proximity of uncles, aunts, and cousins are currently far more the exception than the rule. Many an observer has related the disappearance of this arrangement to a weakening of structural and moral ties, and even has suggested this as an explanation for increased anti-social and violent behavior.

Marriage and Such

Marriages may be made in heaven, but there must be a botch up somewhere before getting to earth. A high percentage of marriages end in divorce. Until recently, marriage was supported by social, moral, and religious sanctions, and its dissolution was inhibited by legal and economic difficulties. Much of this has changed. The need for a legal document to validate a relationship and the imperative for a couple to raise a family have diminished. The mystical contract for better or worse unto death is no longer universally accepted.

Nevertheless, for most, marriage represents an enduring relation between two people. Often, however, people marry for more immediate reasons: marriage can be the most propitious opportunity to leave parents; it can be the easiest and most expected way of responding to pressure from family, society, and peers; it can legitimize sex; it can be an impulsive action tied to a passion that is not seen as temporary; and it can be an impetuous search for an antidote to loneliness and insecurity. These motives often result in disillusion and frustration.

The motive with the most favorable prognosis for a successful marriage is, of course, love. Love is understood in many ways by different people, but it always includes the appreciation of the other person as an equal or complement to the self. If the other is depreciated or idealized, then a lopsided relationship is the consequence. Resentment and strife follow, unless there is a contract to establish a symbiotic relationship, where one agrees to be the caretaker and the other the one cared for. These are neurotic relationships, but sometimes they are workable when the contract is clear. But love is mutuality based on responsibility, caring, understanding, and respect, seasoned with a passion that may at first be lustful but is always rooted in deep feeling.

When two people in love contract to marry, they have many expectations in the contract—implicit as well as explicit. It is the implicit aspect that makes for trouble. We expect the other person to know what our expectations are, to be a mind reader. This is an unrealistic expectation aggravated by the fact that each is a different sex, has had different formative experiences, carries his or her own set of emotional baggage, and has different needs and perceptions of the world. What is necessary is to make the contract explicit—to share openly what we are feeling and expect in a spouse, lover, companion, co-parent, business partner, playmate, and so on. These sharings, confessions, dialogues, dreams, hurts, joys, frustrations, secrets, and clarifications must of necessity be continuous. They require trust, integrity, and effort.

We marry for unconscious as well as conscious motives. Very frequently, we choose someone who resembles our parents, or who is as opposite as possible—which is the same thing for its effect on the new relationship. Almost always, we expect the other to sense and meet all of our needs. This is impossible. Often, we want to possess or be possessed by the other, which only generates a power struggle and jealousy. The child in us exposes us to feeling excluded, ignored, and unappreciated. Jealousy is a form of control because we are afraid of being helpless and rejected. When people marry young, both change and grow, often at different rates, especially as parental, economic, social, and sexual roles change.

No two people have exactly the same emotional and sexual rhythms. For complex reasons, we tend to choose another
who has a distinctly different sexual time and emotional
rhythm. If one partner wants sex frequently and the other less
often, unless this discrepancy is verbalized and explained
tactfully, it can be interpreted as rejection. Not only may the
frequency of desire vary, but the signals sent and responses to
them may be misunderstood. A little tact and communication, however, can go a long way toward clearing up unnecessary misunderstandings. For example, when one person expresses a wish to make love, rather than refuse or make an
excuse such as a headache, a sensitive partner might respond,
"I don't feel like that right now, but I would like to hold you
or cuddle." Similarly, one partner might expect the other to
get ready in half an hour, which literally means thirty minutes, while the other thinks he or she has an hour or so. Their
very perception of time and rate of activity are at odds. In lieu
of gnawing frustration or a violent explosion, it can help to
ask simply, "My time or yours?"

In communication, one mate can be literal and the other
symbolic. "I could kill Junior" means murder and mayhem to
one and a reprimand to the other.

The task for every couple is to understand and reconcile
their experience and expression. The very delicate dilemma
facing both partners is the need to become more like the other
while retaining his or her own individuality. It is team work
in the most complicated but finest sense.

Inevitably, two separate identities rub against each other
and cause friction, but the expression of irritation causes its
own problems. In our society, it appears to be as difficult for
some to express anger as it is love. One therapist reports that
80% of the couples who come to him never fight and avoid
conflict. The result is an emotional divorce. He teaches
couples to fight constructively. The rationale is that rather
than swallowing gall and expressing rage indirectly and
somatically or sealing off feelings, it is beneficial to ventilate
these emotions. A couple or family who fight together at least
relate to each other.

There are many arguments for catharsis, but there are
also disadvantages. The expression of aggression in couples
may not minimize such expression but exacerbate it into violence. The greater the verbal aggression, the greater, often, is
the physical assault. This problem needs to be considered
carefully, and the definition of aggression is a key factor. We
would define it as the direct expression of attitudes, needs,
wishes, and feelings, including anger, not necessarily intended
to hurt. When people are encouraged to reveal their anger, it

should not be to enjoy an orgy of self-indulgent conflict, but to tap, expose, express, clarify, and modulate these feelings. This can be accomplished when the individual owns his or her own feelings with "I" statements ("*I* get upset at you ignoring me," "*I* am angry") and identifies the source of irritation rather than uses "you" statements ("*You* make me furious," or "*You* are a clod").

In general, the conditions for a constructive marriage, as in any intimate relationship, are an ongoing dialogue, the sharing and expression of feelings, an attempt to "see" the other's position—even by exchanging roles—and negotiations and renegotiations of contracts with changing circumstances.

Open Marriage

Some couples, feeling thwarted sexually and otherwise with their mates, experiment with open relationships. This can range from interchanging all or most of the roles in the home to explicit sexual affairs with others. These couples claim that since one person cannot possibly meet all the needs, including the sexual ones, of a partner, then others can fulfill them. After all, this position goes, if two people can experience love with each other, then they can broaden the experience to others and share their gratifications in the primary relationship, thereby enriching it. In theory, this may seem logical, but we personally have not seen any really successful examples. It would take unusual people to carry it off. They would have to be free of possessiveness and jealousy and be sensitive enough to be intimate with several people. It is these very qualities that seem to make for stable relationships which do not require additional sources of gratification.

We must add, though, that with couples in trouble who do cherish their relationship and wish to maintain it but cannot seem to meet each other's needs, an explicit contract, not clouded by mixed motives, to open up the relationship, does help some. Again, in our experience, after a while the mates generally return gratefully to each other—if they haven't broken up in the process. We strongly urge people to avail themselves of therapy or marital counseling before embarking on experimentation. In fact, we recommend marital counseling from time to time even for "good" marriages as a preventive and enriching measure. (See the discussion on marital counseling in the chapter on Change.)

Divorce

It is not surprising from the above discussion, and in view of social turmoil, rapid change, and women's liberation, that in 1975 there were over one million divorces in the United States—twice as many as in 1966. In 1978, the estimate was as high as 41% of all marriages. A 1976 survey of Chicago's northwest suburbs showed that 35% of school children were products of a divorced home. Each year, over one million children under eighteen live in families that are involved in a marital breakup. It is estimated that one out of six children resides in a single parent home and that 16% of all children in the United States have experienced parental divorce. In the period of marital dissolution, children often show marked changes in behavior, particularly in school, and the changes are likely to be in the direction of acting out behavior.

The impact of divorce on children has been studied. Children, particularly younger ones, often respond with pervasive sadness, fear, feelings of deprivation, and some anger. At the end of one year, many still struggle with coming to terms with this change in their lives. Studies have shown that attention is poor for school-related tasks, and intense anger, fear, and a shaken identity and keen sense of loneliness are displayed. At the end of the first year, hostility lingers on, and half of the children who were studied demonstrated a depressive pattern.

In recent years, techniques for dealing with these problems have been proposed. There are transition groups providing emotional support, catharsis, and information regarding this event. And there are specialized workshops for adolescents from divorced homes. A very useful book for children is *The Boys' and Girls' Book About Divorce* by M. A. Gardner, and for teenagers, *How to Get It Together While Your Parents Are Coming Apart* by Arlene Richards and Eileen Wills.

Because children are often presumed to be ignorant of their parents' problems, they are not given an opportunity to discuss their consequent anxiety. Parents, however, are often astonished by the insights and awareness of their youngsters. Professor Meyer Rothberg has studied and worked with the problems of divorced children. He recommends taking a child advocacy role—the point of view of the child. The impact of divorce is similar to other severe losses. There is an initial period of denial and disbelief. Prior to separation, it is necessary to explain to the child the what, why, and how of the events to take place, giving clear assurance of support and continued care. The parents each need to be conscious of their continued role as a parent, rather than as an aggrieved, combatant party. They need to talk at the child's level, soliciting questions and reflecting and clarifying feelings. This means a sensitivity to non-verbal as well as verbal communication from the child. The parents need to understand the conflict of loyalties experienced by the child, his or her hopeless hopes of reconciliation as well as his or her appropriate anger and rage. Though this is a traumatic experience for the child, it may also provide a challenge for personal growth and the development of resilience and autonomy.

It is the rare person who does not know the value of friendship and feel the longing for it. For unmarried people, friends and social life are rated most important for a sense of happiness. This form of relationship is rarer than one thinks. It seems to most of us that others have more and closer friendships than we do. When we probe our own friendships, we see that they are often acquaintanceships or ties born of necessity, work, or geographical location. The intimacy, sharing, and mutuality that define friendship turn out to be limited. Often we know it only with people from our childhood who have moved away or who are prevented by circumstances from being in any basic contact with us. In other words, friendship often exists only as a fantasy, wish fulfillment, or memory.

Some people claim that they do not know how to make friends or that they lack the opportunity to do so. If the truth were known, it is really the risk and energy required that discourages us from making the necessary effort. Friendships pose demands as well as rewards. In our other relationships, whether by blood or role, there is less choice. We may not like to face the issue, but we have few friends because we choose to do so. We may rationalize with excuses that people do not like us and blandly tell ourselves, "That's the way we are." The bases for friendship are simple but extremely difficult, the same as for any other intimate relationship: effort, risk, mutuality, communication, caring, responsibility, understanding, and respect. It is give and take, neither one without the other.

Friendships limited in kind and number suggest alienation and a constriction of personality. Group therapy may be an appropriate measure, but not just passive attendance as in group rapping, tenuous affiliation, or peripheral participation. Rather, what is implied is an active involvement. The alternative usually is isolation, loneliness, and compulsive distractions of work and other busy-time activities.

Apart from this, however, some commonplace, sensible measures can be tried. Almost all people want more and better friends, though few are willing to make the first gestures. Shared interests, the perception of a good sense of humor, or an easy way of handling a difficult situation are good occasions to strike up an acquaintance. People are often embarrassed to pay a compliment, but often taking such a risk can yield large benefits. Listening sympathetically to someone's problem or sharing your own experiences can be as gratifying to the listener as to the other person. Friendship has its obligations, but it is probably one of the easiest of relations, since it is entered into voluntarily because of interest and is relatively free of roles and responsibilities. Having a few good friends enormously enriches life and takes some of the pressure off other relations. One is probably a better spouse and parent if one is also a good friend.

Authority Figures, Subordinates, and Peers

Theoretically, our relationships with authority, subordinates, and peers is less intense and involved than those with our intimates. In practice, however, this is often not true. We tend to transfer onto these relationships experiences from our families. Thus, the boss is perceived at some level as a father or mother figure, with all the expectations that accompany such a perception. If the transference is positive, we expect to be taken care of and our deficiencies understood. If the transference is negative, we may be intimidated, resentful, and rebellious. Our emotional reactions and overt behavior may then have little relation to objective reality. The fact that the authority figure is also irrationally transferring only aggravates the matter. Injured pride, a sense of rejection, and sabotage of the relationships and of our own self-interest too frequently are the consequences.

In a similar vein, we may relate to subordinates as if they were children or in the manner in which we were treated by our parents. Peers can be viewed as siblings with all the related competition, with consequent feelings of resentment and defeat. In short, our view of other adults and ourselves is often warped by a projection of our intense emotional fixation on earlier experiences. It is our experience that such transference pervades interactions that are social, work-related, and economic, in the church, the political arena, the marketplace—everywhere.

The antidote is to test whether we are responding on an adult, rational basis and whether we are pulling for adult responses from the other person. As in all interactions, we need to be clear on the contract and ensure that it is two-sided. A job is not primarily a source of nurturance or a validation of our personal worth. Nor is any other interaction that is not primarily based on intimacy. Misunderstanding this results in the playing of games and in neurotic reactions.

Summary

Our real happiness depends to a great extent on our forming intimate relations with other people. As necessary as this is to our well-being and sense of contentment, it is one of the most difficult of tasks. In opening ourselves up to another, we risk the most crushing and devastating rejection. So we clam up, desperately needing the one thing we struggle to defend ourselves against. In addition, in the most intimate relationships, we must also attempt to preserve our own identity and not be swallowed up by the other.

All satisfactory relations are based on an agreement— whether it is an explicit contract or an unspoken assumption—by which we give and receive, have needs met and fulfill them in others. But because so much of our motivation is unconscious or confused, these agreements often founder. It is important to be very clear, to ourselves and to the other, about what we expect from a relationship and what we are willing and able to give.

The prototype for all our relations is our experience of our families when we were children. Here we learn the basic lessons of trust, autonomy, and communication, or their opposites. Fads of child rearing come and go, but what has become clear is that the actual practices matter less than the attitudes and motives behind them.

Disruptions in family life due to death or (more commonly today) divorce can have profound effects on children, although if these events are handled properly—with honesty, sensitivity, and patience—a child can emerge the stronger because of them. More serious obstacles to the development of a sound psychology are inconsistent or contradictory messages, or double binds, directed at children.

Nowadays, marriage is an institution that is undergoing profound changes. Divorce is extremely common, and although it involves much pain and disruption, it is probably preferable to a marriage that endures only through convenience, timidity, or convention. Marriages are more likely to endure if they are based on love—a mutual caring and respect. Often, differences between two spouses can be handled by frank and ongoing communication.

Friendship is an extremely important source of pleasure and intimacy, but is too often prevented from developing because of shyness or embarrassment.

Our relations with authority and subordinates are often contaminated and frustrated by our projecting onto them our previous experiences with figures in the family. It is a good idea to be aware of whether or not our actions are appropriate to a present situation, or are really carry-overs from previous experiences.

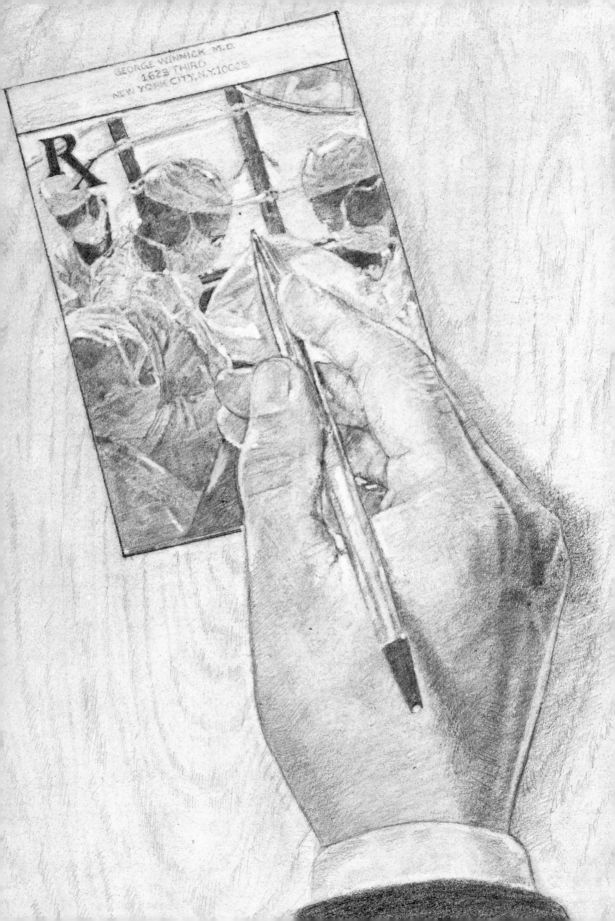

10
Health

To understand an individual, his or her health and behavior, we must look at him or her holistically—somatically, psychologically, and psychosocially—and see how each aspect reciprocally affects the others. Both illness and health must be understood in these terms. For example, there are always at least three factors in every symptom—an agent, a psychological component, and the general status of the individual. For any particular disorder, one factor may be particularly important, but the other two enter into the picture as well.

Let us consider three people: a person who is suffering from tuberculosis, a fatigued person, and a person who suffers headaches. The first has contracted tuberculosis and manifests symptoms primarily because of the effects of the agent, the tuberculosis bacillus. Other people, whose over-all physical status is good, do not come down with this disease, even though the bacillus may be present in their bloodstreams. The first has succumbed, perhaps because he is run-down and fatigued. In addition, his psychological condition may be poor because of stress. The second person feels debilitated and weak because of lack of exercise, sleep, and poor diet. Her psychological condition, while a contributing factor, may be relatively minor. The third has a headache essentially because he is suppressing a great deal of anger. But his physical status and the chemical agents that cause a constriction of capillaries in the head play a part, although a secondary one. In all three cases, all three factors are present.

In physical, or somatic, disorder, we must study all three components as much as we need to do in a psychological disorder. First, let us look at the role of stress in both instances.

Stress

Life stress is the perception of threat—most precisely, the perception of an inability to cope with demands. When we feel such demands, we respond with a tendency to flight or fight, but since such reactions are not always possible, we experience pressure or strain. A life stress can be any number of circumstances—loss of a limb, slum existence or prison life, intense periods of hazard and physical danger, conflict, failure, or rejection. There are several kinds of situations that can cause stress. For example, physical threat can be the perception of actual, anticipated, or imagined physical injury, pain, loss, or death. Psychological threat can be the perception, real or otherwise, of injury or pain to the psychological self.

Stress may also be a reaction to an underload as well as to an overload of stimulation, as in a non-stimulating environment or in the deprivation of sensory input. When external stimuli are minimal, our internal stimulation may become intolerably elevated, thus causing our stress. Individuals respond differently to the same stress condition.

Stress, as we have said, is the perception of threat. Often this involves a negative self-evaluation caused by the previous experience of having failed at similar tasks or situations. This is sometimes referred to as ego threat. Interpersonal threat involves the perception of a disruption of our social relationships. Finally, threat can arise from a constraining or impoverishment or a situation which may cause us some kind of physical deprivation—sleep, food, or movement—or a lack of psychological stimulation, affection, or attention. Conversely, we may fear psychological overstimulation, as in forced intimacy or invasion of our private space.

We may reveal the effects of stress by stammering, a sense of disorientation, or peculiar hostility. A history of vocational, academic, or interpersonal failures may also indicate the same. A sense of not working up to capacity or fulfilling tasks with inadequate quality, speed, or success may also be signs.

Stress and the response to stress vary as a function of experience. Past experience of having mastered stressful situations reduces the perception of threat, while a history of failure reduces the tolerance to stress. Put another way, effective coping with stress leads in the future to less stress, but ineffectual coping with stress leads to continued, if not increased, symptoms.

Helplessness in the face of stress is implicated in a variety of physical diseases, ranging from the common cold to perhaps cancer. Sudden death specifically due to coronary disease frequently occurs in men whose next of kin reported that those men had been depressed anywhere from a week to several months prior to death.

Management of Stress

Stress often becomes unmanageable because of habitual ways of handling it. Following a few guidelines can diminish the effects of stress considerably. It is a good idea to plan our projects sensibly. Disorganization can breed stress. Having too many unfinished projects going simultaneously can lead to confusion, forgetfulness, the feeling that uncompleted projects are hanging over our heads, or the sense that our lives have gotten out of control. If it is possible, we may take projects one at a time and work on them until each is completed. In general, it is best if we recognize and accept limits. Our goals should be reasonable and achievable.

It is also important to surround our hard work with healthy and relaxing activity. Recreation and other forms of gratification are extremely important when we are working hard, and rather than representing wasted time, will actually increase our productivity and effectiveness. So it is a good idea to continue to engage in activities that are absorbing and enjoyable. (See the chapter on Playing.) Regular physical exercise is therefore important for both its physical and psychological benefits. The body and mind cannot tolerate sustained stress, so we must be able to relax without the use of drugs which breed dependency and only add to stress. (See the discussion of medication in the chapter on Sleeping.) Yoga and meditation have proven very useful to many people. It is also important to have an outlet for frustrations. Talking about them to a friend, spouse, clergyman, or professional can be very effective in keeping stress from becoming bottled up.

Finally, our general attitude is very important in the management of stress. We can benefit from avoiding negative, hopeless, or defeated attitudes and from leaving ourselves open to praise and the satisfactions of small achievements. In addition, it is important for us to develop a sense of tolerance for the standards and styles of others. It is counterproductive to perceive situations as unnecessarily competitive. Stressful situations are difficult enough without setting ourselves up against other people.

Psychophysiology

We have seen that stress is implicated in illness. It has been recognized that not only is it possible for psychophysiological changes to alter behavior, but also for psychological events to have physiological reverberations that are both definite and disabling. Anxiety or stress may set in motion a whole train of physiological events. And the converse is equally true. This is most dramatic in hypo- and hyperglycemia—alterations in blood sugar level. Alterations in mood, increased irritability, and vague feelings of apprehension are reported when the blood sugar level is lowered. All these observed changes, in both general behavior and specific mental performance, may be reversed by raising the blood sugar level. The influence of diet in psychophysiological reactions is not restricted to blood sugar level. It is pervasive.

Psychophysiological disorders are physical symptoms that are caused by emotional factors and involve an organ that is usually under the control of the autonomic nervous system. The physiological changes involved are those that normally accompany certain emotional states, but in these disorders, the changes are more intense and sustained. The individual may not be consciously aware of his or her emotional state. Such disorders include certain skin disorders such as pruritis and neurodermatosis; musculoskeletal disorders such as backache, muscle cramps, myalgias, and tension headaches; respiratory disorders such as bronchial asthma; hyperventilation syndromes such as sighing and hiccoughing; cardiovascular disorders; blood and lymph disorders; gastrointestinal disorders such as peptic ulcer, chronic gastritis, ulcerative or mucous colitis, constipation, hyperacidity, heartburn, and irritable colon; genito-urinary disorders such as disturbances in menstruation and urination and impotence and endocrine disorders.

Psychoanalysts believe that there are specific relations between emotional constellations and physical symptoms of psychophysiological reactions. For example, several emotional symptoms are associated with eating. They are said to stem from wishes for love, care, and dependence, repressed sexual wishes, and aggressive and hostile desires. If eating serves to gratify these impulses, the result is overeating. If the impulses are inhibited, undereating or nervous vomiting may result. In gastric ulcers, frustrated desires for love are often involved, while certain kinds of diarrhea are caused by repressed hostile impulses or urges to give or produce. Similarly, hostility may be involved in certain cardiovascular disturbances as well as in hypertension. Asthma is said to represent a fear of separation from mother substitutes. This list can be extended, perhaps to fanciful lengths, but the essential point is the suggestion of the different paths emotional tensions can take.

Psychophysiological reactions may serve as a hint of how our individual history and current environment have impinged upon us and how we are still neurotically dealing with stress. They may be cues, therefore, for improving coping behavior and ameliorating the condition. We tend to learn to respond to stress situations in a typical way, such as by tightening our stomach muscles or holding our breath. Psychologically, the mode in which we resort to body reactions relates to previous, usually childhood, experiences. In addition, most of us have a body that responds to stress more sensitively in certain organs. For example, we may be born with a thin stomach lining. Psychophysiological reactions over a prolonged period of time will result in irreversible damage to the organ system involved.

There are three extremely common psychophysiological reactions that we will discuss in detail because of their importance in their own right and because they may be generalized to other conditions. They are asthma, ulcers, and cardiovascular disturbances that are related to coronary-prone behavior.

Asthma

Somewhere between two and five percent of the population suffers from asthma. It is more common in males than in females. There are three categories of causes of asthma—allergic, infective, and psychological. Pollen and dust are examples of the causes of allergic reactions. Respiratory disorders illustrate the types of infective asthma. Anxiety and tension produced by frustration, anger, depression, and anticipated pleasurable excitement are all examples of psychological factors that may disturb the respiratory system and thus cause asthma. The different causes of asthma vary in importance depending on the age of the individual. Infective factors dominate for those younger than five years. From six to sixteen, psychological factors increase in importance, but are less important than the infective ones. In the age range of sixteen to sixty-five, psychological factors decrease in importance until about the thirty-fifth year, and then again increase in significance.

In one study, 69% of asthmatic patients interviewed reported that their asthma attacks began with an emotional disturbance. Asthma attacks, in another experiment, were produced in the laboratory by reproducing the disturbance in actual or pictorial form. The stimuli to which the subjects were exposed included the national anthem, perfume, the sight of dust, horses, and waterfalls. In yet another study, suggestion alone was sufficient to induce attacks. Various emotional factors in the home seem to contribute to eliciting or aggravating asthma.

Symptoms may be reinforced by catering to the child and treating him or her as fragile. When possible, no special treatment or over-protection is recommended. The asthmatic child is urged to lead as normal a life as possible and to avoid focussing on sickness as the dominant factor in his or her life.

Ulcers

Ulcers occur most often for the first time between the ages of twenty-five and forty, but they have been diagnosed as early as fetal life and as late as the tenth decade. The peak age for ulcers in children is seven to nine. Once ulcers occur, they tend to recur months or years later. The usual symptom of an ulcer is pain, variously described as a gnawing, burning, or hungry sensation, usually in the area just above the navel. The pain commonly occurs half an hour to two hours after eating and sometimes awakens the person during the night. It is frequently relieved by eating or taking an antacid. In children, however, eating may not bring relief. Other complaints, including headache, may accompany the stomachache in children. Many a child's chronic stomachache, often dismissed by parents and even physicians as an excuse for avoiding school, may actually be a symptom of ulcers.

It is possible to have none of these symptoms and still have an ulcer. About one person in ten will get an ulcer sometime in his or her life. Previously, only one in twenty ulcer patients was female. Today nearly one in two is. Possibly this is due to the increasing incidence of smoking and alcohol consumption among women, as well as other changes in women's life styles.

Peptic ulcer is an open sore that results from the eating away of a spot in the lining of the stomach or small intestine by the stomach's highly acidic digestive juices. Most ulcers occur in the small intestine and are called duodenal ulcers. Gastric ulcers, only one tenth as common, occur in the stomach. Duodenal ulcers are associated with the excess production of hydrochloric acid, but gastric ulcers may result from a weakness in the stomach wall.

Factors known to increase the flow of stomach acid include alcohol, coffee, aspirin, and emotional stress. There are people who produce enormous amounts of acid but do not contract ulcers. Heredity apparently plays a part—ulcers are three times more common in the relatives of ulcer patients. Of course, family diet, emotional climate, and similar reactions to stress may be involved.

Ulcers can lead to serious, even fatal, complications. An intestinal obstruction may develop. The ulcer may cause bleeding, resulting in anemia. If a major blood vessel is involved, a severe internal hemorrhage may result. An ulcer may also eat a hole into another organ or into the stomach, causing the contents to spill out with dire consequences. More than 8,000 Americans die each year from ulcer complications. But with treatment, most ulcers heal in two to six weeks. A bland diet is usually recommended for a week until the symptoms subside. Thereafter, patients are advised to avoid smoking heavily and to abstain from caffeinated and decaffeinated coffee, tea, cola, cocoa, and alcohol or to take it only with food. Milk, after an ulcer forms, may be more of an irritant than not. The evidence is still controversial, but there are indications that heavy grains, particularly bran, seem to help prevent gastric disturbances, including ulcers.

Whatever the causes, and whether or not there is an "ulcer personality," there seems little doubt that those who characteristically knot their stomachs, and churn their insides when facing stress are more prone to contracting ulcers, and are more aggravated when they do develop.

Coronary-Prone
Behavior

Certain people, because of their typical patterns of behavior, are more prone to heart attacks than others. Such behavior may lead to success in business or in college, but these people pay an enormous cost in the end. Unfortunately, because of their success, their patterns are rewarded, and the individual may be led indirectly but firmly to a heart attack. Often changing coronary-prone behavior means a major reorganization and reorientation of one's life and a willingness to give up some of the advantages one has been able to achieve by driven behavior. Whatever the rewards are for the coronary-prone individual, as for the ulcer-prone individual, as these people get older, not only do their roles, environment, and patterns of pressure change, but their bodies are less able to cope with both immediate stress and its cumulative effects.

For more than twenty years, the so-called Type A personality has been studied. These are people who, because of their intense and driven patterns of behavior, are especially prone to heart attacks. They are engaged in competition both with the environment and with other people. They are consumed with the ambition to do as much as they can, get as many things as possible, beat as many people who compete with them. They are not at all like certain neurotics who are driven by fear and anxiety, since they are rarely pessimistic about the possibility of losing their chronic struggle. Instead, they show exaggerated traits of aggressiveness, ambition, and competitiveness, a marked preoccupation with deadlines, a pronounced orientation around their work, a long-term impatience, and a sense of time urgency.

People with Type B personality are relatively free of the characteristics that describe Type A. That is, they do not suffer from a sense of time urgency and impatience, do not harbor "free-floating hostility," do not vigorously compete for accomplishment, are able to relax and enjoy without guilt, and can work without agitation.

A study of seemingly healthy Type A men showed that 28% (aged thirty-five to sixty) already had coronary disease—seven times as many as Type B men, despite identical diets and exercise patterns. If a thirty-five to sixty year old man exhibited Type A patterns in the 1960 study, he was almost three times more likely than Type B to get coronary disease in the subsequent decade. Not one man exhibiting Type B behavior who had a normal cholesterol and fat level had yet succumbed to this disease by 1974. Such individuals, no matter how much cholesterol and fat their diet contained, no matter how many cigarettes they smoked, no matter how much they weighed, no matter if one or both parents had coronary disease, and no matter whether they were over- or underweight, still appeared immune to the early advent of heart disease.

It appears that the Type A personality feels the need to control situations. He or she perceives greater threat and therefore reacts to stress "hypersensitively." The Type A behavior pattern seems to be a strategy for coping with uncontrollable stress. In fact, the Type A personality shows greater helplessness than Type B under high stress, although not under moderate stress. Parental standards and an authoritarian discipline style may be associated with the development of pattern A in children, although the parent – child relationship differs according to the sex of the child.

A program has been developed to slow down or change the behavior patterns of Type A personalities. This involves specific changes in typical ways of doing things as well as more subtle shifts in attitudes. At first, these suggestions may seem forced and arbitrary, but after a while, they can become more natural. Type A people should deliberately arrange free periods for themselves when they merely have fun, engage in pet projects, or spend time with those who provide simple support and caring. They should also set up regular periods of time when they have no access to watches, telephones, newspapers, or appointments.

Some of these procedures involve breaking long-term habits of being driven and of acting under pressure. If you find yourself speeding in a car, slow down deliberately for fifteen minutes. If you speed through a yellow light, penalize yourself by driving around the block and waiting for a clear green signal. If you find your mind racing or obsessed with pressures, literally yell "Stop!" Later you can do this subvocally. Even later, this may become second nature.

It is also essential to change habits and attitudes. Formal relaxation procedures may be helpful. Muscle relaxation, biofeedback, transcendental meditation, massage, sauna, yoga, and imagining relaxing situations can help. Truly relaxed, unpressured reading, movies, and TV are also beneficial. At first, it may be necessary to keep telling yourself, "I will keep my cool" or "I will use my anger as a signal." Later, you will be able to reestablish your priorities and reorient yourself to relaxing and to enjoying life. What good is business and financial success if a heart attack incapacitates or kills you before you are fifty?

Friedman and Rosenman, the discoverers of these behavior patterns, present four chapters on "reengineering" the Type A personality in their book, *Type A Behavior and Your Heart*. Many of their recommendations appear to be of considerable value for such individuals.

Psychosomatic Reactions

There are many symptoms of stress or anxiety that may masquerade as physical illness. Some of them are rapid or pounding heartbeat, difficulty in breathing or breathlessness, tremulousness, sweating, dry mouth, tightness in the chest, sweaty palms, dizziness, weakness, nausea, diarrhea, cramps, insomnia, fatigue, tension, headache, loss of appetite and sexual disturbances.

When a physical symptom involves no demonstrable physical cause, it is called a psychosomatic reaction. Unlike psychophysiological disorders, more than one organ system and even logically unconnected parts of the body may be involved. These reactions also have been called hysterical and conversion symptoms. People are expressing through their bodies the anxiety they do not allow themselves to experience or to show others. The symptoms may also represent an unconscious symbol. For example, a conflict resulting from an unconscious wish to strike a family member may result in a paralysis of the arm. Or a forbidden voyeuristic wish may occasion blurred vision or even blindness. Much more common are stomach disorders, sleep problems, and sexual dysfunctions. Often there is a secondary gain. That is, the "illness" is rewarded by getting attention or by permitting avoidance of something perceived as unpleasant, such as work or school. The condition is nevertheless real and not feigned or deliberately induced.

Chronic psychosomatic behavior can result in more serious psychophysiological reactions. Moreover, it is important to distinguish this symptom from a physical disorder. This is often difficult to do, even for medical specialists. Improper diets, vitamin deficiencies, microbiological organisms and subtle endocrine imbalances, for example, may be associated with symptoms that appear to be psychological. It has not been rare for multiple sclerosis to be mistaken for a psychosomatic syndrome.

The important issue in psychosomatic conditions as well as in psychophysiological reactions and even in physical disorders is to be aware of the psychological factors. Once we are aware of them, it is essential that we experience and express them directly rather than indirectly. Every symptom is a mind-body signal of distress—that is, stress that is not being coped with successfully. Symptoms, therefore, are invaluable as cues that more appropriate measures need to be taken. Although there may be a secondary gain, the behavior is indirect and often desperate, and the primary goal or gain may be inefficiently met, if at all. When people under stress avail themselves of brief counseling or psychotherapy, they succumb far less frequently to disabling illness than comparable patients who have no counseling. (See the chapter on Change.)

Physical Disorders

Not only do psychological factors play a role in physical disorders, but different people have varying responses to illness. Some are thrown into the depths of despair and are incapacitated well beyond the necessary consequences of the disease itself. Others refuse to acknowledge the condition at all because it is seen as a stigma or as limiting their sense of omnipotence and grandiosity. They may make themselves sicker. Actually, almost all illness incurs disability to some degree, but is not totally disabling. Even with terminal cancer, some measure of a meaningful life is possible. We learn to deal with illness in various ways as children, often modeling ourselves on our parents. If we are fixated on our bodies narcissistically, any impairment may violate our sense of integrity, and we catastrophize the condition. Some people are practically immobilized by a common cold, whereas others function beautifully with multiple amputations.

The same is true for handicaps and accidents. Basically, we can assume the attitude that they are unfair or that we are being punished. This is, of course, irrational. Fairness has nothing to do with the matter. Or we can assume the attitude that now we deserve and can get unlimited pampering. This is equally irrational. The only rational stance to take is a reassessment of our capabilities and the development of new, even innovative, ways of coping with our condition and our environment. Nowhere is this so clear as with many blind, who, with support and encouragement, not only compensate for their disability but learn to "see" their world better than sighted people.

It is most important with children, as well as with adults and with ourselves, to appreciate the limiting and discomforting implications of illness, handicaps, and accidents and to mobilize support and encouragement. It is equally important not to bend over backwards and thereby reward the symptoms. Instead, reinforce the desirable courage, effort, and innovation involved in coping. The gratification gained in mastery can result in a sense of strength and potency that is appreciable and can even offset to a large degree the disruptive condition.

Summary

Except for philosophical analysis and for purposes of exposition, it is not very helpful, and can be even misleading, to distinguish too sharply between the mind and the body. Each informs and influences the functioning of the other. In effect, they are one. Especially in matters of health, the individual must be thought of as one integrated whole, and any disruption can best be thought of as a convergence of three factors: the disease-causing agent, the psychology of the individual, and his or her general status.

Many psychological and physical disruptions in our lives are caused by the inappropriate or ineffective handling of stress, which is the perception of a real or imagined threat to our well-being. Much of this book consists of suggestions on how to handle stress—an ability all people should develop, since the appropriateness and effectiveness of our response to threat depends to a great extent on our previous experiences. We learn to solve problems or to cave in under pressure.

A whole range of physical disorders, from an annoying headache to a fatal heart attack, is associated with psychological difficulties. While such disorders can be catastrophic, they do serve the invaluable function of pointing to inadequacies in the way we deal with our problems. Asthma, for example, may be primarily a physical illness, but frequently is involved with an inability to handle emotional disturbance. Similarly, ulcers are frequently associated with chronic stress that results in irreversible organic damage.

Significantly, most people who suffer heart attacks manifest a characteristic and chronic pattern of driven, urgent, and competitive behavior. In contrast to people who followed similar diet and exercise patterns, those consumed with ambition or competition with the world around them were very likely to contract heart disease. There are various ways such people can slow down, begin to relax, and enjoy their lives and evade the fate they have been preparing for themselves.

When physical symptoms reveal no physical cause, there is generally a psychological component to the disturbance. Often the symptoms are symbolic and can sometimes lead to a kind of secondary gain, although such benefits are never the most effective way of coping with difficulties. We can use these symptoms, however, to help discover what is at their root. Any psychosomatic complaint is the result of some psychological distress and can best be treated by paying attention to the real cause.

Even disabilities that are purely physical in origin can function psychologically. Few are truly catastrophic and none is really deserved. The best attitude to have in such a situation is a realistic appraisal of our abilities and possibilities and an innovative way of handling our new condition. We can be most helpful to people, particularly children, with such disabilities, if we reinforce their courage, effort, and positive outlook, rather than the symptoms and incapacities.

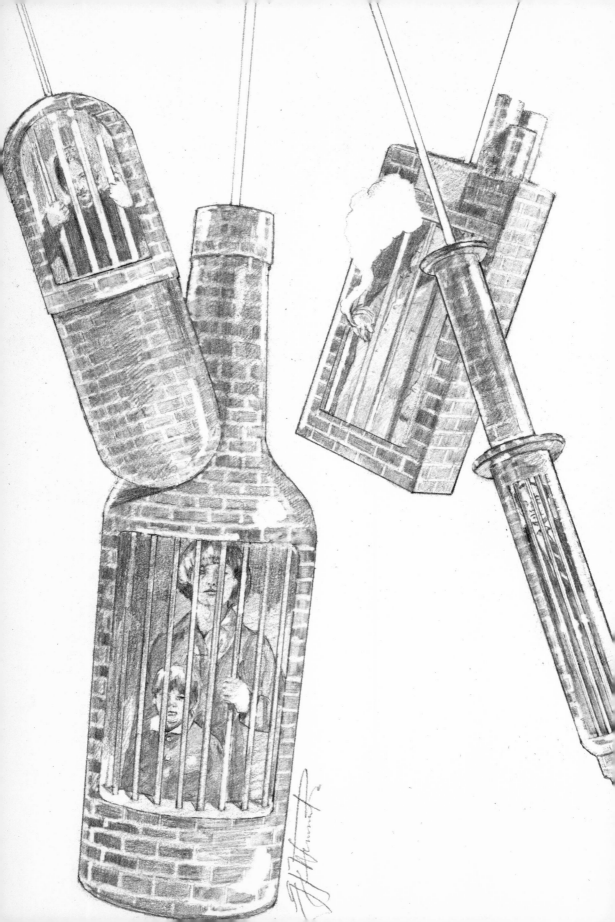

11
Habits

No habits are good. All habits are bad, since they are defined as repetitious behaviors done compulsively. We do not choose such behavior because of its gratifying consequences; instead we are compelled by some stimulus to act in a particular way regardless of the results. We may, and usually do, rationalize our habits, but the choice is dictated by compulsion. With this definition, the range of habit patterns is virtually unlimited. We shall restrict our discussion, however, to compelling behavior that is characterized by addiction or habituation and is associated with malignant results.

Alcoholism

The World Health Organization has defined alcoholics as "excessive drinkers whose dependence on alcohol has attained such a degree that they show noticeable mental disturbance or an interference with their mental and bodily health, their interpersonal relations, and their smooth social and economic functioning; or who show prodromal (incipient) signs of such developments." We would include in this definition those who depend on alcohol to cope with personal or interpersonal stress. This addition includes a significant number of the population, if one considers the businessman's obligatory "couple of drinks at lunch," the routine mid-afternoon nip by the housewife, and the ritual pre-dinner martini, not to mention the behavior that can be observed at any cocktail party.

It has been estimated that in the United States about 80 million people drink alcoholic beverages of one sort or another and that about 5 million are judged to be alcoholic by the above definition. As many as 5% of the total male population qualify as inveterate alcoholics—about three times as many men as women. Approximately 25,000 highway deaths a year are associated with alcohol; 31% of all arrests in the United States are for public drunkenness; and homicide, parental child abuse, and suicide are frequently associated with excessive drinking.

Alcoholics are found in all walks of life, without regard to intelligence, socio-economic status, or occupational level. Alcoholism is a major contributor to divorce, desertion, and family discord, as well as a significant factor in delinquency and crime. Its cost to industry is about 2 billion dollars a year. About 15% of first admissions to mental hospitals are diagnosed as being alcoholic and as suffering from symptoms of an associated mental disease.

Probably because of the virtual universality of alcohol consumption and because of its being interwoven into the social, recreational, and economic fabric, it has been distinguished from drugs. Nonetheless, alcohol is a drug, and it is addicting. Addiction is the ingestion of a drug over a period of time with larger and larger amounts being tolerated and therefore required to maintain previous intoxicating effects. If the frequency or amount is suddenly decreased, the body suffers physiological withdrawal reactions, including acute pain and sometimes even death. The drug alcohol is absorbed into the blood and toxicly affects the brain, central nervous system, liver, and peripheral blood vessels.

Three principle patterns of drinking behavior have been identified. Alpha alcoholism is limited to psychological dependence. People drink too much at the wrong time, but not to the point of losing control over their drinking. They retain their ability to abstain and regulate their drinking. They drink primarily to reduce tension and pain, but persistent drinking leads to impaired work efficiency and disturbed interpersonal relations. Delta alcoholism is characterized by the inability to abstain from drinking—a pattern frequently noted in beer- and wine-drinking countries such as Germany and France. This pattern involves both psychological and physiological dependence. Withdrawal symptoms and craving develop with abstention. Gamma alcoholism is mainly characteristic of Anglo-Saxon and Scandinavian countries where whisky is the prime beverage. It is marked by a loss of control over the amount of alcohol imbibed. Gamma drinkers may abstain for months, but once they start to drink, they may not be able to stop until they pass out. Physiological dependence is involved.

The effects of alcohol include intoxication, relaxation from restraints, a sense of well-being, slurred speech, impaired coordination, memory impairment, impulsiveness, poor judgment, double vision, stupor, and even death. The loss of inhibition may lead to irresponsible behavior, promiscuity, and violence. One of the consequences of withdrawal is delirium tremens, but others include restlessness, irritability, confusion, tremors, illusions, and hallucinations. Chronic alcoholism may result in acute hallucination and brain damage, as in the Korsakoff-Wernicke Syndrome, where there is a loss of memory for recent events and confabulation or transparent, silly lying.

There is a typical progression in developing alcoholism. The first pre-alcoholic stage lasts from several months to two years. In this stage, people drink socially and occasionally heavily to relieve tension. The drinking increases in regularity. In the prodromal stage, drinking may become furtive and possibly marked by blackouts. Drinkers may appear coherent and functioning, but later have no recall. They become preoccupied with drinking, and although they feel guilty, they are concerned with where and when they will have their next drink. The next phase is crucial. They have lost control over their drinking, and once they have one drink, they progress to stupor and to feeling sick. Their social and work lives deteriorate as well as their diet and hygiene. They still have the ability to abstain, but one drink will initiate the pattern all over. In the final chronic stage, drinking is continual. If liquor is not available, they will drink anything that contains alcohol—shaving lotion, hair tonic, medicinal preparations—anything. They suffer from malnutrition and psychological changes. They neglect personal appearance and have lost their self-esteem and sense of responsibility to anyone, including themselves.

Theories of Alcoholism	Psychoanalytic theories explain alcoholism as a fixation on the oral stage of development. Frustrated dependency needs in childhood result in a constant search for satisfaction. Some believe that experience with an over-protective mother contributes to a strong dependency need. When this need is frustrated, the alcoholic becomes angry, aggressive, and guilty. He or she drinks to reduce these impulses and to punish those who withhold affection.

Others theorize that the young male, frustrated by his mother, turns toward his father and develops unconscious homosexual impulses. He indirectly satisfies these repressed impulses by drinking with men in bars and by having his dependency needs met in that way. It is hypothesized that the self-destructive nature of alcoholism might be a means of attempting to destroy a bad mother with whom the alcoholic has identified.

There is little evidence to support these rather fanciful notions, although they often provide therapists with useful working hypotheses. In a similar vein, we should like to propose our own metaphor based on clinical experience. There are many individuals who as children received nurturance that was withdrawn suddenly, was erratic, or was hardly ever forthcoming. They fantasize a giant breast—so to speak— with an unlimited supply of sugar milk. If they can suck on this giant breast and be soothed by a constant supply of milk, they will be soothed and comforted. When frustrated in reality, they narcotize themselves by drinking—literally go to the bottle. When the alcoholics, for one reason or another, face the fact that they must give up this illusion of a "sugar-tit," they are overcome by despair and either kill themselves or resignedly begin to accept the real world and to work for gratification there. We should like to reiterate that we are speaking in metaphors and that they apply in similar if less extreme ways to other people with dependency needs.

Generalizing from animal studies, learning theorists argue that drinking alcohol is a learned response that is reinforced almost immediately by reducing distress, despite the deleterious long-term effects. One problem with this theory is that some individuals who claimed they drank to relieve anxiety and depression reported that they actually felt more anxious and depressed after drinking.

The observation has frequently been made that such ethnic groups as Jews, Italians, and Chinese who specify appropriate ceremonial, nutritional, or festive uses of alcohol have relatively lower rates of alcoholism. These people do not condone over-indulgence. Other national groups, such as the Irish and the English, who do not censor a freer use of alcohol, have higher rates of alcoholism.

One study revealed the importance of the ethnic and cultural backgrounds of drinkers. Investigation of the earlier histories of those who had become alcoholics found no support for theories relating to oral fixation, parental indulgence, or self-destructive tendencies, but ethnic background seemed to be important. More young men with American Indian, Western and Eastern European, and Irish backgrounds were alcoholic than those of Italian and other Latin extractions. There were also more alcoholics from the middle class than from the lower class.

Treatment

Following a prolonged period of intoxication, many patients show symptoms of alcohol poisoning: restlessness, confusion, irritability, belligerence, fright, tremors, and nausea. About half of hospitalized alcoholics have hallucinations, delusions, and memory loss. About 15% have delirium tremens. Treatment includes detoxification—drying out—and the administration of vitamins and a diet high in carbohydrates. Such drugs as paraldehyde, tranquilizers, and antidepressants may also be administered. Toxic symptoms generally remit within two or three days.

After detoxification, the chronic alcoholic may be placed on Antabuse. This is an extremely strong deterrent, because if an alcoholic drink is taken within four days after an Antabuse pill, a throbbing headache, flushing of the face, coughing spasms, vomiting, heart palpitations, labored breath, and blurred vision result. (See the discussion of alcoholism in the section on drug therapy in the chapter on Change.)

Aversive conditioning and other techniques based on learning principles have been employed since 1930 in the treatment of alcoholics. Nausea-producing agents as well as electric shock have been utilized just prior to drinking to establish a conditioned association between drinking and such experiences.

One of the most successful approaches to the treatment of alcoholism is Alcoholics Anonymous. Anyone who admits to a drinking problem is admitted without fee. The group's approach stresses public confession, fellowship, and the support of others. A buddy system is employed, so that at any time a companion may be called for assistance. Group therapy has also proven most effective. Individual and family therapy have had less effective results because of the resistance and frequent relapses of the client. In our experience, many alcoholics seeking help do so under considerable pressure from family and friends, or when they need to ride through a particular crisis. It is necessary to determine and continually mobilize the motivation of the person with alcoholic problems. Then, a combination of AA and individual, group, or family therapy has, in our experience, proven most effective.

Prevention

As innumerable prohibition movements, religious and parental interdictions, and even the Volstead Act have demonstrated, the prevention of alcohol abuse is not easily accomplished, despite the common knowledge of its disastrous effects. There is no doubt that societal and religious attitudes as well as parental modeling can play a part in preventing excessive drinking. But if the young person's family relationships have been fragile or his or her childhood and adolescence repressive, then rebellious behavior may follow. Moreover, the seeds are sown for the effects of peer pressure, which is powerful in any event. Advice to parents is perhaps a cliché, but it is as follows: model but don't dictate; guide but don't tyrannize; and if the adolescent insists on his or her own judgment about drinking alcohol, you can voice your feelings and opinions and establish norms within the home, but outright prohibition will, more likely than not, incur only opposition and secret drinking.

Drugs

In 1914, the Harrison Narcotics Act made the unauthorized use of and traffic in various drugs illegal. It has been established that one person in 3,000 is addicted to narcotics. This does not include addiction to milder drugs and medication, which we shall discuss later. The rate is higher for certain subgroups. For example, it is reported that one out of every hundred physicians is addicted to some sort of drug. Other data gives useful, if general, information on drug addiction: greater numbers of addicts live in large cities, and male addicts outnumber females eight to one.

There are four main categories of drugs. The narcotics or opiates relieve physical and psychological pain, induce a state of euphoria in some individuals, and lead to drowsiness and sleep. The primary drug in this category is opium, from which morphine, heroin, and codeine are derived. The hallucinogens produce perceptual alterations, illusions, visual hallucinations, euphoria, and mood changes. The best known are marijuana, hashish, and lysergic acid diethylmide (LSD). Others are mescaline, peyote, and psilocybin. The stimulants, with the exception of cocaine, are synthetic chemicals and are called amphetamines. They include benzedrine, dexedrine, and methedrine. The amphetamines increase energy level and have an exhilarating effect. They have been used extensively, including by medical prescription, for weight reduction, diminishing fatigue, and repelling sleep. Sedatives include the habit-forming barbiturates, which in mild doses have a relaxing effect and in moderate doses induce sleep; in large doses they are fatal.

Categories

In a comparative study of young narcotics users in the United States and England, the social class background of the English subjects was found to be more varied than that of the Americans, most of whom came from underprivileged environments. The English also had a better work history. In other respects, the two groups were similar. Both were found to have a higher incidence of parental loss through death or separation, family psychoses, persistent childhood truancy, delinquency, and criminal behavior.

Narcotics

Other studies have indicated that drug users in both national groups manifest emotional disturbance (as compared to non-addictive groups of similar socio-economic status), including sociopathic tendencies, depression, tension, insecurity, feelings of inadequacy, and difficulty in forming lasting interpersonal relations.

Opium, heroin, and morphine produce states of euphoria, drowsiness, reverie, and sometimes lack of coordination. All three are addictive. Among the effects of prolonged use are malnutrition because of poor eating habits, loss of sexual interest, and respiratory difficulties. Death due to overdose is frequent. Reactions to abrupt withdrawal can be severe. Within the first twelve hours, muscle pain, sneezing, sweating, and yawning typically occur. Within thirty-six hours, there may be uncontrollable muscle twitching, cramps, restlessness, and a rise in heart rate and blood pressure. The addict may vomit, suffer diarrhea, and be unable to sleep. The symptoms generally persist for about seventy-two hours and then gradually diminish over a five- to ten-day period.

Barbiturates	Barbiturates were synthesized as aids for sleeping and relaxation. Despite their addictive quality, they are prescribed frequently if not freely. In the United States, enough barbiturates are produced to supply each man, woman, and child with thirty pills a year. They are depressants—relaxing the muscles—in small doses and produce a mild euphoria. Excessive doses may make the person irritable and cause him or her to lose weight as well as to suffer impaired reasoning. Very large doses can cause suffocation and be fatal. They are often chosen as a means of suicide. When combined with alcohol, a not uncommon practice, the results can be fatal. Barbiturates are the second most common class of drugs to which people are addicted. Withdrawal symptoms are very severe and long-lasting.
Amphetamines	Commonly known as uppers, amphetamines heighten wakefulness, reduce appetite (and thus are used often in dieting), and produce what feels like boundless energy. Larger doses can make the person nervous, agitated, confused, subject to headaches, dizzy, sleepless, and even paranoid. While not necessarily addictive in the ordinary sense, increased tolerance develops rapidly, so that enormous amounts may be required for stimulating effects. Habituation, or psychological dependence, is quite common. College students cramming for exams, athletes, and professional people with demanding work schedules are among the most common users of amphetamines.
Cocaine	Cocaine has been used since 1844 as a local anesthetic. In 1884, Sigmund Freud used it to combat depression in himself and in his patients. In addition to reducing pain, it may enhance mental processes, induce a state of euphoria, and heighten sexual feelings, self-confidence and well-being. Addiction has not been demonstrated, but an overdose may produce psychotic symptoms, particularly terrifying hallucinations. Drugs, like fashion, move in fads. Nowadays in certain affluent circles, "coke" is in. Its great expense limits its use and probably reinforces a sense of elitism.
Theories of Addiction	A common theory of drug addiction is that the user takes the drug accidentally and through curiosity. He or she then becomes hooked and, to avoid painful withdrawal reactions, takes more and more. This interpretation has been challenged on the basis that withdrawal effects may be no more severe than a bad case of influenza. Synanon, a residential treatment program for drug addiction (before it became a quasi-political, cult-like movement) does not reinforce acute with-

drawal symptoms or at least does not permit them to interfere seriously with daily functions including chores and work.
This approach apparently has had considerable success.

As for psychological factors relevant to drug addicts, the
father in many cases was absent from the home or a shadowy
figure who tended to be hostile and distant. The father frequently had had difficulty with the law and had stormy relations with the mother. Most addicts' initial experiences were
not accidental. Often, they were introduced to drugs by their
peers, commonly in the drug culture or in the drug-ridden
ghetto. While various personality hypotheses may be prof-
fered, such as extreme dependency and a sense of inadequacy in coping with life, cultural and social factors seem to
play a significant if not preeminent part.

Treatment

A common but controversial treatment for heroin addiction
has been the substitution of the synthetic pain killers
methadone and cyclazocine. In effect, a cross-tolerance to
these substitutes is created—that is, the addiction is displaced to the substitute—obviating the need for the far more
expensive and toxic heroin. Being freed from the costly heroin
habit theoretically frees the addicts from the compulsion to
get large amounts of money, often by crime, and from dependence on criminal associations. Governmentally supported
methadone clinics also expose the addict to relevant programs and activities. Favorable results for selected cases have
been reported for methadone and cyclazocine.

The problem with such substitutes as methadone is that
they are equally addictive. Moreover, methadone overdose
and fatality occurs frequently enough to cause concern. When
cross-tolerance is employed with a regulated over-all treatment program, the rationale for its use is more convincing.
Too often this is not the case, however.

What has been effective with addicts has been a comprehensive community-centered program, associated with
and following physiological withdrawal. This includes
psychotherapy, vocational counseling, and assistance in gain-
ing employment, family counseling, financial and housing assistance, and a support system with social programs. This
residential community approach has been offered by Synanon
and Daytop Lodge. Many of these programs employ staff who
themselves have been addicts. They insist on sincerity and
directly assault any rationalizations, excuses, or defenses.
Gut and gutter language is employed, as is fatigue, peer pressure, and intense emotion. Facades are ripped away and what
is offered in return is support and a sense of belonging. Put in
other words, dependent, neurotic, and psychotic behavior is
forcibly negatively reinforced, while positive reward is ac-

corded only to behavior meeting the standards of the program community. This is really a behavior modification program. The "cured" addicts may now, however, be dependent on their new milieu.

Marijuana

Marijuana is derived from the dried and ground leaves of the female hemp plant, cannabis sativa. Hashish, more potent than marijuana, comes from the dried resin of the plant. As of 1972, 24 million Americans—15% of adults and 14% of those twelve to sixteen years of age—were estimated to have used marijuana at least once.

Various allegations have been made about marijuana: that it leads to anti-social and criminal behavior; that it is a stepping stone to heroin and other hard drugs; that it can cause psychotic behavior; that it produces genetic damage; and, although it is not physiologically addictive, long-term use leads to psychological dependence and to loss of interest and withdrawal. The evidence does not support any of these assertions. In fact, intensive studies of Greek and Jamaican people who smoke the much stronger ganja and hashish habitually demonstrate no functional and physical problems as compared to those who do not smoke.

Those who smoke the drug less than once a month reported that they did so primarily out of curiosity and a desire to share a social experience. Those smoking the drug two to ten times a month gave the same reasons but emphasized social and recreational gratification. Moderate and heavy users—eleven times per month to several times a day—mentioned its "kicks" and its use to allay anxiety and boredom. The fact that smoking marijuana is illegal probably titillates the young and the non-conformist. Peer pressure and camaraderie are also strong reinforcers. Considering the lack of evidence for negative effects—it is certainly far more benign than the socially sanctioned smoking of cigarettes and consumption of alcohol—its widespread incidence and the tendency toward decriminalization (that is, removing penalties against possession of small amounts), the inclusion of this habit with drug use is questionable. In fact, a good argument may be made for its legal use, thereby dissociating it for young people from rebellion and anti-social behavior.

LSD

In the 1960s, Timothy Leary and Richard Alpert, two Harvard psychologists, were instrumental in introducing a drug culture in the United States and later in the Western world. Their motto in effect was to tune out the establishment and tune in on drugs. The revulsion over the Vietnam War and corruption in government (and possibly the attainment of maturity of many middle-class children raised in the permissive era of the 1940s) made such a motto appealing to the young. College students especially were thus able to protest and act out their need for excitement and expression at the same time. So acid trips were quite common and still are not rare.

The effects of LSD and other hallucinogenic (psychedelic) drugs are variable and seem, at least in part, to be dependent on the psychological set and climate. Nevertheless, intellectual impairment, confusion, terror, and psychotic behavior may result during and after LSD usage.

While such drugs as narcotics, stimulants, and hallucinogens are used primarily by young people, their seniors have their own drug habits. For example, the use of sedatives such as barbiturates is widespread among the adult and especially older population. Medication for neuritis, arthritis, headaches, assorted aches and pains, digestive disorders, allergies, respiratory problems, skin conditions, and a host of complaints as well as for preventive purposes (birth control pills being the prime example) is not only common, it is endemic. Some are prescribed by physicians—rather too freely, we believe—and more are patent medicines purchased in pharmacies without prescriptions. Some are addictive, such as some of the tranquilizers which are used routinely by millions of people.

Medication

The National Institute on Drug Abuse reported in 1977 that more than 120 million prescriptions were filled in the United States for sleeping pills and tranquilizers alone. An estimated 51 million people have used tranquilizers prescribed for them by a doctor, about 28 million have used sedatives, and 17 million have resorted to stimulants of various kinds. The rate of drug dependence or addiction is so high that an organization, PA or Pills Anonymous, has been formed. Some responsibility for such drug abuse must be ascribed to physicians who are not trained to detect drug abuse or who do not wish to attend to its psychological implications.

Any medication can become habituating, that is, depended upon psychologically. This is apparently what happens with many medicines. Every medication, no matter how benign for most people, has side effects that vary from one individual to another. In some cases, the effects are dramatic. Even aspirin can cause bleeding and allergic reactions. What is now becoming appreciated is the interaction effects of more than one drug taken at a time. Something is known about the interaction of three and practically nothing of four or more. Yet when you stop to consider that a person may be taking something to clear a stuffed nose or for an allergy, is taking something else for an upset stomach, routinely uses something for a skin condition, and is on a tranquilizer or a drug to help him or her sleep, and so forth, the potential interaction effects are rather frightening. It has been estimated that hospitalized mental patients are sometimes on more than twenty medications simultaneously. It would seem that medication is a popular habit for many and is habitually prescribed by doctors.

| Coffee, Tea, and Colas | There are many people who claim they virtually cannot open their eyes until they have their morning cup of coffee. Many feel they could not struggle through the afternoon without a cup. This smacks of an addictive quality, at least of a strong habituation. It is even probable that abrupt cessation of a heavy, chronic use of coffee, tea, or cola has some mild withdrawal effects. These drinks may not be so benign for many. Such reactions to caffeine as restlessness, stomach upset, headache, palpitations, and an inability to go to sleep are commonplace. In certain medical conditions such as heart disorders, these drinks are contraindicated. |

Compulsive Eating

The compulsive aspects of overeating are discussed in the chapter on Eating.

Smoking

For the past twenty years, a series of impressive reports by groups ranging from the World Health Organization to the Surgeon General of the United States and various medical societies have delineated the hazards of cigarette smoking. These have included lung cancer and cardiovascular disturbances. Life expectancy is shorter for smokers. Nevertheless, millions upon millions still smoke. Indeed, while the percentage of American male smokers has decreased from 52% in 1964 to 39% in 1978, the rate of women smokers only decreased from 32% to 29%, and smoking among children is actually increasing. Knowledge about the subject may be necessary as a deterrent, but is not sufficient to stop people from smoking.

In a study of Californian psychologists, it was found that the males tested smoked more than representative American male adults, but about as much as those equally educated. They smoked more than other male health professionals except for psychiatrists (whose sedentary, passive work did not seem to facilitate cessation of smoking). Women psychologists shared a low cessation rate with other female professionals. They reported the stress of work more than males as a reason for persistence in smoking. The other reasons offered for persistence were pleasure, addiction, social influence, and stimulation.

Once a person smokes for a period of time, addiction seems to play a part in the continuation of the habit. Cessation of smoking produces withdrawal symptoms— nervousness, drowsiness and headaches. And people develop a tolerance to nicotine, which induces a physiological arousal and reduces anxiety. It also has the effect of enhancing alertness and concentration. Perhaps that is why psychologists who smoke wrote more books and articles than their non-smoking colleagues. Another explanation is that tension associated with achievement orientation is more conducive to smoking and its purported calming effect.

There are many different measures that may be taken to control smoking, but first and foremost there must be a sincere motivation to stop. The psychologists mentioned above as a group were very knowledgeable about intervention techniques. Neverthelsss, although over 90% expressed a desire to stop, only 61% made a serious effort to do so. And 42% quit for as long as three months before resuming. Of those who stopped, most just quit cold turkey, and only a few utilized a systematic behavior modification technique, despite having a knowledge of and apparent commitment to this approach.

Such programs as Smoke Enders, which utilize behavior modification, seem to be most successful. Like AA, they provide inspiration and group support. But unlike AA, a systematic effort based on learning theory is made in a gradual but increasingly structured way to decondition the smoking habit. For example, smokers must tabulate each cigarette smoked, may begin with quitting in the morning and in such specified situations as eating and driving. When they want a smoke, they are instructed to call a fellow participant in the program to talk it out. As for other attempts to control smoking, there is a high rate of lapsing back into the habit.

The fact that confrontation with the dire consequences of smoking can inspire quitting is borne out by the exceedingly high rate of physicians who no longer smoke, particularly those who specialize in cancer and pathology. But although children now believe that smoking is dangerous, they are not deterred from beginning, partly because the emphasis of anti-smoking messages is on future consequences. Children are more present-oriented.

A program to stop and prevent smoking was conducted with children. They were taught to recognize the pressure to smoke coming from peers, parents, and the media, and were provided with detailed techniques for coping with these pressures. Then, demonstrations of the immediate physiological consequences of smoking were provided, as well as group feedback concerning the incidence of smoking. Ample use was made of videotape and film. Posters, based on interviews with children and demonstrating peer and social pressure, were placed throughout the school. The students were asked to write their reactions to these presentations and to discuss them in small groups. Finally, they were provided with repeated feedback of information and results. The program appeared to be most successful.

In short, we have the tools and techniques to deter and prevent smoking. What remains to be done is to mobilize a systematic effort—in society at large, or at least in the school or family—to counter this pernicious habit.

Gambling

Billions of dollars are gambled each year in the United States. At least a proportional amount is wagered in England. A casual observation of gambling activity among Asiatic people will demonstrate quickly that this is not an occidental quirk. Like drinking and smoking, gambling is participated in by a significant portion of the population. And like these other habits, gambling has a compulsive character.

Compulsive gambling, comparable to alcoholism and inveterate smoking, is the extreme form. Many hundreds of thousands of people in the United States alone suffer its consequences. Compulsive gamblers habitually take chances at every opportunity. This activity precludes all other interests and responsibilities. Gamblers are superficially consummate optimists who never learn from losses, never stop when winning, and despite all reason, risk too much—maybe everything—on one wager.

The literature relevant to gambling is predominantly psychoanalytic, and the consensus is that gambling is a neurotic behavior wherein gamblers have an unconscious wish to lose. They are rebelling against reality, which threatens their grandiose and omnipotent illusions. What they really want is proof of love and esteem, but they need to undergo their inevitable rejection to pay for their unacceptable avarice and taboo sexual impulses and to punish their intimates.

Freudian psychoanalysts theorize that the characteristics of compulsive gamblers embody a fixation on infantile omnipotence, masochism, and oral cravings. For example, a typical analytic characterization is the type who constantly finds injustice and rejection in losing, but establishes relationships with stronger, dominating partners—spouses, friends, etc.

The psychoanalytic theories seem tenuous at points. It would not be easy to predict from these hypotheses who would become a gambler, although they rather conveniently describe someone who is known to be one. Yet these theories do provide useful hints which can be tested out. We believe that it is reasonably pragmatic to observe that compulsive gamblers are attempting to gain a measure of security and control over their environments because their internal security and control are weak. They seek rewards, esteem, and power, but despair of their ability to cope with the effort, persistence, skills, and disappointments required in their everyday lives. Doubtlessly, other rewards are important—the immature, perhaps infantile, thrills, tensions, and illusions of importance and grandiosity in being a winner. A truly compulsive gambler will even play penny ante poker in order to have action, so to speak. Those of us who gamble, not necessarily compulsively, may note that the tension of the game, the displeasure at losing and joy at winning are relatively independent of the stakes—these factors can be present even with valueless chips.

We would agree that the behavior of compulsive gamblers is indicative of character disorders requiring extensive psychotherapy. (See the discussion of character disorders in the chapter on Behavior Disturbances.) Compulsive gamblers, however, may not be motivated to get help until their lives are shattered. As in other compulsive behaviors (all of which seem to be fixations in emotional development around the ages of three to six), support groups and attendance to the entire life style of the individual are indicated. The alcoholic has AA, the drug addict has community-oriented programs, the smoker has Smoke Enders, the compulsive eater has Weight Watchers, and the gambler has Gamblers Anonymous. The point is for the compulsive person and those concerned with him or her to recognize the character and consequences of this behavior and to mobilize the support of counseling, therapy and support groups and to sustain such support. The motivation for compulsive behavior is rarely eradicated. Ability to avoid such behavior and to cope with it, however, is most helpful.

Summary

All habits are bad, because they are compulsive behavior. Although people who are addicted to some behavior or substance may rationalize their compulsion, they have, in fact, little choice about the matter. They do not think about consequences, only the satisfaction of a compulsive craving. Any behavior that is compulsive is neurotic and involves more hardship and cost than benefit.

Alcoholism is an extremely common and destructive habit, made even more pernicious by 'drinking' being a sanctioned social custom. In its extreme form it can lead to total economic, social, familial, psychological, and physical collapse. Many theories have been offered to account for this addiction, but the causes probably have something to do with fixation at the oral stage of development. Similarly, various modes of treatment have been proposed, but the most effective seems to be a combination of individual psychotherapy and group support. Alcoholics Anonymous has had some measure of success in treating this addiction, although here, as elsewhere, the primary requirement is a strong motivation to quit.

Drug addiction is also more common than most people think, and ranges from the hardcore heroin addict to the housewife who can't do without her daily tranquilizer. The four major categories of drugs are the opiates, the hallucinogens, the stimulants, and the sedatives. All of them can be abused and can lead to psychological if not physiological dependence. The frequency of addiction is made all the greater by the rather free prescribing of multiple drugs by careless or ignorant physicians. With severe drug addiction, the best form of treatment again involves a convergence of individual psychotherapy, group support, and family, economic, and vocational counseling. Again, the addict's motivation is the essential factor. Even such commonplace substances as coffee, tea, and cola can have addictive results.

Although the dangers of smoking have been known for twenty years, the frequency of smoking is still alarmingly high. Addiction to cigarettes is at least partly caused by tension and anxiety. The costs to health, however, are enormous. Certain groups like Smoke Enders report considerable success in helping people stop smoking, but only recently has sufficient attention been paid to preventing the formation of this pernicious habit in young people.

Gambling involves billions of dollars a year in the United States, and the cost to an extremely compulsive gambler can be a wrecked life. Compulsive gamblers show certain common characteristics, most of which seem to stem from infantile illusions of omnipotence and grandiosity, often with simultaneous needs to be punished. Such a habit seems characteristic of a personality disorder, a serious condition requiring rather extensive psychotherapy.

All of these compulsive behaviors can be treated best by a combination of approaches—individual therapy, support groups, and various kinds of counseling—provided there is a sincere and sustained desire to change. Still, the unconscious motivation for such compulsion is rarely touched by many kinds of treatment. A healthy psychological development will, of course, prevent such compulsions before they develop.

12
Change

It is extraordinarily difficult to change our own behavior. It is impossible to change someone else's. Of course, it is possible to influence others to alter their behavior, but that is still difficult. Every person's responses are fairly fixed and predictable although the variety of these responses is wide.

This is understandable, say the learning theorists, for we are conditioned to behave the way we do from early in our lives. We keep responses that were rewarded and drop those that were punished. Thus, pleasure and pain shaped our personalities and their expression. Choice had nothing to do with this. The psychoanalytic theorists are in basic agreement with this theory. They also explain our personalities as networks of associations formed early in life. The psychoanalysts ascribe more importance to such drives as sex and aggression, but only in relatively recent years have some of them conceded that choice, will, or ego per se has anything significant to do with behavior.

There are reasons we change our behavior and there are reasons we do not. It is possible and useful to determine the causes that promote or retard change. Different therapies emphasize certain aspects of change or try to arrange for the preconditions of change to develop, but whenever there is an alteration in behavior of any sustained nature, then each and every precondition of change has been met. Which conditions and how many of them are emphasized by a particular therapy determine the speed and quality of the outcome.

What are the components of change? First, there must be an awareness of an unsatisfying condition or state of mind. Second, there must be a willingness to alter this condition or state. Third, there must be a recognition that something has to be surrendered or exchanged. Fourth, there must be a commitment to sustain effort, experience pain, and delay gratification in the service of change. Fifth, there must be experimentation with new modes of behavior and attitudes over a period of time. Finally, there must be a restructuring. With awareness, motivation, surrender of patterns, commitment, experimentation, and restructuring, we can change.

We often want to change. We want to change because someone has told us that there is something wrong. Or we feel unhappy, dissatisfied, upset. But we are not clear about what is bothering us.

Our function as human beings is partly defined by our level of awareness. When we are unconscious, we are barely alive. Conversely, when we are alert and all of our senses are being stimulated and we are being responsive, that is when we are most fully alive. To see, hear, taste, smell, feel—is to live. There is another quality of awareness. And that is to know, puzzle, understand, appreciate, judge, discriminate, and so on. In other words, our cognitive reactions are an essential part of our awareness.

When we are depressed, our senses become jaded, experiences colorless, and our existence virtually lifeless. So we need to be stimulated to be fully alive. The problem is that we can shut off stimuli internally as well as externally. If the environment appears threatening or overwhelming, we can turn off or tune out. But the process of "cutting off" is not that easily reversed. To initiate reversal or change, it is necessary to tune into awareness.

Awareness

Awareness of an unsatisfying condition takes many forms. In its most simple manifestation, it appears as a symptom—a distressing condition. Psychological examples are: the inability to make decisions, obsessive thoughts, irrational fears, a sense of inertia, sadness, irritability, a feeling of futility, emptiness, confusion, loneliness, shame, low self-esteem, a feeling of unfulfillment, etc. Interpersonal examples are: the concern that no one likes us, a difficulty in relating to other people, the sense that others "manipulate" us or us them, problems in dealing effectively with anger, affection, intimacy, or sexuality. Somatic examples are: tics and twitches, insomnia, palpitations, stomach difficulties, heaviness in the chest, headaches, visual and auditory problems, a vague sense of bodily discomfort or generalized anxiety, and a host of psychosomatic disorders.

But to be aware of a symptom is only the beginning of awareness. That is, we may well locate this problem outside ourselves. Or we may ascribe it to causes lying outside of our psychological orbit, residing in our livers, for example. What is necessary is an awareness of the difficulty as it relates to our whole person and our needs, motivations, coping mechanisms, and defenses. Just what does this symptom accomplish for us, what does it prevent, how did it come about, and how may it be related to our over-all behavior, attitudes, and values?

Life-long styles, chronic behavior patterns, and narrowness of experience tend to exclude or weaken the awareness of stimulation. Awareness, for our purpose, is the appreciation of available choices. Full awareness would imply knowledge of all possible options, and unawareness would be limited to a single, already-exercised choice.

It has been demonstrated that it is not the quantity or intensity of stimulation but the patterning of stimulation that is significant. An individual establishes his or her patterning of stimulation and generally responds according to this pattern. This is his or her life style. Whether the pattern is intense, even, or subdued, meaningful and durable gratification may be lacking if the stimulation is not balanced and varied. Thus, often the intense person frenetically seeks even greater intensity, the withdrawn person greater withdrawal, and the seemingly stable individual looks for greater monotony. All deny their lack of gratification. Often it takes a crisis—usually an interpersonal crisis—to make a person aware of his or her dissatisfaction. And sometimes it takes a novel but pleasurable experience to highlight the lack of gratification.

Balanced stimulation, like a balanced diet, implies a diversified intake: emotional, intellectual, interpersonal, and social stimuli. We all have experienced stimulus starvation. After a few rainy days, someone is sure to say, "If something doesn't happen soon, I'll scream." Emotional hunger hurts, but intellectual hunger is experienced as oppression, heaviness, hardening of the cerebral arteries. "I haven't read a good book, seen an interesting movie or held a meaningful conversation for so long, it feels like my brain has gone rusty." Similarly, the hunger for interacting with people and with the group of society can be felt as an itch that grows into an ache.

Once we note a pain, a lack, a malaise, we are at the first stage of awareness. But awareness can range from a vague uneasiness to an acute sense of the conditions causing the discomfort. For meaningful, durable change to occur, it is necessary to be sensitive to the relevant conditions, to have our nerve endings sandpapered, so to speak. Alertness to the factors associated with displeasure and the cues that presage it introduce the possibility for change.

Motivation

Being aware of distress is necessary but not sufficient to eliminate it. It does not follow necessarily that a sensation of displeasure is accompanied by the motivation to rid ourselves of it. Motive implies an urge to *act*. More often than not, even a suffering person merely wishes the suffering to go away. He or she hopes someone else will change things. Maybe he or she can just talk or complain about it, or take a pill, or even cut it out. Perhaps some magic incantation, prayer, or hypnosis will do the trick. All that is wishful thinking, just a step beyond fantasizing how nice things would be if they were different. It is only a passive expectancy, waiting to be acted upon or reacted to. But motivation is a prerequisite for action.

To effect change, we must recognize our power and potency, and we must use this power to alter whatever condition we are unhappy with. People who are unhappy with something about themselves do not necessarily, in our opinion, have sufficient motivation to correct matters. Nor do we believe that telling them to change can be effective if they do not want to change. But we do believe that action can be spurred by confrontation. "So what do *you* propose to do about it?" "What else is new?" "If you're unhappy, what prevents you from doing something about it?"

To many, motivation simply signifies wanting. When they say that they are motivated they mean to say that they want something and hope that something will happen or someone will come along to make it happen. Analysts would describe this as narcissism. "I want, and therefore it will come to pass." "I want, and you should make it occur for me."

But motive implies a force, a motive power, a power to move, to push, to change, to *act*. If we are truly motivated, *we* are willing to act to get what we want. This means we are willing to expend the energy, pay the price, and suffer the inconvenience, pain, or anxiety in the process. In short, motivation is an active rather than passive process. This may mean delaying action while actively planning the most propitious moment to move—far different from stalling, spinning wheels, or rationalizing. On the other hand, impulsive behavior, which often looks like an active response, is nothing more than a narcissistic reaction to passivity. Motivation is ego-oriented and has direction. It is not a diffuse striking out.

Once there is motivation to change, it first may become evident that there is an equally powerful need to hang on to something. At some level of consciousness, there is a felt gain in retaining a current pattern of behavior. There is a payoff in sustaining the status quo despite the expressed discontent. But we most often, on some level, deny, ignore, or selectively inattend to this gain. This advantage may be seen or more precisely sensed as being necessary to survive or to keep anxiety within tolerable limits. It may be a tenacious grip on illusions, conscious or otherwise.

In short, the issue is whether we are willing to give up or exchange something in order to change our behavior. That is what makes behavioral change so difficult. Retaining everything would not be a difficult decision. Nor would choosing between two or more desirable choices. It is the reluctance or fear of losing something we have—some advantage—that makes change so hard. Often this may take the form of a negative advantage—that is, we may try to avoid the *anticipation* of pain, anxiety, or of being overwhelmed with the institution of a new behavioral pattern.

Very frequently, we suffer the illusion that we can trade an imperfect coping mechanism for a perfect one. The reality is that we can trade an imperfect mechanism only for one that is less imperfect. There will always be some disadvantage and stress in our imperfect world, no matter what choice we make. But that is reality, and it is necessary for us to under-

Surrender and Exchange

stand this so that we can tolerate the stress and weigh the pros and cons of the new versus the old.

Commitment

Commitment is an explicit, verbalized pledge or agreement. It is a contract we enter into with ourselves or with others. Commitment for change carries particular force when it is a contract with a therapist. Thus "I am distressed by this symptom, and I will work with you to eliminate it," "I am dissatisfied with my style of life, and I want to learn how to live differently," "My relationship with my spouse is miserable, so I want to see what part I am playing and how I can vary this relationship," etc. In other words, commitment is a contractual statement, as in a therapeutic working relationship. Without it, there is only a complaint. Or there is awareness and perhaps even motivation, but a lack of direction. Surrender of old ways and experimentation surely imply at least partial commitment. But an explicit contract gives direction and pragmatic objectives to shoot for. It is the unifying force which binds the other elements of change into a practical operation.

Of course, commitment is dynamic rather than static. The first commitment may be to get the name of a therapist, and the next real step to make and keep a therapeutic appointment. Next there may be a vague groping: "I want to find out what bothers me." This, then, leads to the elucidation of a problem area: "I see how I push people away, and I am determined not to do this anymore, but I'm beginning to appreciate how little I think of myself, and I want to understand and change that." And so on. So one commitment may lead to another, and, in fact, we would define psychotherapy as a progressive and increasingly comprehensive series of commitments to understand the self and to modify interactions with the self, others, and the environment.

An important component of commitment is responsibility. That is, for change to occur, a person must be willing to be responsible. By this we do not mean moral, legal, or even mental accountability, for that implies a burden or imperative. We do mean the willingness to respond, the foregoing of a passive, reactive stance, and the assumption of an active response. The antithesis of responsibility would be requiring someone else to make us aware, expecting continuous prodding for us to experience and understand, wanting to be provided with reasons for change, looking to the values and expectations of others, and making pseudo-surrenders: "Okay, I give this up because you think it's best for me." Responsibility means the awareness of our own potency, the desire to use this power, the relinquishing of helplessness or passivity, the exercise of our powers to fulfill needs and self-realization, and the unequivocal statement, "It's me who's changing, because *I* want to, and nobody else can do it for me."

Perhaps the most important component of change is experimentation. If there is only a narrow range of behavior available, there is little opportunity to reinforce new modes and extinguish old patterns. On the other hand, if new styles, actions, or responses are ventured, there is always a possibility for change. Experimentation, to prove effective, ordinarily requires activity over a period of time. This is particularly true if the usual bloody nose is experienced—if one risk opens the door to a series of progressive risks, and a sense of loss is felt. Interestingly enough, there seems to be an intrinsic reward in the experimentation itself—the exhilaration of taking action, of mastering and coping. When this pleasure is supported by others, either a friend or a therapist, this reward can more than compensate for fear, anxiety, and rejection.

Experimentation

Once sufficient awareness, motivation, and commitment have been achieved to relinquish fixed ideas, attitudes, and patterns of behavior and response, a restructuring must take place for change to occur. Restructuring is a readiness to explore new options. It can be partial when we say, "Let's try something else," or "Let's see what other possibilities there are." It is holistic when an entirely new orientation emotionally and intellectually redirects a person's response.

Thus, restructuring might range from considering an entirely new life style to deciding to smile or talk more often. Restructuring need not be cognitive, nor even deliberate, for change to occur, but restructuring occurs just prior to behavioral change—it is not the change itself. That is where experimentation comes in. Dreaming, daydreaming, fantasy, wishful thinking—even meditation and prayer—all are restructuring experiences. But they do not necessarily eventuate in change. Indeed, such activities may drain the energy required to galvanize us into changing. For change to be more than promiscuous experimentation, however, and to be purposive and sustained in the service of our needs, the restructuring requires conceptualization.

Restructuring

Successful psychotherapy of any kind is concerned with correcting the distortions individuals have about themselves and others, and about their relation to the world. It also provides support for coping with the frustrations resulting from these

Therapy

distortions. The correction of distortions, dependent on the variety of psychotherapy, may range from explicit verbalization (as in Freudian analysis) to an implicit or even subliminal and mental reorganization (as in behavior modification).

No one creates his or her own suffering, although he or she may do a good deal to contribute to or perpetuate it. People suffer psychologically because they have been exposed to malevolent interpersonal influences and have learned how to protect themselves accordingly. That the protection grows inadequate and anachronistic and that the apprehensions are ill-advised does not at all suggest that the individual is the creator of his or her suffering. The best kind of therapy allows us to become aware of our convoluted attempts to seek gratification, to recognize the payoff in maintaining these hang-ups, and to experiment with new ways of doing things.

Getting Help

We have discussed the components of change. While we have used a psychotherapeutic model, these components are applicable to any facet of life. There are a variety of occasions in life, however, when seeking help is necessary or at least expeditious. When that happens, an important rule to observe is what we call the Triple C—the helper or helping agency should be competent, credentialed, and concerned.

Competency is a most difficult attribute to pin down. It includes credentials, but is much more. In the field of mental health, competency is often gauged by practitioners' visibility and popularity with their colleagues and the public. Their charisma and ability to present, write, and even promote themselves and programs (or to officiate in professional administrative roles) play no small part in this visibility. While these qualities do not necessarily correlate with competency, the maturity and knowledge that impress other colleagues are certainly relevant.

There are certain minimal standards for competency, and these are education and training, particularly postgraduate training in the area of specialization relevant to your problem. Thus a PhD, MD, or MSW accompanied by postgraduate training in individual or group psychotherapy does suggest minimal competency. The disciplines of clinical psychology and psychiatry both have boards which bestow diplomas on experienced practitioners who pass the boards' examinations.

Each of the mental health disciplines has credentialing by licensing in most states. In addition, other specialties, such as marriage counseling, are licensed in several states. Licensing and certification indicate that the practitioner has at least minimal appropriate education, experience, and knowledge.

Credentialing and some indication of competence can be determined, but concern is more difficult to gauge. Your assessment may be strengthened by the recommendation of some professional or friend or by a referral from a professional society or school. In the final analysis, it is incumbent upon you to determine how interested and compassionate the person who is working with you seems to be. You might, perhaps, see an internist or surgeon who acts cold (although we wouldn't recommend it), but this is counterproductive in any psychological work. It is most important to feel comfortable with and have confidence in the person with whom you work. If you don't, and the professional person does not explain his or her behavior to your satisfaction, it probably would be best to sever the relationship.

Psychotherapy

Apart from differences in their theoretical orientations, all types of psychotherapy use language to change another person. These are the talking cures. They assume that talking can achieve certain goals, such as reduction in anxiety or the elimination of undesirable behavior.

There are scores of schools of psychotherapies with extremely variable sets of procedures. What presumably differentiates one from another is a specific, consistent theoretical rationale. Often these theories overlap and do not appear to be that consistent or rational to the outsider or even to an objective researcher. Moreover, despite their apparent differences, practitioners of different schools are often found to utilize the same techniques and procedures. The competency and concern mentioned above, rather than the particular approach, have been found frequently to be the important determinant of successful therpay. That is why we emphasize the importance of the Triple C. Beyond that, finding an approach suitable to your personality and goals is important. Whether the orientation focuses on uncovering unconscious memories and feelings and "restructuring the personality," as in psychoanalysis, or on creating an accepting climate where you can respect yourself, as in Rogerian counseling, it is necessary to determine, on a continuous basis, whether you are truly collaborating with the therapist in meeting your goals. His or her competency and concern in conjunction with your motivation and commitment determine the outcome.

Even the distinction between long-term and short-term therapy is not clear. One has not proven more effective than the other, if only for the fact that it is extremely difficult to compare the needs and motivation of different people. But 70% of people who seek psychotherapy drop out quickly, and those who avail themselves of brief psychotherapy apparently

benefit considerably. Selecting the appropriate psycho-
therapist or the mental health agency, therefore, is crucial to
successful therapy.

There are three major mental health disciplines that
practice psychotherapy. Standards vary, but those that are
acceptable to accrediting organizations are as follows: the
clinical psychologist with a PhD from a school approved by
the American Psychological Association, a year's internship,
and postdoctoral training in psychotherapy (there are also
counseling psychologists whose emphasis is less on research
and more on mild emotional problems); the psychiatrist with
an MD, internship, and a three-year residency in psychiatry
who may prescribe drugs and organic therapy; and the
psychiatric social worker who has an MSW and postgraduate
work in psychotherapy. Referrals may be made by the American Psychological Association, the American Psychiatric Association, or the National Association of Social Workers. Actually, state or local groups are more helpful in making referrals. Even more helpful are multidiscipline associations
whose standards for the practice of psychotherapy are rigorous, such as the American Academy of Psychotherapy, the
American Group Psychotherapy Association, or their regional
and state branches. Any university library will have the ad-
dresses of these organizations.

Group Therapy

In addition to the advantages of efficiency in terms of numbers and fees, group therapy has specific value. The group
serves as a microcosm of society, as a laboratory where you
may experiment with new behavior and learn how others see
you, under relatively structured and safe conditions. The
combined experience and resources of the group and its
power both to support and confront is much greater than any
individual therapist. Potential disadvantages are that the
given chemistry of any group may not be suitable. In addition, you have to learn to assert yourself to work toward your
goals (a positive feature, if accomplished), and there are often
problems with privacy and trust. The choice of the group
therapist is all-important. Every state has a group therapy
association that makes referrals. The American Group
Therapy Association is located in New York City, and through
its affiliation with the International Group Therapy Association, can be of help with suitable referrals throughout most of
the world.

Encounter, Sensitivity Training, and Humanistic Groups

In the last decade, there has been a proliferation of short-
term, intensive group experiences offered to the public. These
may last for several days or for several weeks. As an opportunity to quickly and intensely make contact with emotions,

memories, ideas, and new ways of coping with the self and with others, these groups may be valuable. They are not, however, a substitute for psychotherapy, since there generally is insufficient time for working through issues adequately. For some people, the results may even be injurious if they are not prepared to deal with the intensity and implications of the emotions and insights uncovered. Moreover, many individuals tend to utilize these groups almost in an addictive fashion, substituting group intimacy for the more arduous but gratifying and meaningful commitment to interpersonal relationships. There is such a wide variety of groups and people who assume "leadership" roles that caveat emptor—let the buyer beware. Without additional information—the lay person may often be quite gifted—it would behoove you to ascertain that the group facilitator is a licensed and credentialed mental health professional. The best sources of information about these groups are university psychology and social work departments.

Family Therapy

Although almost all emotional problems originate and persist in family contexts, there are some difficulties that particularly involve the family. These are marital discord, problems with children, and familial crises. Family therapy is uniquely suited for dealing with the impact of the family system on the various individuals involved, for facilitating communication among family members, for revealing the games and neurotic techniques that families employ, and for removing the impediments to personal growth of different family members. While family therapy can be most effective, many individuals require or at least desire to have a relationship with their own therapist. Referrals may be obtained from university and medical school centers as well as from local family service agencies.

Behavior Modification

Behavior modification employs the methodology and principles of experimental psychology. It employs rigorous testing of its procedures and results. In terms of time and results, this form of therapy has proven particularly efficient with such specific disorders as phobias, anxiety reactions, and learning difficulties. Criticism, however, has been leveled at this approach for its focussing largely on symptom alleviation rather than dealing with causes, for its results having limited generalizability, and for its not emphasizing the whole person and his or her humanistic concerns. Much of this criticism has been attended to, especially in such approaches as Lazarus' behavior therapy, which is somewhat more eclectic and attempts to span dynamic theory and more conventional behavior modification. The preponderant number of behavior therapists are university-based psychologists, but some psychiatrists practice these techniques.

| Marriage Counseling | One of the most frequent reasons that people seek help for their personal problems is a marital crisis. Unfortunately, the motive is often to remove the crisis without really dealing with the source of the difficulty. Or there is one highly motivated partner (usually the wife) who practically drags the other in. There are three areas of relationships, however, where it becomes virtually impossible to ignore our own dissatisfaction or that of the other. These are family, job, and marriage. The last is by far the most delicate and the most complicated. |

As has been stated, among the most difficult things in life is an intimate and durable relationship with another. Inevitably, frictions, misunderstandings, and miscommunications arise. Often, considerable grief can be avoided if prior to a crisis in a relationship the assistance of a trained therapist or counselor is sought. It makes as much sense as consulting one's physician and dentist preventively, or seeking spiritual guidance from the clergy. Indeed, even with relatively intact marriages, counseling can prove enriching. Pre-marital counseling has been recognized as so useful that many religious and educational agencies make such referrals.

When people seek marital counseling during a crisis, the relationship may be in deep trouble. In fact, often the marriage has already foundered. One or both may already have decided to separate, although this may not be consciously admitted. The task of the marriage counselor is not to save the marriage but to explore its status—good and bad—with the couple. One consequence may actually be divorce counseling. There are always three options: maintain the status quo with its attendant miseries, strife, or emptiness; split with full examination for all concerned—especially children—in the most mature and meaningful manner; and a commitment by both parties to work diligently to make changes to improve the relationship.

In all cases, the marriage counselor works with the couple to allow them to communicate openly and to appreciate the various options, implications, and viewpoints of the other. This requires motivation and a willingness to be frank and flexible. Often, one or both partners realize that individual or group psychotherapy is required. The American Association of Marriage Counselors has chapters in every state and most large cities. Marriage counselors are licensed in most states, but many people use this title and are ill-trained. Counselors may be psychologists, psychiatrists, social workers, and pastoral counselors. Catholic, Protestant, and Jewish marriage encounters are frequently offered to enrich marriages that are not too seriously in crisis. County family service agencies can usually make a suitable referral.

Sex Therapy

In recent years, because of the liberalization of attitudes toward sex, the work of Masters and Johnson, educational and professionally sponsored workshops, and the proliferation of self-help books, a considerable number of people are interested in and willing to avail themselves of sex therapy. (See the discussion in the chapter on Sexuality.) The extent of sexual dysfunction is fairly broad, and people are less willing nowadays to ignore this problem. Nor should they. There seem to be excellent results from sexual counseling or therapy. Appropriate referrals may be made by university psychology clinics and many medical schools. Some states have licensed sex counselors, but this credentialing is still in its early stages.

Crisis Services

Almost every county has a community mental health center. Contact may be made for emergency service or for prompt referral. In addition, there are suicide prevention centers, frequently associated with the psychiatry departments of medical schools. For referrals anywhere in the country, contact may be made with the Center for Studies of Suicide Prevention of the National Institute of Mental Health in Bethesda, Maryland. Almost every city has hot lines, which can be reached in university psychology departments or in the psychiatry departments of general hospitals. For help with a crisis problem, these telephone numbers may be called anonymously, and trained volunteers will talk to you and make referrals when appropriate. A call to telephone information (ask for a supervisor if the operator does not have the number) will usually provide you with the number of the closest hot line.

Drug Therapies

Modern psychopharmacology is only about twenty years old, but has had a profound effect on the care and treatment of the emotionally disturbed as well as the psychologically distressed. The latter group includes a significant portion, if not most, of the general population at one time or another. There are three major categories of drugs: the minor tranquilizers, the major tranquilizers, and the antidepressants. It is essential to be aware that these drugs are constantly changing, often before their side effects and long-term implications have been adequately investigated. Some medication may be effective for some behavioral disorders (without necessarily addressing the causes and factors behind the symptoms). Moreover, the majority of currently used physical treatments have been discovered by accident; they have not been scientifically determined.

| Minor Tranquilizers | Minor tranquilizers are used to reduce anxiety that is not of major proportions and are usually prescribed for people suffering from anxiety, tension, and mild or moderate depression. The most widely used of these are meprobamate (Miltown and Equanil), chlordiazepoxide (Librium), and diazepam (Valium). |

The tranquilizer industry has so mushroomed that it has become part of our social fabric. "Happy" pills have replaced the "Happy Hour" of local bars in popularity. They are widely used and freely prescribed, but there has been little controlled research on their effects and contraindications. The clinical evidence suggests, however, a calming effect for most people without addressing the basic problems that may have occasioned the symptoms. Care needs to be taken so that even these mild medications, such as Valium, do not become addictive or, in long-term use, create or aggravate physiological disorders.

| Major Tranquilizers | In 1950, chlorpromazine (Thorazine) was synthesized in France for use as an antihistamine. It was found that the drug diminished such psychotic symptoms as hallucinations in mental patients. By 1970, over 85% of all American state mental hospital patients were receiving Thorazine or the related class of drugs called phenothiazines. Their use was almost immediately associated with a dramatic decrease in hospital populations and the opening of many closed custodial wards. As a result, many patients can now be treated in the community. |

The major indication for these compounds is in the treatment of the schizophrenias. They are also useful in treating agitated depressive states and emotionally unstable personalities.

There is impressive evidence that phenothiazine medication is the preferred treatment for hospitalized schizophrenics, although that does not necessarily mean they are "cured." Rather, it may merely signify that they can be stabilized or "maintained" while on this medication. Readmissions are frequent. Long-term institutionalization can be replaced by a "revolving door" pattern of admissions, discharge, and readmissions. Moreover, such side effects as fatigue, dryness of the mouth, blurred vision, and involuntary tremors can result from long-term use of phenothiazines.

Reliance on these drugs in the treatment of the schizo-phrenias can result in the failure to attempt more far-reaching therapy. Such a situation is aggravated by the shortage of funds and personnel, especially in the treatment of the poor. In addition, the revolving door syndrome we have mentioned puts an enormous strain on the communities into which drug-maintained mental patients are released. Especially in high density cities where out-care facilities are inadequate, seriously ill patients are merely shuttled from one place to another.

Antidepressants

The tricyclics (Tofranil, Elevil, and Sinequan) and MAO in-hibitors (Nardil and Parmate) are two subcategories of an-tidepressants. The typical use for antidepressant medication is for retarded (i.e., slowed up psychological and motor re-sponses) depression, but they are also useful in the treatment of agitated depression and phobic anxiety states.

There are various "triggers" for depression, such as be-reavement, infections, prolonged fatigue, debilitation, weight loss, surgery, endocrine disorders, disappointment, or feel-ings of loss. Tricyclics seem to be less helpful for such exoge-nous depression than they are for endogenous cases—people with long-term patterns of seemingly inexplicable depressed states. Their depression may be chronic or come on without any apparent reason. Side effects of tricyclic drugs include dry mouth, constipation, dizziness, palpitations, and blurred vision. Drug therapy with depressed outpatients often results in the risk of suicide.

The therapeutic effectiveness of MAO inhibitors has not been demonstrated. Their use requires extremely careful con-trol of diet. Because of a variety of extremely harmful—even fatal—effects, interest in this medication has waned.

Panic States

When an individual suffers from recurrent, unexplained panic attacks with feelings of impending doom and as-sociated physical symptoms such as heart palpitations, sweating, dizziness, hot and cold flashes, diarrhea, vomiting, and breathing difficulties, Tofranil has proven most effective—even dramatically so. A common error is the use of antidepressant agents (e.g., Librium and Valium) alone.

Sleep Problems

Sleep problems include insomnia, the inability to remain asleep and early waking, as well as such other disturbances as nightmares, sleepwalking and talking while asleep. Fre-quently, these are related to a more general psychological disorder. (See the discussion in the chapter on Sleeping.) In the past, sedatives were prescribed for relief of these symptoms, but the dangers of addiction, abuse, and side effects have caused these drugs to be prescribed less readily. They have been replaced, for the most part, by the benzodiazepines (e.g., Valium), which do not entail such risks.

| Geriatric Medication | Medication for geriatric patients may try to relieve their sluggishness and apathy. Such stimulants as the pentylenetetrazols (e.g., Metrazol) may be effective, but their side effects are undesirable, especially with the old. First of all, they tend to suppress appetite, which may have serious consequences for patients who have difficulty in maintaining adequate nutrition. In addition, stimulants can aggravate a psychosis in a patient who may have some organic brain damage. It has been found that beer may serve adequately as an antiapathetic agent. It promotes increased socialization and also may provide a necessary nutritional supplement. |

| Alcoholism | Chemical treatment of alcoholism per se has not generally proven successful. Antabuse, however, can be used to keep the alcoholic from drinking, although it does not address the reasons or desire for drinking. If a person drinks alcohol after Antabuse, he or she develops truly noxious reactions: rapid heartbeat, fearfulness, headache, rapid breathing, nausea, vomiting, and fainting. These reactions may last for several hours. People on Antabuse should be carefully instructed about the dangers of alcohol in any form—in foods, industrial fumes, etc. For those who drink in order to relieve anxiety, a benzodiazepine antianxiety agent may be prescribed. |

| Placebos | A placebo, typically a sugar pill, is an inactive agent given to a patient who thinks it is a useful medication. Numerous recent studies, however, have shown that placebos have significant, lasting, and even physiological effects. Placebos have relieved pain in 30 to 40% of patients with headaches, arthritis, angina pectoris, and those recovering from surgery.

There seem to be biochemical explanations for the ability of placebos to relieve pain. Substances in the brain that inhibit pain are stimulated by the patient's reactions to the placebo administration. So too are other self-healing mechanisms, including interferon, which fight infections, and steroids that counter inflammation.

In other words, the holistic concept that mind and body continually interact and are, in fact, indistinguishable, seems supported by these placebo effects. After all, through the ages medicine has relied on the confidence of the patient (and the doctor) in the treatment of whatever kind—or in the placebo effect—to result in amelioration or cure.

Placebos even cause side effects characteristic of the real |

drug. Apparently, these side effects are neither "faked" nor mimicked, but rather are actual physiological consequences. Studies have shown that placebo responses are most likely to occur when the symptom being treated is severe, the anxiety high, and the patient has faith in the healer.

The implications for drug therapy (and perhaps nutritional regimes) seem clear. The results (good and bad, incidentally) may be occasioned by placebo responses. Rather than avoid these effects, it is wise to take advantage of them.

In recent years, lithium has been used in the treatment of acute mania. Because of the nature of the treatment and its possible fatal side effects, the administration of this drug must be carefully monitored by a physician and frequent tests must be taken to determine lithium levels in the blood.

Lithium

Lithium cannot be taken on an "as needed" basis, since administration requires long-term maintenance. In fact, the drug will not begin to have an effect until approximately five to ten days after treatment begins. Since mania, however, frequently occurs in episodes and then remits suddenly, it is important that someone suffering from the disturbance continue lithium treatment even while he or she is experiencing no symptoms. Often this is not done, because of the drug's side effects, which can include gastrointestinal difficulties, muscular weakness, sleepiness, dizziness, blurred vision, tremors, and possible seizures. Nevertheless, if the drug is taken, it is essential that the physician's instructions be followed faithfully and that frequent blood tests be done.

In ECT, an electric current of about 150 volts is passed between the temples of a patient for approximately two seconds. This induces a grand mal (epileptic) seizure. It is used primarily for the treatment of severe depression, although some forms of schizophrenias, especially catatonia, also respond. In the past, interest in this form of treatment was decreasing because of patients' dread of it, its occasional use as a punishment, and the physical injury, including broken bones, which the seizure may cause. Recently, however, ECT is being used again with precautions. The use of a muscle relaxant, for example, has reduced the chances of physical injury.

Electroconvulsive Treatment (ECT)

After the induced seizure, the electrical activity of the brain sharply decreases and then slowly returns to normal, often causing the initial depression to lift. Often, however, many treatments are necessary for this to happen. Immediately after treatment, the patient will experience confused thinking, disorientation, and a temporary amnesia. But these signs are reversible and disappear. The advantage of ECT is its relative quickness of effect, as compared with the two to four weeks required for the antidepressant drugs.

Summary

Although the range of human behavior is enormous, and although we are capable of doing things in any number of ways, we tend to settle into one pattern of behavior. When our way of life becomes unsatisfactory, anxiety-ridden, or downright painful, we may want to change, but this is a difficult and complex undertaking. Merely wishing that things were nicer is not sufficient. Instead, several preconditions must be met before we are in a position to really change ourselves.

The first step is becoming aware of how unsatisfactory our condition or state of mind really is, and then we must locate more precisely the source of our malaise. The second step is a real willingness to change. This means taking active responsibility for ourselves instead of passively wishing some person or pill would make things better. The third is our recognition that something must be given up. Even the most unsatisfactory or painful situations and attitudes involve certain benefits, even though they may be unconscious. We must recognize that the state we desire will not be perfect, but only a realistic, less imperfect compromise with reality. The fourth step is our willingness to commit ourselves to new ways of doing things. Often this involves anxiety, pain, disappointment, rejection, and frustration, but there is also an excitement and exhilaration in trying out new patterns of behavior. Finally, a process of restructuring occurs, in which we begin to see new possibilities and options. Real change can now follow, and if all these preconditions have been met, a new, enduring, productive, and satisfying behavior can result.

Often such a process requires or can be facilitated by seeking out professional help. There is a wide range of help available, but in choosing any kind of therapy, it is always wise to evaluate the competency, credentials, and concern of the therapist. Of these three, concern is by far the most important. In addition, a successful therapy depends on the commitment and motivation of the person seeking help. Merely attending sessions or listening passively to advice or interpretation will not solve any problems. Being in therapy is an active and committed undertaking.

Although various psychotherapies like to distinguish themselves from one another, their procedures are more similar than unlike. All involve a "talking cure" which offers the individual insight into his or her condition and habitual ways of doing things. Certain extreme forms of behavior modification and sensitivity training may dispense with most verbal procedures, however.

Group therapy is in certain ways more efficient in terms of money and also offers certain advantages. The group is a microcosm of the society and the family, and permits a person to try out new behaviors as well as learn how others see him or her. Encounter groups offer short-term, intense experiences which can be very helpful in coming to some understanding of oneself. But the experience can be injurious to a person who has no way of understanding and incorporating the powerful insights and experiences to be had there. Family therapy specializes in psychological difficulties that particularly involve the family. It is useful in opening up communication among members of a family and in uncovering the various neurotic games families often sink into.

Behavior modification bases its procedures on rigorous experimental findings. Although it has proven quite effective for the treatment of phobias, anxieties, and learning difficulties, it has been criticized for focussing only on symptoms and not paying sufficient attention to the whole person.

Marriage counseling is useful both for marriages that are in trouble and for those that are in reasonably good shape. The latter can be enriched by opening up channels of communication and revealing the viewpoint of each partner to the other. At times, however, counseling results in divorce. Sex therapy treats sexual dysfunctions and inadequacies and, as a result of recent liberalizations of attitudes and research, is quite effective at doing so.

There is a network of referral agencies that can recommend appropriate therapists. A wide variety of services is available in all cities and in community health centers. Hospitals, university medical centers, and even the phone book are places to start looking for help if no other sources of information are readily available.

13
Behavior
Disturbances

In this chapter, we are describing and discussing common behavior disorders. Treatments for the disorders in this complex and changing field vary; new drugs are constantly being developed, and new knowledge about their effects, particularly in relation to each other, is being discovered at a very rapid rate. Drugs—their effects and side effects—should be carefully discussed with the physician. Here we will only attempt to *familiarize* the reader with some of the most common forms of medication.

Childhood Disorders

Childhood reactions which seem maladaptive do not fall into clearly defined diagnostic categories. Consequently, in 1966 the Committee on Child Psychiatry of the Group for the Advancement of Psychiatry recommended the following working classifications: "healthy" reactions, reactive disorders, developmental deviations, and childhood psychoses.

"Healthy" Responses

This category emphasizes the normality and even appropriateness at certain ages of reactions that might be perceived as symptoms of pathology. For example: sucking in infants, mild separation anxiety exhibited by pre-school children, and frequent confusion of adolescents centering around identity and dependence—independence. (See the discussion of adolescence in the chapter on Stages.) Manifestations of such behaviors may be checked in textbooks of developmental psychology or with pediatricians, child psychologists, and child psychiatrists. It is important to realize that what might be "normal" for one child might not be so for another, particularly in light of varying developments and circumstances that individual children undergo.

Reactive Disorders

These are transient situational behaviors that represent reactions to particular events. Typical situations are illness, hospitalization, birth of siblings, loss of a parent, school pressures, and the attitudes and behaviors of peers. Specific symptoms include loss of appetite, passive or aggressive behavior, regressive enuresis (bed-wetting), unusual preoccupation with fantasy, and overt panic. Generally, reactive disorders are transient, but they can become chronic. Therefore, they need to be attended to, and if necessary, help sought.

Developmental Deviations

Developmental deviations are an interaction of maturational patterns and the experience of learning. As the child grows, these deviations fade away. Typical deviations include delayed speech, delayed toilet training, and poor coordination.

Symptoms may be expressed in hyperactivity, underactivity, impulsiveness, or apathy. The most common cognitive dysfunctions are reading disabilities and impaired proficiency in spelling, writing, and arithmetic. Socially, examples of deviation include shyness, lack of social skills, emotional immaturity, aggressive behavior, and the inability to relate effectively with peers.

Hyperactivity has become so prevalent or, at least so well known, that we are devoting special attention to it here. It is not clear whether it is genetically determined, due to some brain defect, inappropriate learning, specific reactions to dietary and environmental substances, or all of these factors. In any event, hyperactive children deal with life situations in a casual, superficial, and insufficiently focussed fashion. They may arrive at decisions impulsively and prematurely abandon tasks. They crave stimulation and attention, rush into relationships which they maintain superficially, and react to frustration with explosive anger or devious behavior. Often they suffer with respect to physical health, intellectual achievement, and personal relations.

It is not simply that these children move around a lot. Their movements are unpredictable or inconsistent. They are restless, inattentive, and distractable. Often they oppose structure with whining and tantrums, despite all threats and attempts at discipline. They tend to be emotionally unstable, frequently hurting themselves due to carelessness and curiosity. While they can be friendly, they often are grossly insensitive. It has been estimated that 5% of all elementary school children and perhaps as many as 50% of all school behavioral referrals are diagnosed hyperactive.

Stimulant drugs, such as benzedrine, dexadrine, and particularly ritalin have been widely used for hyperactivity. About 2% of these children receive such medication, and in certain groups the figure may be as high as 20%. It is claimed that if the child is properly selected and the dosage carefully administered, the troublesome behavior will disappear. Still, 40% of these children have adverse reactions to stimulant drugs. And even where medication is effective, the timing and duration of dosage must be meticulously suited to the individual. Long-term drug therapy administration, some say through adolescence and beyond, seems necessary for the most beneficial results. Reliance on drug therapy has been challenged by some, who claim that behavior therapy proves more effective in the long term than stimulants in dealing with these problems.

Although the symptoms of hyperactivity may diminish with age, a variety of secondary problems may develop early, persist across time, frequently get worse during adolescence, and seriously interfere with successful academic, social, and emotional development. It is probable that many factors influence the development of hyperactivity, although there may be a single causative factor such as brain injury or inconsistent discipline. What is more probable is an interaction of these factors with other possible ones such as reactions to certain foods, heredity, inhalation of such substances as lead, learning habits, and so on. In any event, the distress to the family is as marked as it is to the hyperactive child. Whatever the etiology, and whether medication is utilized or not, family counseling seems indicated. Much of the hyperactive child's behavior appears to be a reaction to frustration, caused sometimes by his or her physical and mental difficulties. Reinforcing the strengths of the child's positive achievements is all-important.

Recently, it has been proposed that much hyperactivity in children is caused by an allergic reaction either to a chemical found in certain fruits and in artificial food coloring or to sugar. Dr. Benjamin Feingold, a pediatrician, treated hyperactive children by eliminating this chemical from their diet and found an improvement rate of almost half. Subsequent careful studies have not been able to reproduce Dr. Feingold's findings. The evidence seems to indicate that such a complex disturbance is unlikely to be caused by such a simple allergic reaction, although some children benefit from such treatment.

Childhood Psychosis

Approximately 5% of all children under fifteen referred for psychological or psychiatric examination are diagnosed as psychotic—almost always as schizophrenic. The symptoms are severely impaired emotional relations, aloofness and preoccupation with inanimate objects, absence or poor development of speech, disturbance in sensory perception, bizarre behavior and coordination, unpredictable panic, and uneven or fragmented intellectual development.

The term *childhood schizophrenia* is applied to the psychotic behavior of children over five years of age who have regressed in adjustment, although some have manifested this behavior from their earliest months. Schizophrenics often begin their lives apparently normally before regressing at about age four or five. Many respond to long-term, intensive psychological treatment in specialized environments, but prognosis is poor. Childhood schizophrenics are very likely to be diagnosed as adult schizophrenics, but some are still able to function in society, even graduate from college, provided they receive life-long psychiatric support. (See the discussion of juvenile delinquency in the chapter on Stages.)

Infantile autism is a rare but dramatic disorder. There are estimated to be 4.5 cases for every 100,000 births. This condition begins shortly after birth and is detectable by the time the child is two or three years old. These children are usually healthy but characteristically do not begin to respond to the mother and other human beings. Instead, they often relate mechanically to inanimate objects. Speech patterns are bizarre, or speech is entirely absent. There even may be an absence of non-verbal communication. The child may echo like a parrot, reverse words and syllables, and respond with irrelevance. The child is also often extremely upset by the slightest variation of daily routine and environment. He or she may appear insensitive to light, sound, or pain, may bang his or her head, rock rhythmically, and resist any demand or request.

A combination of genetic, organic, and psychological factors seems implicated in autism. The psychological factors, specifically the personality of parents and their ability to relate to their children, are the most vague and probably only aggravate rather than cause autism. In fact, the child's initial inability to respond to his or her mother is likely to result in a high degree of anxiety and insecurity on the part of that parent. About 25% of these children make significant recoveries, and another 25% show some clinical improvement. But even those considered to have recovered continue to show serious impairment in human relationships and social skills and persist in acting in a markedly eccentric fashion. The procedures most often used with such children are permissive residential treatment programs and operant behavior modification.

Adult Psychosis

All the psychoses share the characteristic of a gross, chronic distortion of reality. Often these distortions are flagrant and are easily detected by others as psychotic behavior. Sometimes the convoluted thinking is more subtly expressed and remains concealed for long periods.

Schizophrenia

The basal rate of schizophrenia has been about 1% of the population. Schizophrenics constitute about 20% of all first admissions to public mental hospitals and 50% of their resident populations. Seventy-five percent of adult schizophrenics are diagnosed between the ages of fifteen and forty, with a peak between twenty-five and thirty-five.

These disorders (since schizophrenia seems to be a variety of related conditions) are characterized by gross disturbances in thinking, mood, and behavior. Schizophrenic people distort reality and sometimes experience delusions and hallucinations. In addition, they have frequent, radical mood changes, inappropriate emotional responses, and a lack of empathy with others. Behavior may be withdrawn, regressive, and bizarre. Theoretically, there are two kinds of schizophrenia. The first, process schizophrenia, begins relatively early in life, has a gradual onset, and is characterized by life-long maladjustment. The other, reactive schizophrenia, has a more sudden onset, often is triggered by a life crisis or the demands of the environment, and is preceded and often followed by a reasonably good adjustment. While both process and reactive schizophrenia may be genetically and organically determined, the latter may be induced, or at least aggravated, by psychological factors.

The introduction of phenothiazine drugs (e.g., chlorpromazine) in the 1950s revolutionized the treatment of schizophrenics. Approximately 75% of schizophrenics admitted to mental hospitals and treated with these drugs return to the community within a few months. Another 10% return after a longer stay. About a quarter make fairly successful adjustments. (See the discussion of the major tranquilizers in the chapter on Change.) Behavior modification has favorable results in terms of eliminating or minimizing specific symptoms. Sensitive therapists with extraordinary understanding, empathy, and patience can effect positive changes over a very long period, but this kind of treatment is extremely arduous.

Paranoid States

This is an extremely rare condition characterized by the gradual development of an elaborate system based on and often proceeding logically from the misinterpretation of an actual event. Frequently, paranoids consider themselves endowed with unique and superior abilities. Often their condition does not seem to interfere with the rest of their thinking and personalities.

The more common disorder, paranoid schizophrenia, is characterized primarily by the presence of persecutory or grandiose delusions, often associated with hallucinations. Excessive religiosity is sometimes found. Patients' attitudes are frequently hostile and aggressive, and their behavior tends to be consistent with their delusions. This is by far the most common of the schizophrenias and is the condition usually suffered by those who are implicated in anti-social and bizarre behavior, often of a violent nature.

Manic-Depressive Psychosis

This condition is characterized by extreme mood swings from excessive elation, hyperactivity, accelerated speech, and flight of ideas to a pervasive mood of sadness, motor retardation, poverty of ideas, and retardation of mental activity. The psychosis is differentiated from neurotic or personality disorders by its gross distortions of reality as well as extreme mood shifts. Characteristics of grandiosity, preoccupations with magic and numbers, hilarity, and excessive sexuality are not uncommon in this condition. Interestingly, many so-called normal individuals can be swept up in the wild, manic schemes of these psychotics.

About 13% of all first admissions to state mental hospitals were diagnosed as manic depressives in 1933, but only 2% were so diagnosed by 1968, probably because of refined diagnostic procedures. Initial attacks may occur between the ages of twenty to sixty, peaking in the late thirties. The manic phase (and there may not necessarily be a shift from manic to depressive) is characterized by bursts of energy, euphoria, irritability, and rage. The person seems to be rushing off in all directions at once. Loss of weight and physical exhaustion are common. The depressive reaction consists of feelings of sadness, helplessness, despair, guilt, low esteem, apathy and psychomotor retardation. Attempts at suicide are frequent.

Electric shock treatment has proven effective in reducing the duration of depressive moods, and lithium has been quite successful in mitigating acute manic states. Lithium treatment, however, carries certain risks, and may even be fatal. (See the discussions of lithium and electroconvulsive treatment in the chapter on Change.) When lithium is used, the patient must be under a doctor's watchful supervision to ensure his or her well-being.

An interesting line of recent research has interpreted manic depressive disorders as resulting from a disruption in the functioning of certain "biological clocks." In normal individuals, the cycle of activity and resting, on a daily as well as long-term basis, is controlled by biological processes that work through the body's hormonal system, among others. In manic depressives, it seems that these monitoring and controlling processes are not synchronized with each other or the environment. Treatment, which is still in preliminary stages, involves altering the rate of active and resting cycles. Drugs called tricyclic antidepressants speed up the cycle, while those like lithium slow it down. Future research will attempt to control these cycles more subtly and regularly. In any case, although the most overt symptoms of manic depression are psychological and behavioral, the most promising lines of treatment currently are more chemical and metabolic.

Psychotic Depression

Unlike the depressive phase of manic depressive psychosis, psychotic depressive reactions seem to be related to a significant loss or misfortune. The overreaction to such calamity (often a disappointment rather than a catastrophe) is marked and may far outlast the triggering event. Thus, a predisposition for such a depression appears probable. There are exaggerated feelings of guilt, sin, and deterioration approaching bizarre proportions. Suicidal preoccupation is extremely prevalent, and attempts are common.

Involutional melancholia occurs between the ages of forty-five and sixty-five. It is associated, at least chronologically, with the climacteric period, and in women the changes occasioned by menopause have been assumed to be a contributory factor. Certainly, a change of roles and/or any inability to function as before have a bearing for many. Thus, rigid compulsive personalities tend to be more prone to this disorder. Both before and during involutional melancholia, agitation, insomnia, somatic symptoms, and feelings of guilt prevail and symptoms are further aggravated by delusions during the acute phase.

About 80% of psychotic depressive reactions remit spontaneously in about nine months. To reduce the acute suffering, the threat to health, and the risk of suicide, psychotropic drugs and electric shock treatment can be used. In any event, both supportive and explorative psychotherapy are indicated as follow-up treatment.

We are including *suicide* in our discussion of depression, even though not all suicides are depressed. Of course, an extremely high rate of suicide is to be found among people who are depressed, but there are many reasons why people want to kill themselves. They include extreme and real conditions of hopelessness or a painful terminal disease, although what is considered hopeless is often psychologically colored. Not all suicides, therefore, are provoked by depression or the inability to cope with stress, disappointment, or feelings of anger and frustration.

A conservative estimate has it that there are two suicides every hour in the United States. Suicide is the tenth leading cause of death among adults and third among college students. Three times as many men kill themselves as women, although three times as many women attempt it as men. It is affected by social norms and conditions. Protestants are more likely to commit suicide than Jews, Jews more likely than Catholics. There are more suicides in years of economic depression, fewer during war.

Contrary to common belief, most people who commit suicide do give warning signals, either by an overt threat or by general ruminations about the possibility. Those who attempt suicide and fail may succeed later on. There are no reliable statistics on rates of suicides, since they depend on reported data. It is anyone's guess how many suicides go unreported or how many automobile fatalities, accidents, or drug and alcohol related deaths represent clear or covert attempts to end one's life.

Suicide may represent an attempt simply to end one's life or to escape an intolerable situation or disappointment, frustration, shame, or ambivalence. It may also be an attempt to punish the self as a result of turning anger in on the self. Conversely, it may be directed at causing guilt in those who are left behind, or it can be a desperate attempt to get some measure of attention. All suicide attempts are serious and should be attended to, but often the payoff to such a threat or attempt is the panic and concern it causes in others. The causes for such behavior lie very deep, are complex, and most often cannot be handled by those directly involved. Suicide hot lines can be contacted in almost every university or mental health center and can serve as initial interceptors, but once the danger has passed, professional help should be sought in all cases involving even the threat of a suicide.

Neurosis

The essential characteristic of neurosis is the experience of chronic or periodic anxiety or the employment of defenses against this anxiety. Symptoms may be the expression of unsuccessful coping with anxiety, or secondarily, the means of securing gratification and maintaining security. We all suffer to some degree from neurotic behavior. Estimates of the incidence of chronic neurosis vary considerably, but the authors believe a conservative guess would place it from one-third to two-thirds of the population. The pressures of an increasingly technical and troubled world would amost dictate psychological defenses that result in neurotic stress.

Anxiety Neurosis

This neurosis is characterized by anxious over-concern, extending to panic and frequently associated with somatic symptoms. The symptoms are not necessarily related to any specific threat or danger, but the trigger may be some unconscious personal, social or interpersonal stimulus. Anxiety may reach panic proportions and can involve sweating, dizziness, hot and cold flashes, diarrhea, vomiting, rapid heart beat, fainting, and fear of death. Tricyclic drugs, especially imipramine (Tofranil), usually provide immediate relief. Behavior modification techniques stressing relaxation and desensitization are also helpful. To uncover the causes and resolve the condition, first supportive and then uncovering psychotherapy is recommended.

Hysterical Neurosis	This disorder is characterized by the involuntary loss or impairment of some function without an adequate organic cause being present. Symptoms characteristically begin and end in emotionally charged situations and are symbolic of the underlying conflicts. They often can be modified by suggestion or placebos. In conversion hysteria, the senses or motor functions are affected, causing such symptoms as blindness, deafness, anesthesias, and paralysis. The hysterical person often seems amazingly unconcerned over the symptoms and seems to derive some secondary benefit, as receiving sympathy or being relieved of responsibility. In dissociations, there are altered states of consciousness including amnesia, sleepwalking, and confused identity. Psychotropic drugs can provide a calming effect, but extensive psychotherapy is indicated.
Phobias	This condition is characterized by intense fear of an object or situation which the person consciously recognizes as representing no real danger. For example, there are phobias of high places, open places, closed places, of darkness, crowds, or animals. Antianxiety agents, particularly the benzodiazepines, may significantly reduce the anxiety. Behavior modification, employing schedules of decreasing threat, are most successful with phobic reactions. Sometimes, merely reconditioning the responses to the threatening stimuli ameliorates the condition. In all probability, however, the relevance to the person's over-all psychological functioning is involved and requires exploration for persistent relief and the avoidance of new symptoms.
Obsessive Compulsive Neurosis	This disorder is characterized by the persistent intrusion of unwanted thoughts, urges, or actions that the person is unable to stop. The actions may vary from simple movements to complex rituals such as handwashing. If the person is prevented from performing the action or completing the thought, he or she suffers marked distress. Medication is often not helpful, save as an aid in relaxation. This condition is among the most successfully treated by psychoanalysis and is amenable to the various psychodynamic approaches, although treatment often lasts for years.
Depressive Neurosis	These are mood disorders in which anxiety is often mixed with guilt. Symptoms generally include dejection, helplessness, self-deprecation, hopelessness, restlessness, irritability, insomnia, and loss of appetite. They are usually precipitated by some identifiable loss or failure. Two major categories of antidepressant drugs are the tricyclics (e.g., Tofranil) and

MAO inhibitors (e.g., Parnate and Nardil). When employed with knowledge of the depressed person's over-all physical and psychological history, and in a consistent manner, they have produced considerable alleviation of depressed conditions. Nevertheless, psychotherapy, at least in conjunction with medication, is indicated for long-term results and lack of dependency on drugs.

Although not necessarily a neurosis, *post partum depression* is experienced by some women shortly after the birth of a baby. A variety of factors seem to play a part. First, physical and metabolic changes have been taking place in the mother. For approximately nine months, her physical status has been geared for the nourishment of two individuals, the fetus and herself. After delivery, her biology is suited for the nursing of the infant. This involves such consequences as the suppression of sexual arousal and ovulation. In addition, it has recently been found that the pregnant woman and the new mother have fetal cells and other substances from the fetus in their bloodstreams. It is not known what effect this has on the mother. These changing physical conditions in themselves may dispose the new mother to a depressive reaction. In interaction with psychological factors, there is a greater possibility of such a consequence.

The sheer recognition by a young woman who may not have yet accepted separation from her own mother that she is totally responsible for the life and welfare of a fragile human being may be shattering. The illusion that she still will be mothered must be surrendered for the reality of her responsibility for mothering the infant. This sense of responsibility can be aggravated by a compulsive personality, one which strives for perfection out of guilt or a need to control the environment. The birth of the baby and all that follows—feedings, diapers, and late night wakenings—confront the mother with a change of life style. Gone are the relatively carefree days. New roles must be assumed. This can be very depressing for some new mothers.

The physiological and metabolic factors in post partum depression can best be attended to with medical supervision which may well prescribe special diets and exercise. Preparation for baby care—which includes careful planning for the responsibilities but also such considerations as living space, financial factors, babysitting, role of the husband, recreation, and so on—may forestall post partum depression. Training in such preparation is available at some YWCAs and in conjunction with various hospital maternity programs. Support through the transition period by family, especially the husband, can be all-important. Paid help, if it can be afforded, can be most useful.

The same concatenation of factors—physical, psychological, treatment, and prevention—apply for the mid-life condition, involutional melancholia.

Neuresthenic Neurosis

This condition is characterized by complaints of chronic weakness, persistent fatigue, and sometimes exhaustion. Unlike hysterical neurosis, the person's complaints are genuinely distressing to him or her, and there is no evidence of secondary gain. It is most important to differentiate this condition from one that has such organic involvement as metabolic and dietary insufficiencies. Supportive psychotherapy can prove helpful.

Hypochondriacal Neurosis

This condition is characterized by preoccupation with the body and with a fear of presumed disease. The person is neither delusional nor suffering a loss of function as in hysterical neurosis, but the preoccupation persists despite reassurance. Psychotherapy, whether behavior modification or psychodynamic, is indicated.

Existential Neurosis

The characteristics of this condition are a pervasive sense of the meaningless of one's life, loneliness, apathy, boredom, and aimlessness. The disorder is often precipitated when environmental changes (such as graduation from high school or college, a move from the family, the birth of a child, or the death of a family member) require adaptation. There is reason to believe that prior to this condition, the person had assumed various roles, but had not integrated any value system of his or her own. Psychodynamic therapy, particularly existential and humanistic approaches, is recommended.

Depersonalization Neurosis

This is a dreamlike state of haziness and estrangement. Everything seems unreal, and the person is uncertain of the boundaries separating the self from the world. There is a sense of detachment. A brief experience of depersonalization, however, is not necessarily a symptom of this neurosis.

Personality Disorders

Psychology generally views the varieties of human behavior as existing on a continuum from healthy and normal through neurotic to psychotic at the furthest extreme. The range between normal and neurotic is occupied by the so-called personality disorders. It is often difficult to distinguish them from the neuroses, and in fact, the specific kinds of personality disorders correspond to the specific kinds of neuroses. Generally speaking, the former are characterized by deeply engrained maladaptive behaviors or large flaws in the personality. These may involve marked defects in characteristic modes of responding to situations, self-awareness, perceptions, evaluation, or general orientation.

Personality disorders, then, are not a discrete category of pathology, but a vaguer range of behavior. They do, however, share certain characteristics. People suffering from them characteristically show a restricted and repetitious pattern of behavior, which is manifested in all sorts of situations, no matter how inappropriate and self-defeating. Most frequently, those who have a personality disorder are not particularly disturbed by their condition. It seems normal to them. Consequently, they rarely seek therapy on their own, and if they are pressured to do so by others, they are frequently uncooperative and unresponsive.

All human behavior is influenced by cultural norms. Consequently, some personality disorders are more frequent in certain sub-cultures that reward, encourage, or even require behavior that seems maladaptive and self-defeating in the larger society. The fact that someone has a personality disorder does not mean he or she will go on to develop a more serious neurosis or psychosis. But since such behavior is maladaptive, such people are prone to stress, which if severe, can cause a person to break as he or she is driven to more and more extreme forms of his or her abnormal behavior. Similarly, normal individuals under strain or unusual circumstances can develop behavior that seems characteristic of the personality disorder. But most people are more flexible and adaptive. What is characteristic of the personality disorder is its rigid, unchanging, and stereotypical nature.

The categories of the personality disorders are based on the divisions made in the neuroses and psychoses. The *paranoid personality* is characterized by excessive and unwarranted suspicion, distrust, envy, hypersensitivity, and self-importance, all of which result in a striving for self-reliance and independence. The *schizoid personality* shows a marked detachment from reality, although he or she does not lose touch with it. Such an individual is typically shy, reserved, emotionally cold, spending much time and energy in daydreams, and avoiding real contact and intimacy with others. The *explosive personality* shows a characteristic instability. Although seemingly normal in most circumstances, when frustrated he or she loses control and engages in violent aggressive behavior, which strongly recalls infantile tantrums. Later, the person frequently regrets his or her outburst, but seems unable to control future outbursts. The *obsessive-compulsive personality* shows a high degree of rigidity, neatness, and conformity. He or she insists on perfection and regularity and emphasizes these requirements in eating, sleeping, and other bodily functions. The *hysterical personality* is more common in women, particularly adolescent girls, but is found in men also. Such people are self-dramatizing, excitable, and are role players. Often they seem to be outrageous flirts, although such behavior is not intended to tease or frustrate. Instead, it is a maladaptive attempt to secure the interest of others around them.

Organic Brain Syndromes

Most of the mental disorders we have been discussing have been caused or at least largely aggravated by emotional events—a disruptive early familial experience, chronic or acute stress that could not be coped with adequately, maladaptive learning. Of course, many of these conditions may have had an organic disorder as their bases, but emotional factors have also been important. Consequently, psychotherapy can be useful in their treatment. Another class of disorders, however, is caused entirely by injury or deterioration of the brain. They are called organic brain syndromes, because they are caused by a deficit in the physical organ of the brain. They may result in symptoms of emotional disturbances, but are not caused by them.

Approximately one-quarter of all first admissions to mental hospitals involve an organic brain syndrome. Approximately one-third of these patients are over the age of seventy-five. Thus, the incidence of brain damage is very high for the old. Symptoms can include any or all of the following. The individual can suffer an impairment of his or her sense of orientation and be confused about who or where he or she is, or may lose track of time. His or her memory can be affected, particularly for recent events. Thus, the individual may have vivid and accurate memories of his or her earlier life, but be unable to remember what happened yesterday or fifteen minutes ago. Intellectual functions may also be impaired, and he or she may experience difficulty in understanding, learning, or making plans. Finally, emotional functioning may be disrupted, and the person may show either flattened or exaggerated emotional responses.

In general, the major characteristic of brain damage is the effect on cognitive functions. But because the personality is a complex and unified whole, emotional difficulties may follow as a secondary consequence of cognitive dysfunction. Thus, a person suffering from memory impairment may resort to patent lies and falsifications to make up for gaps in his or her memory. Similarly, some people may be thrown into a panic when they find they are unable to function normally. Tearfulness and hopelessness may also result from the recognition of sudden or encroaching helplessness. Finally, bizarre emotional behavior can be the primary result of brain damage to certain centers of the brain concerned with emotions.

Brain damage can be caused by several events, either sudden or of long duration. Infection, as from encephalitis or syphilis, can cause the selective degeneration of certain places in the brain. With syphilis particularly, it is imperative to detect this disease early so that it can be treated before irreversible damage is done. A physical blow can also damage vital parts of the brain, as can prolonged nutritional deficiencies. *Korsakoff's psychosis*, characterized by loss of recent memory and consequent transparent lying, is frequently caused by the chronic malnutrition experienced by chronic alcoholics. Tumors and strokes may also result in the loss of certain functions. There may be global paralysis or an extremely circumscribed deficit, such as an inability to write, while the ability to read remains intact. Many of these disabilities due to stroke are amenable to successful therapy, depending on the age and motivation of the person suffering from them.

Certain organic diseases are related to advancing age and involve a deterioration of the brain. These may begin in the forties, although quite rarely, in which case they are known as *presenile dementias*. In *Alzheimer's disease*, there is rather rapid brain degeneration. It begins with difficulty in concentration, procedes to absent-mindedness and a failure of memory. The sufferer blames others for his or her difficulties and suffers corresponding delusions. Death follows in four to five years. In *Pick's disease*, the total weight of the brain may be reduced by almost a quarter. The patient has difficulties with memory and abstractions as well as with speech. His or her affect becomes blunted and he or she suffers depressions. Death follows in four to seven years. *Huntington's chorea* usually begins in the thirties and is genetically determined. The offspring of a person with this disease have a 50% chance of suffering it themselves. Early symptoms are slovenliness and disregard for social convention. Emotional outbursts, euphoria, and suicidal ideas also develop, as do involuntary jerky movements. Finally, there is total loss of bodily control, and although death follows, it may be delayed for up to twenty years. *Parkinson's disease* is caused by the degeneration of a group of nerve cells in the brain that help control muscular movement. Its symptoms are tremors in muscles that are at rest, muscular rigidity and a general masklike lack of expression on the face. Depression and intellectual impairment may also follow. This disease can be treated by providing the damaged cells with the chemical they cannot produce naturally.

In true *senility*, or *senile dementia*, general functioning begins to deteriorate. Beginning with a general carelessness about appearance and social convention, there is a developing impairment of memory, alertness, coherence, and a growing rigidity. Senile people become depressed, spend much time in reverie and memory, lose contact with the social world, and may become psychotic. Although the immediate causes are organic brain degeneration, the incidence of senility has been correlated with previous social isolation. Old people who keep active and involved with others stand a smaller chance of becoming senile.

Human behavior can be arranged on a continuum from the normal and healthy through the neurotic to the psychotic. The divisions we make are not really discrete categories, but convenient ways of understanding and dealing with the varieties of human behavior. All people are neurotic in some aspects of their lives, and under sufficient stress, almost all people will "break."

Behavioral disorders of childhood can be divided into several rough categories. "Healthy" responses are those behaviors that, while normal at certain stages, may indicate pathology at others. Individual rates of development make this an extremely difficult category to apply accurately. Reactive disorders are abnormal behaviors occasioned by particular events such as illness, separation, loss, or some other disruption. While they are usually transient, they can become chronic and genuinely pathological. Developmental deviations most often involve delayed learning, although social skills and the ability to relate to others may be involved. Hyperactivity is another common form that has been treated by drugs as well as psychotherapy.

Childhood psychoses account for 5% of all children under fifteen referred for psychological problems. Childhood schizophrenics seem normal for the first four or five years, but they regress. Many are later diagnosed as adult schizophrenics, although with treatment, they are able to function in society. Infantile autism is a rare condition in which an infant does not show the usual responses to human contact. Instead, autistic children seem most content with inanimate objects and repeated, mechanical routines. Many of these infants improve with treatment, although most show serious impairment in their emotional development.

The most common form of adult psychosis in the United States is schizophrenia, which is most likely a variety of related conditions. It is characterized by distortions of reality and gross disturbances in thinking, mood, and behavior, often involving delusions and hallucinations. Process schizophrenia begins rather early in life and has a slow and insidious development. Prognosis for cure is poor. Reactive schizophrenia, on the other hand, is a reaction to a particular event, although the preconditions for this development probably lie deep in the personality. Chances for a reasonably good adjustment are rather good. Other adult psychoses include: paranoid states, which involve delusions of persecution or grandiosity; manic depression, which involves alternating cycles of extreme elation and equally extreme depression; and depression. These conditions are treated by a variety of psychotherapeutic, chemical, and behavior modification techniques.

The neuroses all involve the experience of acute anxiety or extreme unconscious defenses taken against it. Anxiety neurosis is characterized by extreme anxiety attacks, often extending to panic. Hysterical neurosis involves the loss of some function—blindness or paralysis, for example—which is caused by no real organic disturbance. The phobias are intense fears of objects or situations that the individual recognizes as posing no real danger. The obsessive-compulsive neurosis involves the persistence of intrusion of unwanted thoughts or urges or the need to repeat some behavior or ritual, such as handwashing. Depressive neurosis is characterized by the experience of anxiety mixed with guilt and feelings of worthlessness. Neuresthenia is the chronic feeling of weakness, fatigue, and exhaustion without an organic basis for these symptoms. Hypochondria is the excessive preoccupation with the body and disease. Existential neurosis is a pervasive feeling of meaninglessness, loneliness, boredom, and anomie. Depersonalization neurosis involves a dreamlike feeling of haziness and detachment.

The personality disorders occupy the range between the neurotic and the normal. They involve deeply engrained and stereotyped maladaptive behaviors and manifest an inability to change the way one does things or the way one views the self or the world. The varieties correspond to the divisons of the neuroses and the psychoses. Thus the paranoid personality shows excessive and chronic suspicion and envy. The schizoid personality is markedly detached from reality. The explosive personality, although he may regret his emotional outbursts, seems incapable of controlling them when he is frustrated. The obsessive-compulsive personality shows a high degree of rigidity, neatness and conformity. And the hysterical personality, more common in women than men, is excitable, overdramatic and role-playing.

Organic brain syndromes are impairments of function— cognitive, emotional, learning, or behavioral—that are caused by brain damage. Such damage can be caused by infection, injury, or degeneration of brain cells. Impairment to functioning can be very local and limited or diffuse and global. Often, these syndromes result in a secondary emotional disturbance. The most common are such presenile dementias as Alzheimer's disease, Pick's disease, Huntington's chorea and Parkinson's disease. Senility is a special case of brain degeneration brought on by old age in some people, although habits of activity and stimulation seem to contribute to many cases.

Glossary of Psychopharmaceuticals

By Milton R. Bronstein, MD

Below are listed some of the most commonly used medications for mental problems from anxiety to psychosis. The medications are listed by trade names and by groups. The smallest dose for maintenance therapy is recommended. New "tranquilizers" are approved yearly by the score. All medications should not be used by persons driving or in hazardous occupations. These medications cause some decrease in awareness, alertness, reaction time, etc. You are referred to texts for a more complete list of complications. The standard texts are listed in the bibliography.

Patient compliance is most important. Your physician can prescribe medications as he or she feels you need them, but patients control whether or not they decide to take the medication. You as the patient must decide if you want to take the medication and whether or not you will take it as prescribed (one, two, three, or four times a day). You are free to and *should* let your physician know *whether* or *not* you take your medication. This is most important. It is not wise to play games with your health. Do not play games with your physician. Make him or her aware of your feelings.

You should tell your physician and therapist of any other medications you take, including alcohol, aspirin, Tylenol, medications for thyroid, blood pressure, diabetes, heart conditions, etc. This is most important, since many medications may act adversely with tranquilizers. *Remember: as a general and important rule, alcoholic beverages are contraindicated with all tranquilizers.* The action in most cases is cumulative (more potent than the tranquilizers alone or alcohol alone).

If you or a member of your family or a friend is given a medication for nervousness, anxiety, depression, etc., you can look up the medication by trade name in the index and check out what may occur and how the medication works, if this is known. Any side reactions, precautions, and symptoms should be checked to determine if any unusual feelings are related to the medication or other medical problems. Most of the following medications are used routinely, but the complications may be either common or rare. It is known that people react differently to any type of treatment. The listing and information below is not to be used as a guide, but mainly as a *reference*.

After reading some of this you may appreciate your physician's predicament in prescribing medications; the benefit must outweigh the risk. Overuse is to be avoided at all costs. Do not be angry with your physician if he or she will not supply you with more medicine than you should be taking in a week or two. I personally keep very close tabs on the amount of medication supplied to those who are in need of help. I find that many patients find it convenient to overdose themselves. The false theory many use is "if some is good, more is better."

Where feasible, the following medications are grouped into chemically similar families. The reactions are similar. Some preparations in the same group may have advantages or disadvantages over others. Of necessity, the physician takes this into consideration when prescribing.

As a general rule, I advise my patients to store *all* medications out of reach of children. I also emphasize cleaning out medicine cabinets periodically and throwing out all medications when they are not actively being taken. Purses should be treated the same way as medicine cabinets — pocketbooks present a very exciting adventure for children.

Ativan, Librium, Serax, Valium, Azene

Main use: To reduce anxiety.

Contraindications and precautions:
1. Not to be used in patients with sensivity (allergy).
2. Not to be used in patients with glaucoma (acute narrow angle).
3. Drug addicts and alcoholics may become addicted.
4. Not to be used during pregnancy or by nursing mothers and children.
5. Not to be used with alcohol or barbiturates.
6. Not to be used when driving or working with dangerous machinery.
7. Possibility of suicide.
8. Not to be used by patients with impaired kidney or liver function.
9. Blood counts and liver function tests are periodically necessary when on medication long-term (months).

Possible complications:
1. Low white blood count.
2. Sedation, tiredness, sleepiness.
3. Dizziness and unsteadiness.

4. Disorientation, depression, nausea, vomiting, diarrhea, change in appetite, headache.
5. Sleep disturbance, agitation.
6. Skin rashes.
7. Inability to focus eyes.
8. With overdosage: somnolence, confusion, coma, low blood pressure.
9. In patients with liver impairment, the medication will not be 'broken down' chemically for utilization by the body. This will result in excess medication in the blood, such a high blood concentration is thus an overdose. The same problem may be expected in persons with impaired kidney function. If the medication is excreted by the kidney and the kidney is not excreting waste products as it should, an excess of the medication will remain in the blood stream and thereby cause an overdose of medication.
10. Abrupt withdrawal may increase symptoms for which patient is being treated (anxiety, agitation, irritability, tension, insomnia, and occasional convulsions).
11. Withdrawal symptoms may occur when discontinuing: convulsions, tremor, abdominal and muscle cramps, vomiting, and sweating.

Main use: For sedation. Anticonvulsant, depressant.

Dosage: ½ grain to 3 grains per day.

Barbiturates (Seconal, Nembutal, and others)

Contraindications and precautions:
1. Not to be used with alcohol.
2. Not to be used while driving or working in hazardous occupations.
3. Not to be used in patients with allergy to any barbiturate.
4. Not to be used with other tranquilizers.
5. Not recommended for patients with recent head injuries.
6. To be used with care in kidney or liver disorders.
7. Not to be used during child delivery, may manifest disorders to the brain, or lung and heart abnormalities of newborn.
8. To be used with precaution by people with liver and kidney problems.

Possible complications:
1. Drowsiness, tiredness, sleepiness, dizziness, weakness.
2. Overdosage is common and requires prompt treatment.
3. Constipation.
4. Addiction and dependence possible.
5. May depress respiration or other brain functions.
6. May lower blood pressure.

Haldol (Haloperidol)

Main use: Manifestations of psychotic problems. Also to control tics and vocal utterances (Gilles de la Touretts' syndrome).

Dosage: 0.5 mg. to 5 mg. depending on severity of symptoms.

Contraindications and precautions:

1. Not to be used in patients with severe depression or in a coma.
2. Not to be used with alcohol.
3. Not to be used with medications which cause depression as a symptom.
4. Not to be used in patients who have Parkinsonism.
5. Not to be used in patients with allergy to Haldoperidol.
6. Not to be used during pregnancy and for children.
7. Not to be used with Lithium.
8. Not to be used with medications that prevent convulsions.
9. Not to be used when performing hazardous tasks or driving a motor vehicle.
10. To be used with care in people with heart disease. (May cause low blood pressure, chest pain.) Not to be used with Adrenalin-type medication, since it will block these medications.
11. To be used with extreme caution with anticoagulants (blood thinners).
12. Not to be discontinued abruptly.
13. Not to be used in patients with muscle spasm and hyperthyroid (overactive thyroid).

Possible complications:

1. Extrapyramidal reactions, even on low doses (the higher the dose, the greater the problem).
2. Restlessness of body muscles.
3. Tardive dyskinesia symptoms.
4. Insomnia, anxiety, agitation, drowsiness, depression, headache, confusion, dizziness, seizures ("fits"), and hallucinations.
5. Fast heart beat and/or low blood pressure.
6. Low white blood count, anemia, and other blood abnormalities (checked by blood count).
7. Abnormal liver tests and/or jaundice.
8. Skin rashes and loss of hair.
9. Breast enlargement, menstrual irregularities, impotence or increased libido, high or low blood sugar.
10. Loss of appetite, constipation, diarrhea, "acid" stomach, nausea and vomiting.
11. Dry mouth, blurred vision, excessive sweating, inability to pass urine.
12. Tightening of throat, larynx, and bronchial tubes.

Main use: Manic episodes of manic-depressive illness. **Lithium**

Dosage: 200 mg. to 600 mg. or 10 ml. (2 tsp.) three times a day. Blood level between .6 and 1.2 meq/l. level is measured periodically to avoid overdose.

Contraindications and precautions:
1. Not to be used during pregnancy or for children.
2. To be used with care when on diuretics (medication that increases urine excretion), since this can increase the concentration in serum (the blood).
3. To be used with care in kidney or urinary excretion problems since Lithium is mainly excreted in the urine, and may build up in high concentrations in the blood.
4. Adequate fluid intake necessary (2 to 3 quarts of fluid per 24 hours).
5. Diarrhea, excess sweating, or high temperature may increase concentrations in the blood.
6. To be used with care in combination with other tranquilizers (or anti-psychotic medications).

Possible complications:
1. Fine hand tremor, increased urination, nausea, and thirst (may disappear after 1 to 2 weeks on medication).
2. Diarrhea, vomiting, drowsiness, muscular weakness, and lack of coordination may be early signs of overdose.
3. At higher levels may cause giddiness, loss of balance, blurred vision, ringing in ears, and increased urine output.
4. Twitching of muscles, uncontrolled hand movements, blackouts, seizures, slurred speech, uncontrolled loss of urine and feces.
5. Irregular heart beat, low blood pressure, and collapse.
6. Elevated sugar in urine.
7. Drying and thinning of hair, numbness of skin.
8. Blurred vision, dry mouth, tiredness, tendency to sleep, weight loss.
9. Changes in thyroid blood tests, changes in electrocardiograms (ECG) and electroencephalograms (EEG).
10. Headaches, high blood sugar, itching with or without rash, skin ulcers (sores), excessive weight gain, swelling of ankles or wrists, coldness of hands or feet.

Main use: Antidepressant. Recommended for depression not helped or for patients who cannot take the tricyclic group of medications. **MAO Inhibitors: (Marplan, Nardil, Parnate) Monamine Oxidase Inhibitor**

Dosage: 30mg. per day to start and reduced to 10 to 20 mg. as soon as improvement is noted.

Contraindications and precautions:

1. Not to be used in patients with allergy to medication.
2. Not to be used in patients with severe liver and/or kidney problems.
3. Not to be used in patients with heart failure.
4. Not to be used with amphetamines, epinephrine, and drugs in this group.
5. Not to be used with foods such as broad beans, cheese, beer, wines, pickled herring, chicken liver, yeast extract, and excessive amounts of caffeine. These can all cause severe high blood pressure, which may be fatal.
6. Not to be used in patients who are going to have elective surgery requiring general anesthesia. Discontinue 10 days prior to surgery.
7. Not to be used with alcohol or barbiturates.
8. To be avoided in elderly people, especially with high blood pressure, heart and brain circulatory diseases.
9. Not to be used with common cold and hay fever medications.
10. Not to be used for children under 16 years of age or in pregnancy or while breast feeding.
11. Not recommended for use with other psychotropic medications.
12. To be used with caution in combination with medications for high blood pressure.
13. Should be discontinued with high blood pressure symptoms (headaches, palpitations, etc.).
14. If a change in medication is needed, the MAO inhibitors should be stopped for at least 10 days before other medication is begun.
15. Liver function should be monitored by blood tests.
16. To be used with care in diabetes, since low blood sugars are possible.

Possible complications:

1. Hypertensive crisis (sudden and severe rise in blood pressure). Collapse, brain hemorrhage, severe headache, nausea, vomiting, eyes sensitive to light, sweating, elevated temperature, coldness, clamminess, palpitations, fast or slow heart rate, and chest pain. Low blood pressure also possible.
2. Combination with other tranquilizers may produce hypertension, excitation, delerium, tremor, twitching, convulsions, and coma.
3. Jaundice and hepatitis.
4. With epilepsy may have increased or decreased seizures.
5. May cause excess stimulation or agitation.
6. Dizziness, loss of balance, constipation, muscle twitching, confusion, memory impairment, inability to sleep,

weakness, fatigue, dry mouth, blurred vision, loss of
appetite, skin rashes, intestinal disturbance (nausea,
vomiting), black tongue, coma, involuntary loss of
urine or inability to pass urine, sexual disturbances,
and hallucinations.

Main use: To reduce tension, anxiety.

**Meprobamate,
Miltown, Equanil**

Dosage: 200 – 400 mg. three to four times a day.

Contraindications and precautions:
1. Not to be used in patients with allergy.
2. Not to be used in patients with diagnosed intermittent
   porphyria.
3. Possible drug dependence and abuse.
4. Not to be used with alcohol.
5. Reduce dosage slowly.
6. Not to be used when driving or in hazardous occupations.
7. Not to be used in pregnancy.
8. Not to be used for children.
9. Not to be used in patients with liver and kidney mal-
   function.

Possible complications:
1. Loss of equilibrium, slurred speech, dizziness, overstimulation.
2. Nausea, vomiting, diarrhea.
3. Palpitations, fast heart beat, irregular rhythm, low
   blood pressure, fainting.
4. Allergic itching, rash.
5. Decreased white blood cells (by blood count), hemorrhage, black and blue marks, swelling of hands and
   feet, elevated temperature, enlarged glands, high temperature, chills, hives, decreased urination, and inflammation of rectum, tongue, and skin.
6. Withdrawal symptoms: vomiting, tremors, muscle
   twitching, confusion, hallucinations, and seizures.

*Main use: To reduce excitement, agitation, tension, depression,
and for alcohol withdrawal and intractable pain.*

**Phenothiazenes
(Mellaril, Stelazine,
Thorazine, Trilafon,
Prolixin,
Compazine)**

*Dosage: 25 to 100 mg. three times a day to maximum of 800 mg.
per day if needed (Mellaril). Other medications used in different dosages.*

Contraindications and precautions:
1. Not to be used in patients with severe nervous system
   depression or coma.

2. Not to be used in patients with high or low blood pressure.
3. Not to be used in patients with hypersensitivity, allergy, jaundice, blood problems.
4. Not to be used with alcohol and/or anesthetics.
5. Not recommended in pregnancy or for children.
6. Not to be used when operating a motor vehicle or when engaged in a hazardous occupation.
7. Liver dysfunction should be checked by blood tests.
8. When used for nausea and vomiting, intestinal diseases may be masked.

Possible complications:
1. Decreased vision, brown color to vision, blurred vision.
2. Low blood pressure, decreased blood count.
3. Convulsions, drowsiness, extrapyramidal symptoms, restlessness, headache, confusion, tardive dyskinesia.
4. Nasal stuffiness, nausea, vomiting, diarrhea, bloating.
5. Loss of menses (periods), breast engorgement, swelling of ankles, weight gain, may inhibit ejaculation.
6. Skin rashes.
7. Swelling of salivary glands.
8. Parkinsonism symptoms.
9. Allergic reaction such as swelling of throat, tongue, face, asthma.
10. Electrocardiograph changes with possible cardiac arrest and death.
11. High fever, bizarre dreams, skin and eye pigmentation change.

Ritalin

Main use: Used with other modalities of treatment in minimal brain dysfunction in children (may be discontinued after puberty), narcolepsy (condition of falling asleep with no control), mild depression, withdrawn senile behavior. The exact action is unknown.

Dosage: In children 5 mg. two to three times a day. Not more than 60 mg. three times a day.

Contraindications and precautions:
1. Not to be used in patients with marked anxiety, tension, and agitation.
2. Not to be used in patients who are hypersensitive or allergic to the medication.
3. Not to be used under the age of 6.
4. Not to be used in depression.
5. Not to be used in pregnancy.
6. To be used with care in patients with high blood pressure.

7. To be used with caution with MAO inhibitors and with high blood pressure medications.
8. May interfere with some blood thinner, anticonvulsion, and tricyclics medications.
9. To be used carefully in patients with a history of drug dependency or alcoholism (they are very liable to raise dosage themselves).
10. Blood counts should be checked periodically.

Possible complications:
1. Suppression of growth.
2. Convulsions, muscle twitching, dry mouth.
3. Visual disturbance such as blurred vision.
4. Psychotic episodes.
5. Depression, nervousness, inability to sleep.
6. Skin rash, fever, joint pain, black and blue marks on skin.
7. Nausea, loss of appetite, dizziness, palpitations, headaches, drowsiness, blood pressure and pulse up or down, irregular heart rhythm, abdominal pain.
8. Scalp hair loss.

Main use: Antidepressant. Also may have a depressant effect.

Tricyclics (Aventyl, Elavil, Endep, Daxolin, Loxitane, Norpramin, Sinequan, Tofranil, Adapin).

Contraindications and precautions:
1. Not to be used with MAO inhibitors (stop MAO 2 weeks before starting tricyclics).
2. To be used with care after a heart attack.
3. May block action of certain hypertensive medication.
4. To be used with care in glaucoma, urinary retention, seizures (epilepsy), overactive thyroid or while on thyroid medication.
5. Not recommended with pregnancy or for children.
6. Not recommended for use while driving or when engaged in hazardous occupations.

Possible complications:
1. High or low blood pressure, fast or slow heart beat. Coronary thrombosis (heart attack), strokes, and abnormal heart rhythm.
2. May activate latent schizophrenia, exacerbate psychosis, increase manic phase of manic-depression, cause nightmares, panic, insomnia, agitation, hallucinations, delusions.
3. Numbness, tingling, loss of coordination, ataxia (off balance), tremors, and seizures.
4. Dry mouth, blurred vision, urinary retention.
5. Bone marrow depression, anemia, purpura (black and blue marks).

6. Nausea, vomiting, loss of appetite, diarrhea, peculiar taste, cramps, black tongue.
7. Increase or decrease of libido, enlarged breast (male and female), breast discharge in women, testicle swelling, and elevation or lowering of blood sugar.
8. Altered liver function, jaundice, perspiration, flushing, drowsiness, dizziness, weakness, headache, swelling of salivary gland, loss of hair.
9. If abruptly discontinued, may produce nausea, heache, and weakness.

Bibliography

A.M.A. Drug Evaluations, 3rd edition, 1977, Publishing Sciences Group, Inc. Littleton, Mass.

Physicians Desk Reference, 33rd edition, 1979, Medical Economics Co., A. Litton Division, Oradell, New Jersey.

The Pharmacological Basis of Therapeutics, Louis S. Goodman and Alfred Gilman, 5th edition, 1975, Macmillan Publishing Co., Inc. New York.

Milton R. Bronstein, M.D.

Born

July 4, 1924, New York City

Presently

Physician, Internal Medicine and Nephrology. Private practice since 1953 at 12 Carlton Street, Edison, New Jersey, 08817, 201-826-5606.

Editor and Founder:
Journal of Perth Amboy General Hospital, Perth Amboy, N.J.

Hospital Affiliations:
Senior Attending, Internal Medicine-Nephrology, Perth Amboy General Hospital, Perth Amboy, N.J.
Assistant Director, Regional Hemodialysis Unit, Perth Amboy General Hospital.

Assoc. Attending, Internal Medicine-Nephrology, John F. Kennedy Medical Center, Edison, N.J.
Director of Medical Education, John F. Kennedy Medical Center

Courtesy Staff, Internal Medicine-Nephrology, Roosevelt Hospital, Metuchen, N.J.

Medical Associations

Middlesex County Medical Society
Medical Society of New Jersey
American Medical Association

Fellow, National Board of Medical Examiners
Medical Writers Association
Renal Physicians Assoc.
New Jersey Renal Physicians Assoc.
New Jersey Dialysis Assoc.

A. B. 1947 New York University   **Educational**
M.B. 1949 Chicago Medical School   **Background**
M.D. 1950 Chicago Medical School
1949– 1950 Rotating Internship, Newark
           City Hospital, Newark, N.J.
1950– 1952 Resident Internal Medicine,
           Newark City Hospital, Newark, N.J.
1952– 1953 Chief of Medicine, U.S. Army Hospital, Fort
           Hamilton, New York

New Jersey Medical Society Journal   **Publications**
American Medical Journal
Journal of Perth Amboy General Hospital

Middlesex County Medical Society   **Past President**
1976– 1977.

Associate Professor of Clinical Medicine-Fairleigh Dickinson
University, School of Dentistry

Clinical Instructor of Medicine
CMDNJ – Rutgers Medical School

References

"Stages":

Bry, B. "The Impact of Parents on their Adolescent Sons' 'Identity Crisis'." *The Clinical Psychologist*, 1978, *32*, 12–13.

Butler, R. *Why Survive? Being Old in America*. New York: Harper and Row, 1975.

Charaton, F. "Depression in Old Age." *New Jersey State Journal of Medicine*, 1975, *25*, 2505–09.

Erickson, E. "Eight Ages of Man." In *Readings in Child Behavior and Development*. Ed. C. Stindler. New York: Harcourt, Brace and World, 1964.

———. *Childhood and Society*. New York: Norton, 1967.

Flanagan, J. "A Research Approach to Improving our Quality of Life." *The American Psychologist*, 1978, *33*, 138–47.

Fromm, E. *Escape from Freedom*. New York: Rinehart, 1945.

——— *The Art of Loving*. New York: Harper, 1956.

Hunt, D. "Modifications of Therapeutic Procedures to the Needs of the Elderly." Paper read at the meeting of the American Psychological Association, Toronto, August, 1978.

Irwin, O. "Infant Speech: Effects of Systematic Reading of Stories." *Journal of Speech and Hearing Research*, 1960, *3*, 187–90.

Jenkins, R., and Glickman, S. "Patterns of Personality Organization among Delinquents." *The Nervous Child*, 1947, *6*, 329–39.

Jones, N. "Care of the Aging: A New View." *Psychotherapy*, 1977, *14*, 379–85.

Kessler, J. *Psychopathology of Childhood*. Englewood Cliffs, New Jersey: Prentice-Hall, 1966.

Klagsburn, F. *Too Young to Die: Youth and Suicide*. Cambridge, Massachusetts: Houghton-Mifflin, 1976.

Krasner, J. "Loss of Dignity—Courtesy of Modern Science." *Psychotherapy: Theory, Research, and Practice*, 1977, *14*, 309–18.

LeBoyer, F. *Birth without Violence*. New York Random House, 1975.

McGee, J., and Lakin, M. "Social Perspectives on Psychotherapy with the Aged." *Psychotherapy*, 1977, *14*, 333–41.

Sheehy, G. *Passages*. New York: Dutton, 1974.

Sullivan, H. *The Interpersonal Theory of Psychiatry*. New York: Norton, 1963.

Teri, L. "Depression in Adolescence." Paper read at the meeting of the American Psychological Association, Toronto, August, 1978.

Toolan, J. "Depression in Adolescence." In *Modern Perspectives in Adolescent Psychiatry*. Ed. J. Howells. London: Oliver and Boyd, 1971.

Vincent, C. "Trends in Infant Care Ideas." *Child Development*, 1951, *23*, 197–209.

Wolferstein, M. "Trends in Infant Care." *American Journal of Orthopsychiatry*, 1953, *23*, 120–30.

"Eating":

Bjorntorp, P. "Disturbances in the Regulation of Food Intake." *Advances in Psychosomatic Medicine*, 1972, *7*, 116–27.

Doleys, D. "Behavioral Treatment for Nocturnal Enuresis in Children: A Review of the Recent Literature." *Psychological Review*, 1977, *84*, 30–54.

Erikson, E. "Eight Ages of Man." In *Readings in Child Behavior and Development*. Ed. C. Stendler. New York: Harcourt, Brace and World, 1954.

Feingold, B. *Why Your Child is Hyperactive*. New York: Random House, 1975.

Herman, C., and Polivy, J. "Anxiety Restraint and Eating Behavior." *Journal of Abnormal Psychology*, 1975, *84*, 666–72.

Jones, H. "The Behavioral Treatment of Eneuresis Nocturna." In *Behavior Therapy and the Neuroses.* Ed. H. Eysenck. Oxford: Pergamon, 1960.

Kessler, J. *Psychopathology of Childhood.* Englewood Cliffs, New Jersey: Prentice-Hall, 1966.

Lakin, M. "Personality Factors in Mothers of Excessively Crying (Colicky) Infants." *Monographs in Social Research and Child Development,* 1957, *22,* ser. 64, no. 1.

Mayer, J. *Overweight: Causes, Cost and Control.* Englewood Cliffs, New Jersey: Prentice-Hall, 1968.

McCandless, B. *Children, Behavior and Development.* New York: Holt, Rinehart and Winston, 1967.

Mowrer, O., and Mowrer, W. "Eneuresis: A Method for its Study and Treatment." *American Journal of Orthopsychiatry,* 1938, *8,* 426–54.

Nisbett, R. "Hunger, Obesity and the Ventromedial Hypothalamus." *Psychological Review,* 1972, *79,*433-53.

Polivy, J. "Anorexics as Overly Restrained Eaters." Paper read at the meeting of the American Psychological Association, Toronto, August, 1978.

Rodale, J., ed. *Encyclopedia for Healthful Living.* Emmaus, Pennsylvania, 1972.

Schachter, S. "Eat, Eat." *Psychology Today,* 1971, *4,* 44–48.

————. *Emotions, Obesity and Crime.* New York: Academic Press, 1971.

Sears, R., *et al. Patterns of Child Rearing.* Evanston, Illinois: Peterson, and Co., 1957.

Verville, E. *Behavioral Problems of Children.* Philadelphia: Saunders, 1967.

Williams, R., *et al.* "Induced Thiamine (B1) Deficiency and the Thiamine Requirements of Man. Further Observations." *Archives of Internal Medicine,* 1942, *69,* 721.

"Sleeping":

Aserinsky, E., and Kleitman, N. "Regularly Occurring Periods of Eye Mobility and Concomitant Phenomena during Sleep." *Science,* 1953, *118,* 273–74.

Cartwright, R. "Happy Endings for Our Dreams." *Psychology Today,* December, 1978, 66 *ff.*

Coates, T., and Thoresen, C. *How to Sleep Better: A Non-Drug Program for Overcoming Insomnia.* Englewood Cliffs, New Jersey: Prentice-Hall, 1977.

Dement, W., and Mitler, M. "An Overview of Sleep Research: Past, Present and Future," in Hamburt, D., and Brodie, H., eds, *American Handbook of Psychiatry.* Vol. 6. New York: Basic Books, 1975.

Edwards, A. "Effects of the Loss of One Hundred Hours of Sleep." *American Journal of Psychology,* 1941, *54,* 80–91.

Foulkes, D. "Dreams of Innocence." *Psychology Today,* December, 1978, 78 *ff.*

Freud, S. *The Interpretation of Dreams.* London: Hogarth, 1960.

Garfield, P. *Creative Dreaming.* New York: Simon and Schuster, 1975.

Gesell, A., and Ilg, F. *Infant and Child in the Culture of Today.* New York: Harper and Row, 1943.

Greenleaf, E. "Senoi Dream Groups." *Psychotherapy: Theory, Research and Practice,* 1973, *10,* 218–22.

Hill, W. "Activity as an Autonomous Drive." *Journal of Comparative and Physiological Psychology,* 1956, *49,* 15–19.

Jung, C. *Man and His Symbols.* New York: Dell, 1968.

Kahn, E., and Fischer, C. "Sleep Characteristics of the Normal Aged Male." *Journal of Nervous and Mental Diseases,* 1969, *148,* 477–94.

Kessler, J. *Psychopathology of Childhood.* Englewood Cliffs, New Jersey: Prentice-Hall, 1966.

Kleitman, N. "Sleep." *Physiological Review,* 1929, *9,* 624–65.

Lazarus, C. "The Drug-Free Way to Sleep Soundly." Cassette tape. Relaxation Dynamics, Ltd. Valley Stream, New York.

McCarley, R. "Where Dreams Come From: A New Theory." *Psychology Today,* December, 1978, 54, *ff.*

New York Times. "U.S. Study of Sleep Drugs Finds Risks and Overuse." April 5, 1979, A1.

————. "Sleeping Pills May Aggravate the Very Problems They are Supposed to Be Solving." April 11, 1979, C10.

Perls, F. *Gestalt Therapy Verbatim.* New York: Bantam Books, 1971.

Price, V., *et al.* "Prevalence and Correlates of Poor Sleep among Adolescents." *American Journal of Diseases of Children,* 1978, *132,* 583–6.

Roffwarg, H., *et al.* "Ontogenic Development of the Human Sleeping Cycle." *Science,* 1966, *152,* 29.

Rosen, G. *Relaxation.* Englewood Cliffs, New Jersey: Prentice-Hall, 1977.

Voices, 1978, *64.*

"Thinking, Feeling and Fantasy":

Erikson, E. *Childhood and Society.* New York: Norton, 1967.

Freud, S. *The Ego and the Id.* New York: Norton, 1960.

————. *The Interpretation of Dreams*. London: Hogarth, 1960.

Fromm, E. *Man for Himself*. New York: Holt, Rinehart and Winston, 1947.

————. *The Art of Loving*. New York: Harper and Row, 1956.

Gaylin. W. *Feelings: Our Vital Signs*. New York: Harper and Row, 1978.

Horner, M. "Fail: Bright Women." *Psychology Today*, November, 1969, 36 *ff.*

Janov, A. *The Primal Scream*. New York: Dell, 1970.

Jung, C. *Analytical Psychology: Its Theory and Practice*. New York: Random House, 1968.

Kohlberg, L. "Moral and Religious Education and the Public Schools: A Developmental View." In *Religion and Public Education*. Ed. T. Sizer. Boston: Houghton and Mifflin, 1967.

Muson, H. "Moral Thinking: Can It be Taught?" *Psychology Today*, February, 1979, 48 *ff.*

Perls, F. *Gestalt Therapy Verbatim*. New York: Bantam Books, 1971.

Piaget, J. *Genetic Epistemology*. New York: Columbia University Press, 1970.

Shaffer, L., and Schober, E. *The Psychology of Adjustment*. Boston: Houghton and Mifflin, 1956.

Sullivan, H. *The Interpersonal Theory of Psychiatry*. New York: Norton, 1963.

Whorf, B. *Language, Thought and Reality*. New York: Wiley, 1956.

"Sexuality":

Bach, G., and Deutsch, R. *Pairing*. New York: Avon, 1970.

————, **and Wyden, P.** *The Intimate Enemy*. New York: Avon, 1969.

Belliveau, F., and Richter, L. *Understanding Human Sexual Inadequacy*. Boston: Little, Brown, 1970.

Boston Women's Health Book Collective. *Our Bodies, Ourselves*. New York: Simon and Schuster, 1976.

Clinebell, H., and Clinebell, C. *The Intimate Marriage*. New York: Harper and Row, 1970.

Comfort, A. *The Joy of Sex*. New York: Simon and Schuster, 1972.

Fasteau, M. *The Male Machine*. New York: McGraw-Hill, 1974.

Fromm E. *The Art of Loving*. New York: Bantam Books, 1956.

Haeberle, E. *The Sex Atlas*. New York: Seabury Press, 1978.

Harris, T. *I'm OK, You're OK*. New York: Avon, 1973.

Katchadourian, H., and Lunde, D. *Fundamentals of Human Sexuality*. New York: Holt, Rinehart and Winston, 1972.

Kinsey, A., *et al*. *Sexual Behavior in the Human Male*. Philadelphia: Saunders, 1948.

————, *et al. Sexual Behavior in the Human Female*. Philadelphia: Saunders, 1953.

Klaich, D. *Woman Plus Woman: Attitudes Towards Lesbianism*. New York: Simon and Schuster, 1974.

May, R. *Love and Will*. New York: Dell, 1969.

McBride, W. *Show Me: A Picture Book of Sex for Children and Parents*. New York: St. Martin Press, 1975.

McCary, J. *Human Sexuality*. New York: Van Nostrand, 1973.

National Sex Forum. *The SARguide for a Better Sex Life*. 1978.

Pomeroy, W. *Boys and Sex*. New York: Dell, 1971.

————. **Pomeroy, W.** *Girls and Sex*. New York: Dell, 1973.

Rogers, C. *Becoming Partners*. New York: Dell, 1973.

Silverstein, C. *A Family Matter: A Parents' Guide to Homosexuality*. New York: McGraw-Hill, 1977.

Tripp, C. *The Homosexual Matrix*. New York: McGraw-Hill, 1975.

"Relating":

Bach, G., and Wyden, P. *Intimate Enemy: How to Fight Fair in Love and Marriage*. New York: Morrow, 1969.

Berne, E. *Games People Play*. New York: Grove, 1964.

Cantor, D. "School-Based Groups for Children of Divorce." *Journal of Divorce*. 1977, *1*, 183–87.

————. "Collaboration Between Community Mental Health Centers and School Psychological Services." Paper presented at the meeting of the American Psychological Association, Toronto, August, 1978.

Clanton, J., and Smith, L. *Jealousy*. Englewood Cliffs, New Jersey: Prentice-Hall, 1977.

Eisenstatt, J. "Parental Loss and Genius." *American Psychologist*, 1978, *33*, 211–23.

Etaugh, C. "Effects of Non-Maternal Care in Children." Paper presented at the meeting of the American Psychological Association, Toronto, August, 1978.

Felser, R., *et al*. "Crisis Events and School Mental Health Referral Patterns of Young Children." *Journal of Consulting and Clinical Psychology*, 1975, *43*, 305–10.

Fraiberg, S. *The Magic Years*. New York: Scribner, 1959.

Freedman, J. *Happy People*.

Ganley, A., and Harris, L. "Domestic Violence: Issues in Designing and Implementing Programs for Male Batterers." Paper presented at the meeting of the American Psychological Association, Toronto, August, 1978.

Gardner, R. *Psychotherapy with Children of Divorce*. New York: Jason Aronson, 1976.

Gelles, R. *Conjugal Violence.* Beverly Hills: Sage, 1974.

Gesell, A., and Ilg, F. *Infant and Child in the Culture of Today.* New York: Harper and Row, 1943.

Harris, T. *I'm OK, You're OK.* New York: Harper and Row, 1969.

Kelly, J., and Wallerstein, J. "Brief Intervention with Children in Divorcing Families." *American Journal of Orthopsychiatry,* 1977, *47,* 23 – 35.

Kessler, J., and Bostwick, S. *Beyond Divorce: Coping Skills for Minors.* Atlanta: National Institute for Professional Training in Divorce Counseling, 1977.

Kotelchuck, M. "The Nature of the Child's Tie to his Father." Doctoral dissertation, Harvard University, 1972.

Livingston, C. *Why Was I Adopted?* New York: Lyle Stuart, 1978.

McDermott, J. "Parental Divorce in Early Childhood." *American Journal of Psychiatry,* 1968, *124,* 1424 – 32.

———. "Divorce and its Psychiatric Sequellae in Childhood," *Archives of General Psychiatry,* 1970, *23,* 421 – 27.

Morrison, J. "Parental Divorce as a Factor in Childhood Psychiatric Illness." *Comprehensive Psychiatry,* 1974, *15,* 95 – 102.

O'Neill, N., and O'Neill, G. *Open Marriage: A New Life Style for Couples.* New York: Evans, 1972.

Parke, R. "Socialization into Child Abuse." In *Law, Justice and the Individual in Society: Psychological and Legal Issues.* Ed. J. Topp and F. Levine. New York: Holt, Rinehart and Winston, 1977.

Schwartz, M. "Situation/Transition Groups: A Conceptualization and Review." *American Journal of Orthopsychiatry,* 1975, *45,* 744 – 45.

Spock, B. *The Common Sense Book of Baby and Child Care.* New York: Duell, Sloane and Pearce, 1946.

———. *Baby and Child Care.* New York: Pocket Book, 1962.

Steinmetz, S., and Strauss, M., ed. *Violence in the Family.* New York: Harper and Row, 1974.

Strauss, M. "Leveling, Civility and Violence in the Family." *Journal of Marriage: The Family,* 1974, *36,* 13 – 29.

Weinraub, M., and Lewis, M. "Determinants of Children's Responses to Separation." *Monographs of the Society for Research in Child Development,* (in press).

Wolfenstein, M. "Loss, Rage, and Repetition." *Psychoanalytic Studies of the Child,* 1969, *24,* 432 – 60.

"Health":

Appley, M., and Trumbull R. *Physiological Stress.* New York: Appleton, 1967.

Cofer, C., and Appley, M. *Motivation: Theory and Research.* New York: Wiley, 1964.

Davison, G., and Neale, J. *Abnormal Psychology.* New York: Wiley, 1974.

Dembroski, T., ed. *Proceedings of the Forum on Coronary-Prone Behavior.* DHEW Publication no. (NIH) 78-1451, 1977.

Dohrenwind, B., and Dohrenwind, B. *Stressful Life Events: Their Nature and Effect.* New York: Wiley, 1974.

Engel, G. "A Life Setting Conducive to Illness: The Giving Up Complex." *Annals of Internal Medicine,* 1968, *69,* 293 – 300.

Freedman, M., and Rosenman, R. *Type A Behavior and Your Heart.* New York: Knopf, 1974.

Gaylin, W. *Feelings: Our Vital Signs.* New York: Harper and Row, 1974.

Glass, D. *Behavior Patterns, Stress and Coronary Disease.* Hillsdale, New York: Lawrence Erebaum Associates, 1977.

———. "Stress, Behavior Patterns and Coronary Disease." *American Scientist,* 1977, *65,* 177 – 87.

Greene, W., et al. "Psychosocial Aspects of Sudden Death: A Preliminary Report." *Archives of Internal Medicine,* 1972, *129,* 725 – 31.

Lazarus, R. *Psychological Stress and the Coping Process.* New York: McGraw-Hill, 1966.

McGrath, J., ed. *Social and Psychological Stress.* New York: Holt, Rinehart and Winston, 1970.

Mirsky, I. "Physiologic, Psychologic and Social Determinants in the Etiology of Duodenal Ulcer." *American Journal of Digestive Diseases,* 1958, *3,* 285 – 314.

Rees, L. "The Significance of Parental Attitudes in Childhood Asthma." *Journal of Psychosomatic Research,* 1964, *7,* 253 – 62.

Saul, L. "The Effects of Emotional Tension." In *Personality and the Behavior Disorders.* Vol. I. Ed. J. Hunt. New York: Ronald Press, 1944.

Selye, H. *The Stress of Life.* New York: McGraw-Hill, 1956.

Small, A. "Giving Up as a Final Pathway to Change in Health." *Advances in Psychosomatic Medicine,* 1972, *8,* 18 – 38.

Weiner, H., et al. "Etiology of Duodenal Ulcer: Relations to Specific Physiological Characteristics and Rate of Gastric Excretion." *Psychosomatic Medicine,* 1957, *19,* 1 – 10.

Woolfolk, R., and Richardson, F. *Stress, Sanity and Survival.* New York: Monarch, 1978.

"Habits":

Ausabel, D. "Causes and Types of Narcotic Addictions." *Psychiatric Quarterly,* 1961, *35,* 523 – 31.

Barber, T. *LSD, Marijuana and Hypnosis.* Chicago: Aldine, 1970.

Bergler, E. "Personality Traits of Alcohol Addicts." *Quarterly Journal of Studies in Alcohol,* 1946, *2,* 356–61.

———. *The Psychology of Gambling.* London: International University Press, 1958.

Bernstein, D., and McAlister, A. "The Modification of Smoking Behavior: Progress and Problems." *Addictive Behavior,* 1976, *1,* 89–102.

Brecher, E. *Licit and Illicit Drugs.* Mt. Vernon, New York: Consumers Union, 1972.

Brill, L., *et al. Rehabilitation in Drug Addiction.* HEW Mental Health Monograph, no. 3, 1963.

Cantanzoro, R., ed. *Alcoholism: The Total Treatment Approaches.* Springfield, Illinois: Charles Thomas, 1968.

Chafetz, M. "Addiction II. Alcoholism." In *Comprehensive Textbook of Psychiatry.* Ed. A. Freedman and H. Kaplan. Baltimore: Williams and Williams, 1967.

Cherin, I., *et al. The Road to H: Narcotics, Delinquency and Social Policy.* New York: Basic Books, 1964.

Department of Health, Education and Welfare, Public Health Service. *Teenage Smoking: National Patterns of Cigarette Smoking, Age 12 Through 18, in 1972 and 1974.* DHEW Publication no. (NIH) 76-931, 1976.

Dicken, C., and Bryson, R. "The Smoking of Psychology." *American Psychologist,* 1978, *33,* 504–07.

Dole, V., and Nyswander, M. "The Use of Methadone for Narcotic Blockade." *British Journal of Addiction,* 1968, *3,* 55–57.

Evans, R., *et al.* "Deterring the Onset of Smoking in Children." *Journal of Applied Social Psychology,* 1977, *8,* 126–35.

Fenichel, O. *The Psychoanalytic Theory of Neurosis.* New York: Norton, 1945.

Franks, C. "Behavior Modification and the Treatment of the Alcoholic." In *Alcoholism: Behavioral Research.* Ed. R. Fox. New York: Springer, 1967.

Gilbert, J., and Lombardi, D. "Personality Characteristics of Young Male Narcotic Addicts." *Journal of Consulting Psychology,* 1967, *31,* 536–38.

Goodman, L., and Gilman, A. *The Pharmacological Basis of Therapeutics.* New York: Macmillan, 1972.

Hall, R., *et al.* "Tobacco and Evoked Potential." *Science,* 1973, *180,* 212–14.

Hill, H. *et al.* "Personality Characteristics of Narcotics Addicts as Indicated by the MMPI." *Journal of Genetic Psychology,* 1960, *62,* 127–39.

Jellinek, E. "Phases of Alcohol Addiction." *Quarterly Journal of Studies in Alcohol,* 1952, *13,* 673–84.

———. *The Disease Concept of Alcoholism.* New Haven: Hillhouse Press, 1960.

Kessel, N., and Walton, A. *Alcoholism.* Baltimore: Penguin, 1965

Klee, G., *et al.* "The Influence of Varying Dosages on the Effects of Lysergic Acid Diethylamide (LSD-25)." *Journal of Nervous and Mental Disease,* 1961, *32,* 404–09.

Knight, R. "The Dynamics of Chronic Alcoholism." *Journal of Nervous and Mental Disease,* 1937, *86,* 538–48.

McCord. W., *et al. Origins of Alcoholism.* Stanford, California: Stanford University Press, 1960.

Nathan, P., *et al.* "Behavioral Analysis of Chronic Alcoholism." *Archives of General Psychiatry,* 1970, *22,* 419–30.

National Commission on Marijuana and Drug Abuse. *Marijuana: A Signal of Misunderstanding.* New York: New American Library, 1972.

Nesbitt, P. "Smoking, Physiological Arousal and Emotional Response." *Journal of Personality and Social Psychology,* 1973, *25,* 137–44.

Page, J. *Psychopathology: The Science of Understanding Deviance.* New York: Aldine-Atherton, 1971.

Resnick, R., *et al.* "A Cyclazocine Typology in Opiate Dependence." *American Journal of Psychiatry,* 1970, *126,* 1256–60.

Salzberger, G. "The Acute Alcohol Debauch." *Diseases of the Nervous System,* 1967, *28,* 387–89.

Shelley, J., and Bassin, A. "Daytop Lodge: A New Treatment Approach for Drug Addicts." *Corrective Psychiatry and Journal of Social Therapy,* 1965, *2,* 186–95.

Von Felsinger, J., *et al.* "The Response of Normal Men to Lysergic Acid Derivatives." *Journal of Clinical and Experimental Psychopathology,* 1956, *17,* 414–28.

Wanberg, K., and Horn, J. "Alcoholism Symptom Patterns of Men and Women: A Comparative Study." *Quarterly Journal of Studies on Alcohol,* 1970, *31,* 40–61.

Willis, J. "Drug Dependence: Some Demographic and Psychiatric Aspects in United Kingdom and United States Subjects." *British Journal of Addiction,* 1969, *64,* 135–46.

World Health Organization. *International Conferences on Smoking Cessation.* 1978.

Yablonsky, L *Synanon: The Tunnel Back.* Baltimore: Penguin, 1961.

Zadikow, C. "A Professional Poker Player: A Psychoanalytically Oriented Psychodiagnostic Orientation." Doctoral thesis, Rutgers University, 1978.

"Change":

Blank, L., *et al.,* ed. *Confrontation: Encounters in Self and Interpersonal Awareness.* New York: Macmillan, 1971.

Cummings, N., and Vanden Bos, G. "The Gen

eral Practice of Psychology." Paper read at the meeting of the American Psychological Association Division of Psychotherapy, Mexico City, March, 1979.

Davison, G., and Neale, J. *Abnormal Psychology.* New York: Wiley, 1974.

Honigfeld, G., and Howard, G. *Psychiatric Drugs.* New York: Academic Press, 1973.

Lazarus, A. *Behavior Therapy and Beyond.* New York: McGraw Hill, 1971.

New York Times. April 3, 1979, Cl.

"Behavior Disturbances":

American Psychiatric Association. *Diagnostic and Statistical Manual.* 2nd ed. Washington, D.C., 1968.

Bender, L. "The Life Course of Schizophrenic Children." *Biological Psychiatry,* 1970, *2,* 165 – 72.

Davison, G., and Neale, J. *Abnormal Psychology.* New York: Wiley, 1974.

Feingold, B. *Why Your Child is Hyperactive.* New York: Random House, 1975.

Harley, J. "Food Additives and Hyperactivity." Unpublished ms., University of Wisconsin, 1976.

Honigfeld, G., and Howard, G. *Psychiatric Drugs.* New York: Academic Press, 1973.

Kinsbourne, M., and Swanson, J. "Hyperactivity." Quebec: Quebec Association for Children with Learning Disabilities, (in press).

Lotter, V. "Epidemiology of Autistic Conditions in Young Children Prevalence." *Social Psychiatry,* 1966, *1,* 124 – 37.

Milbrich, R., and Losey, J. "The Role of Hyperactive and Aggressive Symptomatology in Predicting Adolescent Outcome among Hyperactive Children." Department of Psychiatry, University of Iowa, 1978.

New York Times. "Manic-Depressive Cycle Tied to 'Clock' Defect." December 5, 1978, Cl.

O'Leary, K. "The Etiology of Hyperactivity." Paper presented at the Second Annual Italian Behavior Therapy Association Meeting, Venice, June, 1978.

————, **and O'Leary, S.** "Behavioral Treatment for Hyperactive Children." Paper read at the meeting of the American Association for the Advancement of Behavior Therapy, Atlanta, 1977.

Page, J. *Psychopathology: The Science of Understanding Deviance.* Chicago: Aldine, 1971.

Palmer, S., *et al.* "Food Additives and Hyperactivity." *Clinical Pediatrics,* 1975, *10,* 956 – 59.

Rimland, B. "The Differentiation of Childhood Psychoses: An Analysis of Checklists for 2,218 Psychotic Children." *Journal of Autism and Childhood Schizophrenia,* 1971, *1,* 161 – 74.

Swanson, J., and Kinsbourne, M. *Procedures to Prevent the Overdiagnosis of Hyperactivity and to Optimize its Treatment with Stimulant Drugs.* The Neuropsychology Research Laboratory, The Hospital for Sick Children, Toronto, August, 1978.

Index